GW00645102

FIRE OVER ENGLAND

FIRE OVER ENGLAND

*The German Air
Raids of World War I*

H. G. CASTLE

A Leo Cooper Book

Secker & Warburg · London

First published in Great Britain 1982 by
Leo Cooper in association with
Martin Secker & Warburg Limited, 54 Poland Street, London W1V 3DF
Copyright © 1982 H. G. Castle

ISBN 0 436 08900 9

Photoset in Great Britain by
Rowland Phototypesetting Limited, Bury St Edmunds, Suffolk
and printed by St Edmundsbury Press
Bury St Edmunds, Suffolk

Contents

ACKNOWLEDGEMENTS

Any author who writes about aviation in the First World War is indebted to the official history, *The War in the Air*, which was begun by Sir Walter Raleigh and completed by H. A. Jones. I gratefully acknowledge my use of this most accurate and reliable source.

Another impeccable source for the brief outline of activities up to 1914 is the late Charles H. Gibbs-Smith whose comprehensive *Aviation: An Historical Survey from its Origins to World War II*, is an indispensable reference work.

I am also indebted to the staffs of the reference and photographic libraries of the Imperial War Museum who were generous not only with their time but also their expert knowledge.

The Imperial War Museum also gave permission to reproduce the photographs marked IWM. The diagrammatic drawing of the Zeppelin is reproduced by permission of *The Illustrated London News* Picture Library.

A rather more distant acknowledgement is due to the former Air Ministry who gave me access to *Air Raids*, the intelligence reports for 1915–1918. In the writing of this book they have been an invaluable corrective to less reliable sources.

My thanks are due to Faber & Faber for permission to reprint the extract on page 184 from *Memoirs of an Infantry Officer* by Siegfried Sassoon. Thanks are also due to Heinemann Educational for permission to re-produce the map on pages viii and ix.

Less formally, I would like to mention my father, who inspired a childhood interest in aviation and encouraged me to follow its war time development.

List of Illustrations

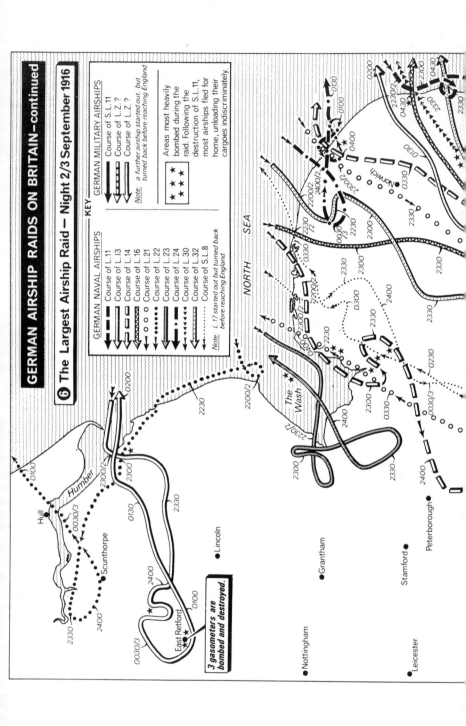

GERMAN AIRSHIP RAIDS ON BRITAIN—continued

❻ The Largest Airship Raid – Night 2/3 September 1916

KEY

GERMAN NAVAL AIRSHIPS

- Course of L.11
- Course of L.13
- Course of L.14
- Course of L.16
- Course of L.21
- Course of L.22
- Course of L.23
- Course of L.24
- Course of L.30
- Course of L.32
- Course of S.L.8

Note: L.17 started out but turned back before reaching England

GERMAN MILITARY AIRSHIPS

- Course of S.L.11
- Course of L.Z.?
- Course of L.Z.?

Note: a further airship started out, but turned back before reaching England

★★★
★★★
Areas most heavily bombed during the raid. Following the destruction of S.L.11, most airships fled for home, unloading their cargoes indiscriminately.

NORTH SEA

3 gasometers are bombed and destroyed.

Hull

Humber

Scunthorpe

Lincoln

East Retford

The Wash

Nottingham

Grantham

Stamford

Peterborough

Leicester

Norwich

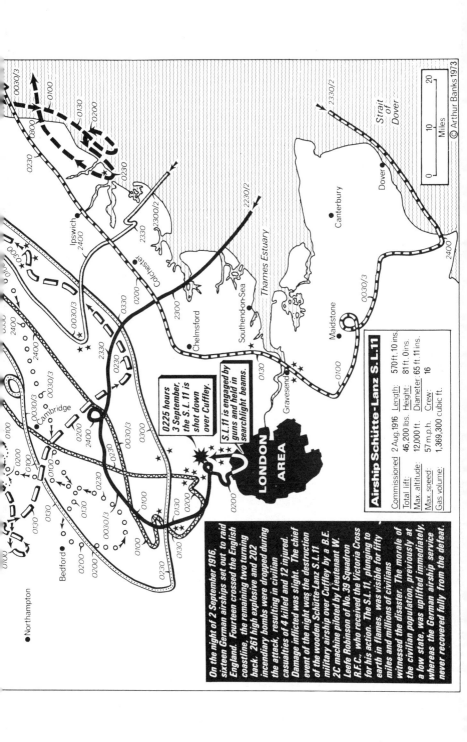

Northampton

Bedford

Cambridge

Ipswich

Colchester

Chelmsford

Southend-on-Sea

Thames Estuary

Gravesend

Maidstone

Canterbury

Dover

LONDON AREA

Strait of Dover

0225 hours 3 September, the S.L.11 is shot down over Cuffley.

S.L.11 is engaged by guns and held in searchlight beams.

Airship Schütte-Lanz S.L.11

Commissioned	2 Aug. 1916	Length:	570 ft. 10 ins.
Total lift:	46,200 lbs.	Height:	81 ft. 0 ins.
Max. altitude:	12,000 ft.	Diameter:	65 ft. 11 ins.
Max. speed:	57 m.p.h.	Crew:	16
Gas volume:	1,369,300 cubic ft.		

On the night of 2 September 1916, sixteen German airships set out to raid England. Fourteen crossed the English coastline, the remaining two turning back. 261 high explosive and 202 incendiary bombs were dropped during the attack, resulting in civilian casualties of 4 killed and 12 injured. Damage inflicted was slight. The chief event of the night was the destruction of the wooden Schütte-Lanz S.L.11 military airship over Cuffley by a B.E. 2C machine piloted by Lieutenant W. Leefe Robinson of No. 39 Squadron R.F.C., who received the Victoria Cross for his action. The S.L.11, plunging to earth in flames, was visible for fifty miles and millions of civilians witnessed the disaster. The morale of the civilian population, previously at a low state, was uplifted immediately, whereas the German airship service never recovered fully from the defeat.

© Arthur Banks 1973

0 10 20
Miles

CHAPTER 1

A Slow Take-Off

When Germany made the first air attacks on Britain in December, 1914, only a few people realized that the 'island fortress' was a thing of the past and that the nation was soon to become the first country in history to endure aerial bombardment.

The attacks were accepted with curiosity, indifference and a touch of local pride and excitement. The effects did nothing to justify the predictions of the scaremongers who had forecast that Britain would be overwhelmed by this new form of warfare.

The first attack took place at 1 pm on 21 December when a German Albatross seaplane flew over the south-east coast at Dover, dropped two 20-lb bombs offshore at Dover Pier and returned to its Belgian base. Three days later a Taube aeroplane dropped the first bomb ever to fall on British territory, near Dover Castle. There were no casualties; a few windows were broken. Undisturbed, the Taube flew off.

On the following day another Albatross made a more ambitious and audacious sortie. Just after 12.30 pm on Christmas morning it flew in from the sea over the Isle of Sheppey, in Kent, crossed the River Medway and followed the Thames to Erith, on the very edge of London itself. It then turned back downriver to the estuary and dropped two bombs which caused minor damage to the village of Cliffe.

Three Royal Flying Corps aeroplanes and three Royal Naval Air Service aircraft from Eastchurch and Grain followed the Albatross on a fruitless pursuit. A gun at Sheerness was equally unsuccessful. Another gun, at Cliffe Fort, fired at the intruder on its return journey but the Albatross mocked this token gesture by dropping two bombs on the railway station.

Scarcely anyone then believed that ramshackle aeroplanes could ever be the new, decisive, third arm of warfare. If there was to be one, then it must be the Zeppelin airship. Constant propaganda, worldwide publicity, and a unique contribution to the conquest of the air had made the Zeppelin an awesome prospect; but there was the comforting thought that peacetime achievements could not be compared with the unknown hazards of war.

There was a persistently held conviction that at least one Zeppelin had made a secret flight over England before the war. But for active service raids the weather could not be hand-picked to ensure ideal conditions. And no propaganda nor good publicity could hide those disasters which unexpected weather changes had brought to the Zeppelins. Moreover, there was now the safeguard of the Royal Navy at sea and the defences on land—or so it was believed.

When the First World War began Britain had some 280 aircraft and seven airships. The Royal Flying Corps had about 190 aeroplanes; the Royal Naval Air Service had thirty-nine aeroplanes, fifty-two seaplanes, one flying boat, and seven airships. But the operational strength of the Royal Flying Corps consisted of, at best, sixty-three machines. Twenty-four were ready for service when the British Expeditionary Force embarked for France in August. In addition, 116 non-operational aeroplanes were, on paper at any rate, available for training. But a senior Royal Flying Corps commander, Lieutenant-Colonel F. H. (later Major-General Sir Frederick) Sykes, confessed that only about twenty of them were fit for the task.

Similarly, only about half of the Royal Naval Air Service strength can be said to have been operational. Because accurate figures for both the Royal Flying Corps and the Royal Naval Air Service were inadequately kept—or frequently not kept at all—reliable strength records do not exist. No one ever knew how many aircraft were ready for operational service, even on a day-to-day basis.

Winston Churchill, First Lord of the Admiralty in 1914 and therefore responsible for naval aviation, wrote in *The World Crisis 1911–1914*: 'I had in my own hand on the eve of war fifty efficient naval machines.'

No one had deliberately deceived Churchill; nor indeed had he deceived himself. The early aviators and mechanics existed on daily optimism. The aeroplane or seaplane that could not take off in the morning could be airborne by the afternoon and perhaps grounded again by the evening. And who was to say that training aircraft could not be used operationally?

Records of strengths of other principal air forces at the outbreak of war are equally unreliable but they provide a rough comparison: France is said to have had 136 aeroplanes; Belgium twenty-four; Germany between 250 and 260.

Balancing strengths by numbers, however, is misleading. Strategically, Germany had temporarily relegated, but not isolated, the aeroplane in favour of the Zeppelin. German determination to march faster and better than anyone else in the event of war brought a highly emotional, patriotic response. And the Zeppelin was at the heart of it.

Long before 1914 German aviation, and the Zeppelin in particular, was being prepared for war. It had unequivocal Government support. There was a positive attitude and a clear-sighted plan for its development. The German people, at least in cities and large towns, were certain that the Zeppelin was not only the vanguard of a new kind of warfare but also a war-winner in its own right.

The British Government—especially the Liberal administrations—and the War Office have been castigated by the hindsight historians for their negative attitude, for Britain's weak air service, and for having left the country vulnerable to aerial bombardment. They are accused of having ignored expert advice that the aeroplane and the airship would be the decisive third arm; the 'insistent voice of the British people' was ignored; attempts to improve 'a desperate situation were made too late' and under pressure of a 'public outcry'.

The reality is different. Like any other historical event, the aerial bombardment of Britain needs to be seen in its correct and indivisible political and social setting.

Once the First World War had begun the Government and the War Office were indeed guilty of muddle, vacillation and ignorance over the air defence of Britain. Before that, however, they were victims rather than villains, reflecting public opinion and attitudes. With good reason most Service chiefs were reluctant to accept the fragile aeroplane and the flimsy seaplane. To the army, in particular, the aeroplane was no more than an extra 'eye in the sky', a subordinate to cavalry scouting and reconnaissance.

Nevertheless, in 1912, with the formation of the Royal Flying

Corps with its Naval and Military Wings, Britain was apparently the only nation which had a co-ordinated air service. But it was doomed from the outset. Three years and three months later, in July, 1914, the Siamese twins of a single air force were separated by the creation of the Royal Naval Air Service. The separation was inevitable but it was to have a significant effect on the aerial bombardment of Britain.

As we shall see, there were good reasons for the Navy's decision. For one thing, its attitude to service aviation was bold and progressive, whereas that of the Army was cautious and lacking in confidence. The pilots and observers of the Royal Flying Corps were no less enthusiastic, dedicated, or efficient than those of the Royal Naval Air Service, but the naval aviators had the powerful, personal support of Winston Churchill. Left to themselves their Lordships at the Admiralty would doubtless have been as lukewarm as were the generals. No one in the War Office had the same influence as Churchill nor the aggressive determination of officers such as Captain Murray Sueter and Commander Samson, the pioneers of naval aviation.

The army had accepted the aeroplane reluctantly. The Air Battalion was formed in 1911. A year later, in April, 1912, it was replaced by the Royal Flying Corps. The Central Flying School was opened in the same year. Despite this apparent progress, there was some justification for the criticism of the scathing but able editor of *The Aeroplane*, Charles Grey. He accused the War Office of treating the aeroplane as no more than a mechanized version of the reconnaissance balloon which had been used on active service for the first time in 1884 and as recently as the South African War of 1899–1902.

In retropsect it is easy to compare the Army unfavourably with the Navy and to charge the War Office with neglect. But the cold logic of hindsight ignores the facts of the contemporary scene and the differences in the people who made the policies.

War Office interest in powered flight went back to the very first of its kind. In 1904 Lieutenant-Colonel Capper, Royal Engineers, (later Major-General Sir John Capper) was sent to America to report on aviation progress. The only progress was that of Orville and Wilbur Wright. Capper saw them ten months after they had made the world's first powered, controlled aeroplane flight at Kill Devil Hills, Kitty Hawk, Ohio, in their Flyer I.

Although their first flight and those which followed it proved to be one of man's major achievements, they were like Doctor Johnson's reference to a dog walking on its hind legs, 'It is not done well; but you are surprised to find it done at all'. When Capper met the Wright brothers they had a new aeroplane, a slightly modified version of Flyer I. A 15 h.p. engine had replaced the original 12 h.p. unit. In effect, however, the machine which Capper saw was the same as Flyer I—a biplane with a span of 40 feet 4 inches. But it was fragile in the extreme and dangerously unstable.

Nevertheless, Colonel Capper had an immediate understanding of the principles on which the brothers were working. Remarkably, from those crude beginnings he foresaw the practical military application of the aeroplane. He asked Orville and Wilbur Wright if they would come to Britain. They demanded £20,000 for four years' work and guaranteed the exclusive use of their experience, unless the United States invited them to return home. Their achievements had not impressed official circles in their own country, especially the Board of Ordnance, whose recognition would have made America the first nation to develop military aviation.

At the beginning of 1905 Capper wrote to the War Office:

> I wish to invite very special attention to the wonderful advance made in aviation by the brothers Wright . . . It is a fact that they have flown and operated personally a flying machine for a distance of over three miles, at a speed of 35 m.p.h.

The proposal was rejected, as was another when the Wrights offered to sell an aeroplane to the War Office and themselves give flying instruction. These rejections have echoed down the corridors of time, leaving a loud impression of neglect. Britain, it has been said, missed a unique opportunity to become the first country in the world to have a practical aeroplane and the nucleus of a military air service. The bizarre claim that this might have shortened the First World War is still made.

The negotiations with the War Office were abortive because of the Wrights' insistence that no one could examine their aeroplane in detail until a sale was made. Justifiably, they were afraid that their unpatented designs would be discreetly copied or blatantly stolen. In 1905 no one in the War Office had ever seen a powered aeroplane and rejection was inevitable.

There was scarcely any significant progress in the development of the aeroplane until 1908, when Wilbur and Orville Wright made their first public flights: Wilbur in France and Orville in America. On 8 August Wilbur was in the air for no more than 1 minute 45 seconds, but his complete control and the perfect stability of his machine at first dumbfounded and then converted a crowd of sceptical onlookers.

Three weeks later Orville made the first of a series of public flights at Fort Myer, Washington, DC. He created new altitude records of 200 and 310 feet, and a new duration record of 1 hour 2 minutes 13 seconds. A more melancholy record was also established during the series when his machine crashed and his passenger, Lieutenant T. E. Selfridge, became the first fatal casualty of powered flight.

Coincidentally and directly, the Wrights' displays, particularly those by Wilbur in France, set off a surge of aviation activity. In October, 1908, the American, Colonel S. F. Cody, made the first officially recognized powered flight in Britain. But the following year became the most momentous in pre-war aviation, the outstanding event, though not the most important, being the first crossing of the English Channel by the Frenchman, Louis Blériot.

As a result, many dire warnings and much gratuitous advice were given to the Government. The popular newspapers, led by the *Daily Mail*—which had offered a £1,000 prize for the first Channel crossing by air—were sensationally alarmist about Britain's new vulnerability. In the *Daily Mail* H. G. Wells began to lay down a well-trodden path of portentous warnings. 'In spite of our fleet,' he wrote, 'this is no longer, from the military point of view, an inaccessible island.'

Six years were to pass before the significance of that flight was realized. Its immediate effect on the Government, the War Office and, most of all, the British people has been greatly exaggerated. The public, at any rate, was not 'deeply disturbed' or 'gravely concerned' or 'fearful of a new menace that threatens our lives'. To most people the flight was an exciting sporting curiosity, like Captain Webb's cross-Channel swim in 1875.

The Blériot No. XI monoplane was seen by an estimated 120,000 people at Selfridge's store in Oxford Street, London. It would have been hard to find anyone, outside the world of aviation, who believed that this puny machine, with its open-framework fuselage, was anything more than a dangerous toy, let alone a potential threat to national security or a new third arm of warfare.

Everyone knew that Blériot had only just completed the crossing. Having neither a compass nor a watch, and having out-distanced his escort vessel, he had temporarily lost his way in mid-Channel. Even the landing in Northfield Meadow, by Dover Castle, was not free from mishap and the engine and undercarriage were damaged.

The newspapers made much of Blériot's courage, skill and determination, all of which was true, but the very qualities for which they praised him convinced most people that he was a very lucky record-maker indeed. This was confirmed by the two failures of the French aviator, Hubert Latham. Six days before Blériot's success, Latham's attempt to win the £1,000 prize had ended in the sea when the engine of his Antoinette IV stopped when he was about eight miles from Sangatte, near Calais. Two days after Blériot's crossing he had come down in the water again, this time only a mile from the English coast.

Although Blériot's flight did not have a serious impact on the British people, it did impress the world of aviation. But this was an esoteric world of experts and enthusiasts. It excluded most generals, admirals and politicians, whose indifference reflected the public attitude right up to the beginning of the First World War.

There was some official recognition that the aeroplane might have a long-term future, but in 1909 there was no support for it as a military weapon. Even the most important event of the year, and indeed the most important event in the development of the aeroplane—the first-ever international aviation meeting at Rheims a month after Blériot's feat—did not change this attitude. David Lloyd George was among the many distinguished spectators who were deeply impressed by 'Rheims Week'.

'I feel, as a Britisher,' he said, 'rather ashamed that we are out of it.' He was then Chancellor of the Exchequer, but his 'shame' did not inspire him to encourage substantial expenditure on military aviation.

Although Britain did make some notable progress in aeronautics and aviation during the years before the First World War, very little of it was translated into an effective air service. The Royal Aircraft Factory at Farnborough—the Royal Air-

craft Establishment of today—became internationally respected for its research and development. 'The Factory', as it
was generally referred to, had evolved from the Balloon Factory, which in turn had grown from the Balloon Committee set
up at Woolwich Arsenal in 1878.

An unhappy division between Farnborough and the various
independent designers and constructors was a serious handicap
in those formative years between 1909 and 1914. The independents had two major grievances which seemed to be contradictory. Some complained that they were deprived of Government
help and excluded from the benefits of Farnborough research
and development. On the other hand, most of them refused to
work with the Factory. They were convinced that bureaucracy
would emasculate their freedom and lead to a stagnant
monopoly. The Factory considered itself to be an exclusive and
superior organization, which it undoubtedly was.

An accurate account of why British military aviation was so
weak in 1914 is impossible without the paradox of its success.
To say that Farnborough was at the heart of that success does
not diminish the work of the independents. The Factory's sole
object was that of research, development and testing, mostly for
a still reluctant army. For a time an incredibly obtuse ruling
prevented it from making original aircraft. To overcome this
embargo, foreign aeroplanes were dismantled, examined and
'reconstructed'. Early Farnborough types carried prefix letters
such as B.E. for Blériot Experimental, S.E. for Santos Experimental, B.S. for Blériot Scout.

This absurd reconstruction pretence did not last. Although
some of the prefixes remained, the aeroplanes became in effect
Farnborough productions which, with some of the Factory's
'pure' types, were among the foundation lines of British aviation.

In his indispensable reference work, *Aviation: An Historical
Survey from its Origins to World War II*, the distinguished aviation
historian C. H. Gibbs-Smith wrote:

> Farnborough was now [in 1913] rapidly becoming the
> foremost of the world's aeronautical research establish-
> ments; it was developing both aircraft and aero engines,
> methods of inspection and testing, as well as conducting
> basic aerodynamic research.

It had the closest co-operation with the National Physical Laboratory. Its quest for safety was unremitting. It insisted on the highest engineering standards. It was a contradiction in terms: it carried out radical and original research, and was the epitome of caution and conservatism in its application. With some justification it was said that the more daring feats and experiments carried on elsewhere were perfected by Farnborough.

The most serious aspect of pre-war non-co-operation was that of the aero engine. The Factory did not actually build engines, but those which were built elsewhere were unreliable, with faults which could be dangerous, if not fatal, mainly through lack of adequate testing facilities. When the Factory did have an engine laboratory it included a test bed with a wind tunnel in which flying conditions could be simulated, but most manufacturers neglected it and the Royal Flying Corps had to rely almost entirely on foreign engines when war began in 1914.

In those pre-war years the independents faced formidable difficulties. The lack of a substantial market for aeroplanes meant a shortage of money. Because aviation had a speculative future, except in the eyes of its beholders, and because it was undeniably dangerous, investment capital was scarce.

A few independents survived as a result of far-seeing sponsorships and the dedication of wealthy and determined men such as T. O. M. Sopwith, Alliott Verdon Roe, Robert Blackburn, Claude Grahame-White, H. G. (Harry) Hawker, the partnership of H. P. Martin and C. H. Handayside and that of Horace, Eustace, and Oswald Shortt, as well as firms such as Bristol and Vickers. For good and perverse reasons the Admiralty reinforced this support, mainly through the efforts of Winston Churchill and the Director of the Admiralty Air Department, Captain (later Rear Admiral Sir Murray) Sueter.

With distinguished designers and test pilots at Farnborough like Geoffrey de Havilland, R. C. Kemp, S. C. Wingfield-Smith, Henry Folland, F. T. Busk and Frank Gooden—under the direction of the Factory's Superintendent Mervyn O'Gorman—the burgeoning industry had an unsurpassed array of talent. It included equally distinguished people among the independents. They were all individualists. All held sensible, sound, eccentric, wild, noncomformist ideas which this unique development needed. It was impossible to weld all these disparate talents into a co-operative mould. Nevertheless, if aviation needed Farnborough, it needed the independents as well. The growing threat of the First World War brought about a marriage that was arranged but not always happy.

The newspaper owner Lord Northcliffe was the boldest and most imaginative of the sponsors. His conviction that military and civil aircraft had a serious future was powerfully reinforced by his newspapers, in particular the *Daily Mail*. His flamboyant publicity for the cause was not without self-interest in his papers' circulations; but, unlike its flashier, more ephemeral promoters, aviation had in him the personal support of a man who combined self-interest with genuine faith. He did more than anyone else, or anything else, to foster public interest and excitement.

As early as 1910—only one year after Blériot's precarious Channel crossing and only two years after S. F. Cody's first recognized sustained flight in Britain—Northcliffe offered the sensationally large prize of £10,000 for the first non-stop crossing of the North Atlantic. Even some of the serious believers in the future of aviation dismissed this offer as a 'stunt', to use a jargon word of the time. There were others, including his Fleet Street rivals, who said he had offered it simply for the publicity in the sure knowledge that such a flight could not succeed.

In 1910 it was impossible, but Northcliffe's intention was to inspire the pioneers to achieve something which was then no more than a distant horizon. It had its effect, however, and only the advent of the First World War postponed the realization of the dream.

Among those who responded to the challenge was Frederick Handley Page, who would almost certainly have been the first contender for the prize with his 0/100. He was building it specially for the transatlantic attempt when war prevented its completion. Handley Page is a corner-stone of British aviation with an immortal place in its history, but he always regretted that the prize was won in 1919 by Captain John Alcock and Lieutenant Whitten Brown of the Royal Air Force in a Vickers Vimy.

Other *Daily Mail* prizes included £1,000 in 1909 for the First Circular Mile in an all-British aeroplane; £10,000 for the London to Manchester Air Race in 1910; another £10,000 in 1912 for the First Circuit of Britain (popularly known as the 'Round Britain' race); a surprisingly small prize of £250, and a trophy valued at 100 guineas, for the First Aerial Derby in 1912.

Between 1909 and 1914 there were numerous other competitions, open and closed, for speed, endurance and altitude, nearly all of which should have gained serious acceptance for the aeroplane, and to a lesser degree, the seaplane, by the public.

Aviation become a spectator sport. In the summers between 1910 and 1914 many thousands of people went to shows, exhibitions, races and meetings. Unlike the almost exclusively masculine sports of cricket, professional football and horse racing, flying attracted the whole family. The acrid smell of burnt castor oil became as familiar as the sound of bat against ball or the thump of a kicked football.

For what were then expensive fees—for the big events as high as 2/- or 2/6d 'not admitting to grandstand, half price for children'—hitherto unknown thrills and the very real prospect of crashes were on offer every weekend during those five pre-war summers. There were exciting races and breathtaking aerobatics. The more spectacular pilots were as famous as the film stars of later years. The names rivalled those of the best known football and cricket heroes: Claude Grahame-White, Harry Hawker, the Hon. C. S. Rolls, S. F. Cody, Louis Paulhan, Hubert Latham, Adolphe Pégoud—whose loops and 'upside-down flying' made him the first of the 'stunt' pilots— and Frank Gooden.

This competitive striving for better results inevitably made flying even more dangerous. Thirty-two people were killed in various parts of the world in 1910. They included the first British pilot to lose his life, C. S. Rolls. He held Pilot's Licence No. 2, was a partner with F. H. Royce in the Rolls-Royce Company, a former racing driver and the first aviator to make a double crossing of the English Channel without landing. Some five weeks after that he was killed in a crash at Bournemouth. Rolls's death meant not only the loss of someone who belonged to a now vanished class, that of the wealthy, aristocratic sportsman who was admired by all levels of society; it was also a severe setback to the acceptance of the aeroplane by the public. His Blériot/Wright biplane crashed because of a structural fault in the tailplane and several thousand spectators saw the accident.

No less serious was the death of S. F. Cody who was killed in August, 1913, while flight-testing his biplane. A self-taught designer and pilot, he produced and flew several notable aeroplanes. His first became British Army Aeroplane No. 1. He had been associated with aviation since the beginning of the century when he designed and patented a box-kite glider, which was later used by the British Army. He also made public flights with man-carrying gliders. As natural a showman as he was a pilot, Cody always made sure that his name was at the top of the publicity list. An American who became a British citizen, he was immensely popular. By any standards his death was a major loss to aviation. To the public it was like the removal of the last plank of safety.

It is another paradox that the greater the public interest in displays, races and aerobatics, the less seriously was the aeroplane taken. It remained no more than a curiosity until the First World War, now only a year away. And this in spite of a sustained campaign by some politicians, newspapers and aviators to arouse public concern. In 1912 Claude Grahame-White ran a 'Wake Up England!' campaign on his 'flying circus' tour at the peak of the holiday season.

The Conservative Member of Parliament, William Joynson-Hicks (later Lord Brentford), did his best to warn an indifferent public of the danger of a weak air service and of 'the Zeppelin menace'. He was a persistent critic of the Secretary for War, Colonel J. E. B. Seeley, and of Winston Churchill, First Lord of the Admiralty. To the Secretary for War in particular he asked pointed questions about the true state and strength of the Royal Flying Corps. He disputed answers and rightly suspected that the strengths included aircraft which could not conceivably be described as operational.

In the House of Lords Lord Montagu of Beaulieu was a scarcely less persistent critic, and he and Joynson-Hicks had powerful support in the popular press. Most people, however, looked on them as scaremongers who were spoiling whatever case they might have by exaggeration, sensationalism and some distortion of facts.

Typical of the public's indifference and its unwillingness to take the aeroplane seriously was the failure of an appeal by the resoundingly-named Aerial League of the British Empire for £500,000 or, more popularly, 'a million shillings', to buy aeroplanes for the Royal Flying Corps. As someone said of it, the response was 'below expectations'.

Most people thought that more than enough money was being spent on Service aviation. In the 1913–1914 Army

Estimates £50,000 was allocated for the Royal Flying Corps and the Navy Estimates had a figure of £350,000.

The popular newspapers, reflecting their readers' indifference to foreign news, published only the most dramatic, sensational or trivial information, so that there was little general interest in international progress. Even at home emphasis was on eye-catching feats, like that of the first man to fly at more than 100 miles per hour—the Frenchman, Jules Védrines, in 1912. Another great aviation pioneer and dedicated financial supporter, Frank McClean, became better known for an illegal (but well-intentioned) flight under the Thames bridges than for his generous and more serious efforts.

Newspapers with an educated and restricted readership gave a more complete coverage to international and domestic aviation, as did magazines such as *The Aeroplane*—edited by the influential Charles Grey—*Flight* (now *Flight International*) and *The Aero*, but they had a mostly specialist readership.

Progress at home and overseas did not convince the Government, the Treasury or most admirals and generals that the aeroplane was the new offensive arm. But a popular, and sometimes alarmist, press campaign drew to it a few members of both Houses of Parliament. Some sincerely believed in the future of military and civil aviation. To others it was used as a convenient opposition tactic. A few had vested commercial interests. Some, like Winston Churchill, credited the aeroplane with a potential that was then beyond it.

But Churchill's vision and belief were decisive for naval aviation. Before 1914 the War Office had planned that the active service rôle of the Royal Flying Corps would be the passive one of reconnaissance. Ever since he had become First Lord in 1912 Churchill had been determined that the Naval Wing should have an offensive rôle as well. After the formation of the Royal Flying Corps he plotted and intrigued and used all his considerable influence to create an independent naval air service. He had the unanimous support of his admirals and other senior officers. Most of them derided aeroplanes and seaplanes; but if naval officers were to fly them, then they must be controlled by the Navy.

The Admiralty signalled its non-co-operation from the very beginning. With an arrogance and impudence that startled everyone, the Royal Navy ran its Wing as if a combined air force had never even been discussed. Its hostility was not

merely the consequence of its fiercely jealous pride and determination to be independent, which were real enough; the
objectives of the two wings were incompatible. Neither could do
the other's reconnaissance, and with the appointment of Winston Churchill as First Lord the philosophy was different too.
He was totally unsympathetic to any policy which put the
offensive in second place.

Although the Central Flying School at Upavon had been set
up for both Wings, in 1912 the Navy opened its own school at
Eastchurch, on the Isle of Sheppey, under Commander Samson. The pioneer pilots were inspired by Churchill who took
flying lessons there himself. In the early days he knew personally all the men who were to help him to create a truly independent Naval Air Service. They shared his views on the superiority of the aeroplane over the airship.

Dirigibles, in fact, had no place in Churchill's plans. He was
contemptuous of the ineffective non-rigid airships, *Nulli Secun-
dus*, *Beta*, and *Gamma*. They had preceded the construction of the
first British rigid airship, the singularly ill-named and ill-fated
Mayfly, which was destroyed on the ground before she made her
trial flight.

Churchill was to leave the Admiralty in 1915; had he remained he would have stopped construction of all naval operational airships. In *The World Crisis 1911–1914* he wrote that the
decision to build them after his departure meant that 'forty
millions of money were squandered . . . in building British
Zeppelins, not one of which on any occasion ever rendered any
effective fighting service.'

Throughout the summer of 1914 Churchill was expectantly
and enjoyably alert. To most other people, including members
of the Government, war was still unthinkable. Instead, the
imminence of civil war in Ireland was the major preoccupation;
but not to Churchill.

By definition, a Liberal administration was not a militarist
one. Churchill was a maverick war lord in a pacifically-
convinced, although not a pacifist, Government, which had the
support of three general elections. He alone in the Asquith
cabinet saw the aeroplane as a decisive weapon of the future,
and one that was, as he believed, immediately available for the
war which he thought to be inevitable. Naval air stations had
already been established round the coast. Almost all of them
were under strength; some had only a token strength. But the

concentration of what strength there was had a different objective from that of being the first line of aerial defence.

Describing the events of 4 August, 1914, in his *War Memoirs*, David Lloyd George wrote:

> Twenty minutes after the hour Mr Winston Churchill came in and informed us that the wires had been sent to British ships of war in every sea announcing . . . that war had been declared and that they were to act accordingly.

The Royal Naval Air Service received the same message. With the Royal Flying Corps committed to its passive rôle, the Navy flyers were to make the first strikes. To Winston Churchill the air defence of Great Britain began at the Zeppelin bases in the enemy's heartland.

The displays, meetings, races, aerial Derbys and circuses were over. The take-off became faster. Aviation was to be forced into an unrecognizable maturity. A new kind of gladiator was born. The Royal Naval Air Service became the founding father of aerial bombardment.

CHAPTER 2

The Aerial Battleship

In August, 1914, Britain gave the British Expeditionary Force an emotional send-off and waited eagerly for news of a great naval victory, while Germany waited with hysterical impatience for the destruction of England by the Zeppelin.

The first Zeppelin had left an indelible impression on the German people. LZ 1 (Luftschiff Zeppelin 1) had made her maiden flight three years before the Wright brothers achieved their first tentative lift-off. The story of the conquest of the air has no chapter to equal that of the birth and development of the Zeppelin. The birth, or rather the baptism, took place at Lake Constance, near Friedrichshafen, on 2 July, 1900, when Count von Zeppelin demonstrated the world's first practical rigid airship.

Details of that first Zeppelin, and of its successors, can be found in numerous reference books. But they are dead figures on a page which can be brought to life only when set against the contemporary aviation scene: a world of balloons, man-lifting kites, and the patient struggles to build an engine which could take the kites into the sky.

LZ 1 was a giant among pygmies. She created the basic principle of the rigid airship. Developments and modifications did not change it. Count Zeppelin had acquired the patent of an Austrian engineer, David Schwartz, and replaced the single streamlined gas-bag of his non-rigid ship with seventeen separate hydrogen-filled gas cells. These were enclosed in one large fabric-covered frame built of aluminium girders with broad transverse rings. If gas escaped from one or two of the gas-bags the ship could still remain airborne and descend safely.

LZ 1 was 420 feet long and 38 feet 6 inches in diameter. She was driven by two 15 h.p. Daimler petrol engines placed in each of her two gondolas below the keel. They drove two four-bladed propellers. The seventeen cells carried 400,000 cubic feet of hydrogen. Although her estimated speed was 28 miles per hour she achieved only 16. She had several design and construction weaknesses, not the least of which were her underpowered engines.

After her third flight Count Zeppelin's company ran short of money and LZ 1 was broken up and the engines, the floating shed on Lake Constance, the workshops and equipment were sold to pay off the creditors. The original design and plans were Count Zeppelin's only assets.

But LZ 1 was more than a curiosity of aviation history. Although six years passed before a second Zeppelin was launched, few people had forgotten her. Unlike the crude kites and gliders she looked safe and reliable from the outset. She was a true original. While the current aviators and motor cars were objects of ribaldry the Zeppelin was accepted as a ship of the skies whose future was already in the present.

The extent of this remarkable faith is reflected in the events which followed the break-up of LZ 1. In 1906 Count Zeppelin launched his second ship, LZ 2. She was wrecked in a storm while she was moored. LZ 3, which was also launched in 1906, impressed even those sternest critics who knew that the Zeppelin needed better construction and design, and greater power. In 1907 she flew for eight hours. Outside Germany there had been scepticism and disbelief about the Zeppelin and some of the claims made for it. But this new endurance record could not be ignored and it gave the Zeppelin an international reputation. The Count received a government grant for research and development. No less important, and certainly more significant, the Army ordered an airship—on condition that it made a round-trip, 24-hour flight of some 430 miles.

To meet this order Count Zeppelin designed and built LZ 4, which was completed in 1908. She was 450 feet long, had a capacity of 530,000 cubic feet and was driven by two 105 h.p. engines. But the Count's hopes ended in disaster. Engine failure caused her to make a forced landing after eleven hours in the air. The engine was repaired but there were further troubles and she landed at Echterdingen, near Stuttgart, where a violent storm tore her from her moorings. She rose, drifted helplessly in the sky, burst into flames and was destroyed.

A sharp impression of what the Zeppelin meant to the German people was captured by Britain's Chancellor of the Exchequer, David Lloyd George, who arrived just after the accident. In his *War Memoirs* he wrote:

> Of course we were deeply disappointed, but disappoint-
> ment was a totally inadequate word for the grief and
> dismay which swept over the massed Germans who wit-
> nessed the catastrophe. There was no loss of life to account
> for it. Hopes and ambitions far wider than those concerned
> with a scientific and mechanical success appeared to have
> shared the wreck of the dirigible. Then the crowd swung
> into the chanting of *Deutschland über Alles*, with a frantic
> fervour of patriotism. What spearpoint of Imperial adv-
> ance did the airship portend?

Four airships built in eight years, two of them wrecked, was scarcely a testimonial for success. But the Zeppelin was a success. Losses were dismissed as misfortunes. It was a living, flying reality, seen by thousands of people. On her flight for Army acceptance LZ 4 had carried about a dozen very important passengers. Before she made her second and fatal forced landing she had flown about 340 miles.

To the German people the Zeppelin was one of the wonders of the world. Despite the Wrights' achievement, the aeroplane went nowhere and accomplished nothing that was realistic. The Zeppelin travelled comparatively long distances. It could carry passengers. None of the failures had diminished the principle, the design and the engineering.

As it moved slowly and apparently effortlessly high in a cloudless sky, the Zeppelin had a dramatic beauty. It did not look like something to be feared or welcomed as a vehicle of death and destruction, the flagship of a new strategic application. Yet it became the symbol of the aggressive patriotism, the desire for world leadership, which had so impressed Lloyd George.

The public's attitude is exemplified by its response to an appeal for money after the loss of LZ 4. The campaign was run by Dr Hugo Eckener, an economist and sociologist, who was also a newspaper editor. He was to become Count Zeppelin's partner, collaborator and successor, and one of the greatest names in airship history.

The response to the appeal was astonishing—six hundred million marks (then about £300,000) was contributed. Comparison with the failure of the appeal by the Aerial League of the British Empire is not merely inescapable, but sums up a fundamental difference in national attitudes.

After the appeal Count Zeppelin formed four companies: one to manufacture airships; a second to manufacture engines; a third to manufacture equipment; and a fourth, DELAG (*Deutsche Luftschiffahrts-Aktien-Gesellschaft*) became the first commercial air line.

There were successes, failures and setbacks. The German army bought LZ 3 and LZ 5. In 1909 LZ 5 made a record flight of more than 600 miles in just under eight hours. Germany was sure that in the event of war the Zeppelin would prove a devastating new weapon. If there was no war then it would lead the way to a new kind of international travel.

Progress justified the high hopes and the faith. Zeppelins flew over the sea and across the frontiers to Austria and Switzerland. LZ 10—the *Schwaben*—built in 1911 and commanded by Dr Eckener, made 218 flights and carried a total of some 1,500 passengers before she was destroyed by fire in 1912. *Viktoria Luise, Hansa,* and *Sachsen* were added to the DELAG fleet. By July, 1914, Zeppelins had made some 1,500 sorties and flown more than 107,000 miles. Over 10,000 passengers were safely carried. They travelled in comfort, with wicker chairs, a viewing gondola, cold buffet and wines.

These widely-publicized flights had long had a more serious object than pleasure-cruising or promoting the Zeppelin's commercial prospects. Count Zeppelin himself had always intended that his airships should eventually be designed and built for use in war. He was the first man, although certainly not the last, who believed that aerial bombardment by itself could bring victory.

If the Army did not share his belief in the supremacy of the airship, it supported him by its use of Zeppelins for scouting and reconnaissance. But a small and subsequently influential group in the Imperial Navy had early dreams of conquest by aerial bombardment.

When he began to sell his airships to the Army and then to the Navy Count Zeppelin acquired customers who became ever more demanding: the principal demand was for larger airships for long-range reconnaissance and the bombing of enemy military territory. The cosy, enclosed world of the manufacturing company was invaded by naval architects and constructors, engineers, tactical advisers and the inevitable civil servants. Fundamental principles of design and construction were unchanged, but the customers' requirements influenced the application of those principles.

Experience had taught Count Zeppelin to make haste slowly. But 1912, when the Imperial Navy ordered its first Zeppelin, was no year for leisurely progress. Germany believed that she was threatened, first by the Franco-Russian Alliance of 1893–4 –5, then by the Entente Cordiale between Britain and France in 1904; lastly by the Anglo-Russian Treaty of 1907. On the other hand, Britain, France and Russia believed they were threatened by Germany's growing military power and her expansionist ambitions. Germany herself was still suffering from the humiliating defeat in the Franco-Prussian War of 1870–1871.

If she had to fight again her Zeppelins could strike early and decisively. That, at any rate, was an opinion which gained an immovable foot in the door of the argument about the strategic and tactical use of the Zeppelin. Advocates of its suitability as a war-winning weapon believed that the Naval Airship Division, which was formed in 1912, should be the vanguard of a great offensive.

Another famous name in airship history, who was to be the Naval Airship Division's operational commander until 1916 and, as Leader of Airships, still responsible for it almost until the end of the war, was *Korvettenkapitän* (later *Fregattenkapitän*) Peter Strasser. His bold, aggressive personality is inseparable from the Zeppelin's part in the aerial bombardment of England. His place in that history was the result of two terrible disasters. Without them, and without him, the aerial bombardment would have taken a different course.

The first disaster began with the Imperial Navy's first Zeppelin, designated as its own L 1. She was 518 feet 2 inches long, had a diameter of 48 feet 6 inches, and a capacity of 793,600 cubic feet of hydrogen. She had three 495 h.p. engines, four propellers, and a speed of approximately 47 miles per hour.

Her maiden flight in October, 1912 was a triumphant success. She carried twenty passengers and Count Zeppelin himself commanded her. She flew some 900 miles on a cruise which lasted more than 30 hours, six of which at an altitude of 5,000 feet. This impressive performance won increased support in the Imperial Navy for the Zeppelin and convinced a previously sceptical Minister of the Navy, Grand Admiral von Tirpitz.

An overjoyed German public was also convinced that L 1 would be the forerunner of an armada of the air. Tirpitz did not build an armada but he did persuade the German Emperor, Kaiser Wilhelm II, to agree to a five-year building programme of ten Zeppelins.

The first ship in that programme, and the Navy's second, L 2, was ordered in 1913. Although similar to her sister, she had several important differences which her naval architect virtually imposed on the Zeppelin company. Among them was the requirement that she must be large enough to carry bombs to England.

With a gas volume of 953,000 cubic feet and four 165 h.p. Maybach engines in two gondolas, she was the largest pre-war Zeppelin. The increasing size demanded by the Navy called for a permanent base. A site was acquired at Nordholz, near Cuxhaven, on the River Elbe. Its plans included the construction of double revolving sheds from which a Zeppelin could be launched whatever the direction of the wind. These would be in addition to the fixed sheds. The preparation and completion of the base was a long-term project anyway, but in fact it was not ready until the beginning of 1915. In the meantime, the Navy rented the DELAG hangar at Fuhlsbüttel, near Hamburg.

It was from there on the clear sunny morning of 9 September that L 1 took off to scout for the Navy. By mid-afternoon she received a wireless warning of bad weather. Her captain, Carl-Ernst Hanne, turned back, but he was too late. L 1 was trapped in a violent storm and within minutes she crashed into the sea. Only the midships section stayed afloat with four crew members clinging to it. They and two others were the only survivors.

It was the first fatal accident to a Zeppelin. Among the dead was the commander of the Naval Airship Division, *Korvettenkapitän* Friedrich Metzing. His replacement was *Korvettenkapitän* Peter Strasser.

On that same day L 2 made her first flight at Friedrichshafen. Eleven days later she arrived at Johannisthal, near Berlin, for acceptance trials. On 17 October she took off with twenty-eight people on board, including a naval crew of fourteen. The other passengers represented the best brains, skill and experience that were left after the loss of L 1. Among them was the designer, Felix Pietzker.

Not long after she had taken off the forward engine gondola caught fire and L 2 exploded. A mass of flames from end to end, she crashed to the ground. There were no ultimate survivors; three who were found alive died from burns.

Recriminations and accusations followed. Dr Eckener attacked the Admirality for having allowed Pietzker to impose unwelcome, and perhaps unwanted, ideas on the Zeppelin Company. Old Count Zeppelin also blamed the dead Pietzker. Tragedy, humiliation and jealousy brought bitter personal clashes.

The wider repercussions of this double disaster were more serious. A later inquiry confirmed that faulty design had been the principal cause of the loss of L 2. The embittered, disillusioned von Zeppelin ceased to play an effective part in policymaking or design. The Naval Airship Division was left without a single airship and only a few trained personnel. (Peter Strasser was still learning how to fly and handle a dirigible.) The five-year, ten-ship programme was halted and was in danger of being abandoned altogether, along with the Naval Airship Division itself.

As soon as he heard of the L 2 disaster Strasser left his training course to try and sustain the morale of those men who were left. Grief and distress, fear and uncertainty, were ruthlessly suppressed by Strasser's dominating will and by his immediate plans for a future in which at that moment perhaps only he believed. Less than a week later three crews were in training.

Although he was a senior naval officer, he was also a junior among his own seniors. However, in a Service where rank and protocol were paramount, Strasser managed to impose his will on the top layer of the hierarchy. The Naval Airship Division was no more than a Commander's post but he pushed his ideas—formally and through the rank structure—to the top layer. He may have saved the Division from extinction; he certainly saved it from permanent relegation as a subordinate handmaiden of the surface fleet.

As a result of his leadership the Naval Airship Division was transformed. The old pleasure cruisers *Sachsen* and *Viktoria Luise* were acquired for training. Dr Eckener and *Kapitan* Ernst A. Lehmann were borrowed from DELAG to carry out the training and put it to practical use: no one in the Division could then fly an airship, let alone command one. Designs for more airships were prepared. Men and money became freely available. The thread of faith which had been sewn in 1900 had been woven into a permanent fabric.

The Naval Airship Division might have been nicknamed 'Strasser's Own'. A harsh disciplinarian, he was hero-worshipped by his men. Those who survived his rigorous standards reached the apex of efficiency. Most of his captains became fearless leaders whose resolution and courage were to be tested to extreme limits.

In less than a month after the war began L 4 was added to his fleet. Meanwhile, he watched with morbid pleasure the misuse of the Army airships. The mutual rivalry and jealousy intensified the overriding ambition to be the first to bomb England.

The Army had not relied on the Zeppelin Company for its early airships. Instead, it had commissioned the Schütte-Lanz organization, which, with Army support, had set up in business in 1909. Its first ship, SL 1, made her maiden flight in 1911 and was bought by the Army, which also bought SL 2 in February, 1914. SL 3 was to be acquired by the Navy in 1915.

Schütte-Lanz airships had a plywood framework for the envelope in preference to the Zeppelin's use of aluminium. They were first-rate ships, and some of their features were incorporated into Zeppelins after the beginning of the war when Schütte-Lanz was taken over by the Government.

Although the Imperial Navy bought SLs, Strasser disliked the plywood construction. In any event they were never intended to be the equal of the Zeppelin as a long-range raider. And to the German public the *only* airship was the Zeppelin. But one SL was to make history during the aerial bombardment of England.

The Army airships had the dubious honour of being the first to go into battle at the beginning of the war. Because Schütte-Lanz did not have the resources to meet its demands, the Army turned to its first supplier. At the outbreak of war it had seven operational Zeppelins. Three were on the Eastern Front; four— Z 6, Z 7, Z 8 and Z 9—were on the Western Front, where they took part in the bombing of Antwerp and acted as low-level infantry support. The loss of three of those four Zeppelins illustrates the tactical misuse of the Army dirigibles.

Two days after the war began Z 6 made an infantry-support

attack on a fort at Liège. Bad weather, her bomb load and the need to fly low over the target took her close to the defending guns. She was hit and crashed on her way back to Germany. Z 7 and Z 8 were both put out of action by ground defence fire on the same day. On the Eastern Front a Zeppelin came down behind the Russian lines, another victim of ground defence fire.

Temporarily the Army Zeppelins were no longer an effective force and Strasser saw a chance to become supreme commander of a combined Navy and Army strike unit. Not surprisingly the proposal was rejected, but the weakness of the Army airship service ensured that he and his Naval Airship Division would win the race to bomb England.

But the way ahead was not easy. Strasser needed more Zeppelins; there were conflicting ideas about their strategic rôle and tactical use; there was the seemingly inflexible decision by the Kaiser that England must not be bombed. Strasser was sure that the Emperor's instransigence would soon disappear under pressure from the Naval High Command, which was emerging from a long subservience to him, and the fear that Germany would be bombed by enemy aeroplanes.

The war was more than five months old before Strasser and his crews could attack and, as they believed, destroy England by aerial bombardment. Meanwhile, they were restless and fretful but not, as boastful British propaganda suggested, afraid to cross the North Sea. They were impatient to prove that the Zeppelin was a master weapon and the future third arm.

Apart from the inescapable natural hazards, there was no reason for apprehension. There would never be a better opportunity. No British aeroplane or seaplane could climb fast enough to reach a Zeppelin flying at 10,000 feet or more. The fastest attacking aeroplane took about 45 minutes to reach that altitude, by which time the airship would have escaped or flown to another target. On the ground, weapons masquerading as anti-aircraft guns could not effectively reach that height either.

The German people were no less impatient. Before the war newspapers, magazines and books extolled the Zeppelin as a super destroyer. It was described in melodramatic detail, 'huge cigar-shaped engine of death'. There was a lurid forecast of 'panic-stricken civilians fleeing from their homes'. Readers were invited to 'picture the havoc a dozen such vultures could create attacking a city like London'.

In Britain there were mixed feelings about the Zeppelin.

Some self-styled experts pointed to previous accidents and the airships' fatal vulnerability to natural hazards: the passage across the North Sea, with its unpredictable weather, could bring disaster. There were those other experts, the scaremongers, who believed that the Zeppelins' impressive safety record had been ignored in the concentration on accidents. Some students of war were convinced that Germany must strike from the air while Britain's defences and counterattack were weak.

The Zeppelin certainly acquired a macabre reputation, but, as always in the face of threats to their national security, the British people generally were phlegmatic about the warnings. There was a kind of morbid enjoyment in the descriptions of the 'menace', although most people did not believe in it because they did not believe in the possibility of war.

There were many unconfirmed pre-war rumours of Zeppelins, 'unseen monsters of the dark', flying high over Britain's night sky: they had been over London; crossed the east and north-east coasts; been identified in the English Channel; 'flashing signal lights' had been seen, sometimes in the most unlikely places. Newspaper and magazine speculation carried ominous warnings of the Zeppelins' 'total supremacy'. Vivid 'artists' impressions' fed a rumour-hungry appetite.

One rumour at least had some substance. It came from the naval dockyard at Sheerness. There were reliable reports that a Zeppelin had been there on the night of 13 October, 1912. It was believed to have been L 1, which was carrying out endurance tests. The rumour was so persistent that Count Zeppelin himself publicly denied that she had crossed the English coast.

It is not surprising that these rumours, and that of the Sheerness intruder in particular, were believed. A Zeppelin captain cruising over the North Sea might find it hard to resist the temptation to sneak into English airspace. Moreover, as events were to prove, even the most experienced captains could make navigation errors.

Winston Churchill emphatically rejected any idea of the Zeppelins' invincibility. In *The World Crisis 1911–1914* he wrote:

> I rated the Zeppelin much lower as a weapon of war than almost any one else. I believed that this enormous bladder of combustible and explosive gas would prove to be easily destructible. I was sure the fighting aeroplane, rising lightly laden from its own base, armed with incendiary

bullets, would harry, rout and burn these gaseous monsters. I had proclaimed this opinion in the House of Commons in 1913.

It was not his fault that this dogmatic opinion found a place
in the long record of inaccurate military forecasts. He was to
modify it when he had to defend Britain against 'this enormous
bladder'.

CHAPTER 3

First Strike

The war was only a month old when Lord Kitchener, Secretary of War, asked the Admiralty to take over Britain's air defence, but it was in no better state than the Army for the job.

Two days later, Major-General Heath, Commander of the South Midlands Division, returned from a War Office conference to tell a meeting of civilians at Cromer that London was 'bristling with guns for defence against the Zeppelins'.

There were guns in London. No one knew how many, but it was certain that none of them was an authentic anti-aircraft weapon. Instead, there were 1-pounder pom-poms—relics of the South African War—which had been modified for high-angle firing and had an effective range of perhaps 3,000 feet; 3-in, 20-cwt, high-angle guns which fired a 12½-pound shrapnel shell; 3-pounder and 6-pounder quick-firing Hotchkiss; Vickers 3-pounders; and the veteran, if not ancient, coastal guns.

These were Churchill's 'aerial guns' when the Admiralty took charge on 5 September. Some of them belonged to the Navy, some to the Army. None could hit a Zeppelin at 10,000 feet.

The Royal Naval Air Service had an assortment of aircraft which included B.E. 2s, B.E. 8s, Sopwiths, Avro 504s, Bristol T.B. 8s, Short seaplanes, a Vickers Gun Bus, a few Blériots and Henry Farmans. Even those which were operational had neither the speed, altitude nor fire power with which to attack a Zeppelin at its operational height.

Despite the poverty of their resources the First Lord and his advisers laid the foundations of the defence against the Zeppelin, whose threat Churchill now took more seriously. 'No one', he wrote in one of his Minutes, 'can doubt that aerial attack upon England must be a feature of the near future'.

On the day after assuming responsibility for the aerial defence of England, he issued a comprehensive plan for thwarting the attack. Zeppelins must be attacked not only in their bases but also by aeroplanes over the French and Belgian coasts: 'We should maintain an aerial control over the area approximately 100 miles radius from Dunkirk.' Armoured cars were to defend the Royal Naval Air Service base at Dunkirk itself and its perimeter against 'small parties of Uhlans [which] have made their way freely about the country'.

For the defence of the mainland he demanded an aerial strike force 'at some convenient point within a range of a line drawn from Dover to London, and local defence flights at Eastchurch and Calshot'. In addition, the Zeppelins must be attacked 'not only with shells from guns, but with incendiary bullets or grenades from aeroplanes'.

Any Zeppelins which did avoid the patrolling aeroplanes or ground defences would be met by the last line of defence, aircraft from Hendon. Communication with Hendon and the other stations was essential to avoid confusion. 'It is', Churchill wrote in one of his numerous Minutes, 'indispensable that airmen from the Hendon flight should be able to fly by night, and their machines must be fitted with the necessary lights and instruments.'

New aerodromes were planned. Landing grounds were to be laid out in London parks. Searchlights were to be used in conjunction with the aerial guns. 'Propose me without delay', he requested, 'the quickest means of meeting this need.' In a phrase which was to become a hallmark of his leadership twenty-six years later he asked for a return 'on one sheet of paper showing all anti-aircraft guns, regular or improvised, available afloat and ashore at the present time; and what deliveries may be expected in the next two months. Let me have any suggestions for increasing their number.'

The Minutes still read as if they were written by someone with all the resources to carry out a grand design. Churchill knew, however, that he had only a ramshackle assortment of guns and too few aircraft, even if all of them had been operational. But his inspiration in 1914 drove people to achieve what they believed to be beyond their capacities and so ensured that the possible parts of an impossible plan were carried out.

We shall see how much of his grand design was realized either immediately or later, how much was altered, and how much was never carried out at all. Some of it was in operation within the month. The Anti-Aircraft Corps of the Royal Naval Volunteer Reserve—composed almost entirely of part-time civilians enrolled as Special Constables—manned most of the guns and shared observation duties with the police. Not one of them could know how difficult it would be to see a Zeppelin at night. If any policemen within a 60-mile radius of London *did* spot one they had orders to telephone the warning 'Anti-Aircraft London' to the Admiralty Control room.

The emergency grounds were prepared in Battersea Park and Regent's Park. Street lamps throughout the country were supposed to be dimmed, painted black on their tops and sides so that only a small circle of light was projected on streets and pavements. It was done with varying degrees of efficiency. In some areas, especially those near London and on the East Coast, it was so effective that the illuminated space was no more than a few yards in diameter. Elsewhere, the paint was carelessly applied and a lay-out of streets could be picked out from the sky.

Domestic and industrial lighting caused more serious problems. It was difficult to hide the illuminations in many night-shift munitions factories, and impossible to do so where there were blast furnaces and the like. Decisions about restrictions in the provinces were left to local authorities, with the inevitable result that some places gave up a dazzling glare while others showed only flickers of light. Citizens were ordered by Special Constables to close their (often ill-fitting) curtains so that no particle of light could be seen. Some people hurried to drapers' shops to buy thicker or more appropriate curtains. Many 'good lines' quickly disappeared, to be brought out again with a heavy price increase because of 'shortage due to unexpected war time demands'. The word 'profiteer' resumed its place in life.

Much of the vigilance weakened as the autumn passed without a raid. The high tension of threatened attacks could not be sustained. Almost everywhere the lights became brighter.

To Winston Churchill home defence, although essential, was the passive part of his design. He demanded an early offensive.

He was ably assisted and, when necessary, subtly restrained by officers such as Captain Murray Sueter (Director of the Air Department) and Commander Samson (commanding the Royal Naval Air Service forward base at Antwerp).

Despite credit claimed by others, especially by Murray Sueter, it was Churchill who led the way. No one could match the unique inspiration which was to hold the nation twenty-six years later. Of all the countless words written about him, none are more appropriate to 1914 than those by the distinguished editor and journalist, A. G. Gardner:

> He sees himself moving through the smoke of battle . . . his legions looking to him for victory and not looking in vain.

In 1914 his legions were the Royal Navy and in particular the Royal Naval Air Service. In audacity, resolution and courage, at any rate, it did not fail him.

He and the RNAS were made for each other. The flying machine could produce immediate and spectacular results. It did not need complex logistics or long lines of communication. It could take the fight to the enemy's bases more swiftly than ever before. To the man who had seen active service in the Sudan, in Cuba, on the North-West Frontier of India, in Egypt and in the South African war, the aeroplane was the newest toy in the war game.

However, the number of aeroplanes available for the defence of Britain was restricted because the Royal Flying Corps had sent four of its five squadrons to France with the British Expeditionary Force. The remaining squadron was ordered to undertake coastal patrol duties.

Understandably there were vigorous protests from the Director-General of Military Aircraft, Brigadier-General Sir David Henderson, who claimed that the squadron was indispensable for training. A face-saving compromise was found and the RFC agreed to help 'when it had more aeroplanes'. This meant that, for the time being, there would be no help at all.

Outside London the Army was responsible for anti-aircraft defence, but this was no more than a token. The capital was the only place with a concentration of weapons. Some naval ports and establishments and other vital points had a few guns. But none of them anywhere were of the slightest use.

The additional defence responsibilities did not weaken

Churchill's determination to destroy Zeppelins in their strong-holds. Four raids were made before the year was out. In strictly military terms they were a failure. Only one Zeppelin was destroyed, but the total effect, and that of one raid in particular, gives them a special significance.

The first attempt – made on 23 September by two Sopwith Tabloid aeroplanes of the RNAS at Antwerp—consisted of two separate raids on Cologne and Düsseldorf. It was notably only for the skill and gallantry of the pilots who took part in it. They were handicapped by bad weather, casual planning and insufficient target identification information.

The second raid on 22/23 October was also carried out by Sopwith Tabloids from Antwerp. The new Army Zeppelin Z IX was destroyed in her Düsseldorf shed. The attack was almost fatal to the Army's airship strength. Four had already been lost on the Western Front and a fifth in Russia. Even more serious than the loss itself was the message for the future. Z IX had been in an apparently impregnable base.

With twenty-five trained flight crews, new Zeppelins under construction and others being designed, Strasser knew that the Naval Airship Division was vulnerable too. It was imperative that the Zeppelins begin their campaign against England before the Royal Naval Air Service struck again and reduced the Naval Airship Division's efforts to small, sporadic sorties which would annoy but not destroy. Apart from the destruction of Z IX the raids had achieved nothing. Nevertheless, enemy aircraft had penetrated the home defences and dropped bombs which had put civilians in danger. This must surely bring an immediate demand for reprisals and a reversal of the Emperor's policy. But he was still intransigent.

Even the astute Strasser did not foresee that the British would take the boldest and most daring of the courses open to them, a raid on Friedrichshafen itself.

Friedrichshafen—over 400 miles from England—was a more highly prized target than any operational base. It was not only the Zeppelins' birthplace but was also the strategic centre for research, design, construction and test flying.

The raid itself was an epic of wartime aviation. Its daring concept and secret preparation read like a boys' adventure story. By the merest chance it lacked the conventional happy ending. Nevertheless it is part of the classic literature of First World War aviation and because of its effect on future events it needs more than a passing reference in a history of the aerial bombardment of England.

The imminent capture of the doomed city of Antwerp had prevented even the most elementary preparations for the previous raids. But for Friedrichshafen a base was established on the French aerodrome at Belfort, 125 miles from the objective and only five miles from the German frontier. Surprise, secrecy and first-hand information were essential for success and, although the raid failed, it was not the fault of anyone directly concerned with it, least of all a pugnacious character, Noel Pemberton Billing, then a temporary Flight Sub-Lieutenant in the Royal Naval Air Service. He is said to have learned to fly and to have gained his pilot's certificate in a single day. Before the war he was associated with a company engaged in the construction of flying boats and had been among the loudest-mouthed of the scaremongers.

He had an influence and authority which belied his very junior rank. He would not have discouraged a romantic guess that it was a cover for his work as a spy. In 1916 he was to resign his commission to become a Liberal Member of Parliament. In the House of Commons he was a militant protagonist of Service aviation (and of the RNAS in particular), a scourging critic who accused the Government of neglect and senior commanders of ignorance.

In the Friedrichshafen raid he undertook a daring, one-man reconnaissance, but he was at the heart of the planning from the outset. The boldness of the reconnaissance itself underlines the importance of the object—to inflict the maximum damage on, and perhaps destroy, the power-house of Zeppelin operations.

Disguised as a civilian, certain to be executed as a spy if he was captured, he crossed Lake Constance by boat from the Swiss side. When he returned he reported that two Zeppelins were under construction and gave a detailed study of the plant layout and an assessment of the ground defences.

This remarkable and heroic deed was officially unrecognized. Each of the participants in the raid received the Distinguished Service Order, but there was no award or decoration for the man who had been the pathfinder.

Four aeroplanes of a type that became an aviation classic, the Avro 504 biplane, were selected for the raid. With their mechanics they were sent in the greatest secrecy from Manchester to Belfort. They were powered by 80 h.p. Gnome rotary engines, had a maximum speed of 80 miles per hour and each carried four 20-lb explosive bombs.

In the event only three of them took part in the raid on 21 November. Nevertheless, the attack was pressed home with determination and unflinching courage against heavy anti-aircraft fire. All three aeroplanes dived to 500 feet over the objective. Eleven of the twelve bombs were released. Direct hits were made on a shed, the workshops and a nearby gasworks. Two of the Avros returned safely; the third was shot down and the pilot was captured, although he escaped later in the war.

Winston Churchill could be proud of his legions. But it was not only their bravery which made the Friedrichshafen raid a great achievement. It was also a tribute to Alliott Verdon Roe and his 504s. They were not built as bombers or for long distance flying.

Sir Walter Raleigh, in the official history, *War in the Air*, wrote:

> There have been many longer and greater raids but this flight of 250 miles into gunfire, across enemy territory, in the frail little Avro with its humble horsepower, can be compared as an achievement with the best of them.

Everyone concerned with the raid was certain that one Zeppelin had been destroyed and that the plant had been seriously damaged. But the Germans' quick rebuttal of the claims proved to be correct and the Admiralty soon learnt that the operation had been a total failure. Miraculously, a newly-completed Zeppelin had escaped with only minor damage and was soon to be in action.

All the same the attack set a pattern for further raids on Friedrichshafen. Another attempt, supported with the same meticulous planning, with a larger force of aeroplanes and heavier bombs would surely not suffer the cruel mischance of another near miss. It could still have a decisive effect on a Zeppelin campaign against England.

But there were no more raids. The Germans expected them. Shocked and astounded by this daring long-range penetration, they reinforced the defences and strengthened the permanent garrison. A particular reason for not attacking Friedrichshafen again was a protest by the neutral Swiss Government that at least one of the Avros had flown over its territory. Indirectly, the British Government acknowledged the 'error' but would not risk another violation and its repercussions.

If one of the war's most glittering prizes had been missed, there was a consolation prize nearer home: the newly-constructed, revolving shed at Nordholz. Its destruction before it could house a Zeppelin, and before the Kaiser cancelled his embargo, would destroy a base vital for attacks on England.

The raid on Nordholz and Cuxhaven was different in conception and philosophy from that on Friedrichshafen. The objects were to destroy the shed and make a reconnaissance of German warships in the Schillig Roads at Wilhelmshaven. In theory the raid had the advantage of powerful seaborne support. It was the first-ever combined sea and air offensive. In practice it lacked single-mindedness. The objectives were not explicit because the object was not exclusive. The attack was set for 25 December.

Two light cruisers and eight destroyers escorted the seaplane carriers, *Riviera*, *Engadine*, and *Empress*. These converted cross-Channel packets each had a hangar aft for three Short seaplanes, which were manned by a pilot and observer, carried two 20-lb bombs and were armed with a machine gun. Ten submarines were to patrol off the German coast, and the Grand Fleet waited optimistically for the Imperial Navy to put to sea.

The security of the raid was broken during the night passage to the Heligoland Bight, when the carriers were seen by U-boats. After hours of confused action the Royal Navy task force withdrew soon after midday. There were subsequent claims and counterclaims, but the operation was a fiasco. Seven of the nine seaplanes took off. Partly because of a sudden fog they failed even to see the shed, although they did cause some alarm and confusion as they flew over the Schillig Roads.

Only two of the seaplanes were able to return to their floating aerodromes. Three of their crews were rescued by the submarine E II, which submerged to escape bombs from the Zeppelin L 5. A fourth crew was saved by a destroyer, and the fifth was taken on board a Dutch trawler and temporarily interned. The Zeppelin L 6 was slightly damaged by shell fire from one of the cruisers and small arms fire from *Empress*.

This was the last attempt to keep the island fortress safe from aerial bombardment. The half-truths, subtle emphasis and censored, selective news of the four raids had a welcome effect on the morale of a nation which was facing a new and bewildering experience.

Never before had there been embracing citizen participation in a war. Military conscription was still about a year away but thousands of men had, to use the contemporary phrase, 'joined up' or were in the Territorial Army or the Royal Naval Volunteer Reserve. Previously the nation's wars had been fought by professional soldiers supported, as in the South African War of 1899–1902, by enthusiastic amateurs.

Now, like an alien sea breaching a hitherto safe hinterland, there was the citizens's war. All classes were in uniform. The fatuous optimism that claimed 'it would be over by Christmas' had been destroyed by Britain's greatest public figure, Field-Marshal Viscount Kitchener of Khartoum. As Secretary for War he had told the Cabinet at its very first hostilities meeting that the conflict would last for at least three years.

The thunderbolts of war fell almost immediately. On the Western Front the British Expeditionary Force had retreated to Mons. The German advance was halted at the Battle of the Marne. The Battle of the Aisne was inconclusive. Almost impregnable trench systems—to become the graveyards of the Western Front—replaced the more familiar mobile warfare. The 'first battle of the trenches', the First Battle of Ypres, lasted a month. In his *English History 1914–1945*, A. J. P. Taylor wrote:

> It marked the end of the old British army. The B.E.F. fought the Germans to a standstill and itself out of existence. More than half of those who had crossed to France in August were now casualties; one in ten had been killed (three-quarters of them at Ypres). The old army was gone beyond recall.

There was puzzled disappointment that the Royal Navy had not lived up to expectations. Although it had not fought a major sea action since Trafalgar, 109 years earlier, there was a classless pride in it, a certainty that it was a sure shield in home waters and throughout the Seven Seas. The Army was part of Britain. The Royal Navy belonged to it. The *Manchester Guardian History of the War* summed it up:

Whatever anticipation he may have had of the war on land, it is certain that the average man expected at sea a decision both summary and swift.

The clamping censorship imposed at the beginning of the war suppressed the truth about some serious naval losses and disasters; but the events themselves could not be hidden. The early Royal Navy losses were accepted with surprised calm and were put aside when there were the kind of successes which the nation expected, like that of the Battle of the Falkland Islands on 8 December, 1914.

Nothing, however, astonished, disturbed and alarmed people more than the first strike by the Imperial Navy against the home shores, on the north-east and east coast. It raised fears of an invasion and brought the Zeppelin threat into sharper focus.

On 3 November there was an unsuccessful attempt by four German battle-cruisers and four light cruisers to shell Yarmouth, in Norfolk. But on 16 December five battle-cruisers emerged from the thick early morning mist to bombard Hartlepool, Scarborough and Whitby. Civilian casualties were estimated at 230 dead and more than 500 injured. Some contemporary figures put them even higher.

It was not only the raid itself which caused public dismay, anger and bewilderment. It was also the ease with which Admiral Hipper's squadron had avoided the British Second and Third Battle-Cruiser Squadrons, had been able to freeboot up and down the north-east coast and escape without mortal damage.

Sensational forecasts of German plans to invade Britain had competed with the Zeppelin scare for the best alarmist stories of the years before the war. The Government, however, gave very serious thought to the possibility.

Invasion was a carelessly-used word. It did not even remotely resemble the D-Day operation of 1944. A nearer, if unfortunate, comparison would be that of the Dieppe Raid in 1942. Nevertheless, the word was part of home defence vocabulary. An Invasion Inquiry had been set up in 1908 (and preparations against an invasion were not abandoned until 1917). The possibility was reviewed regularly by the Committee of Imperial Defence and received more urgent attention by the War Cabinet in the war's opening weeks.

Neither the Government nor the Service chiefs believed that

an 'occupation invasion' was either intended or possible. The military appreciation of the situation allowed for simultaneous raids, involving up to 20,000 troops. They would have naval support; and the immediate hinterland would be heavily bombed by Zeppelins in squadrons.

This precise appreciation was not accepted by everyone. Why, many thoughtful people asked, should the Germans go to all the trouble of mounting a major combined offensive and then disembark? There was a widely and seriously held conviction, especially on the East Coast, that if the Germans landed they would create a permanent bridgehead. The war could be on everyone's doorstep. The British Expeditionary Force could be isolated.

Back in August, 1914, H. G. Wells wrote a letter to *The Times* in which he called for a citizens' army, equipped to repel the invader; and he made the curious proposal that if the authorities opposed it then the citizens should shoot the authorities.

Ports, harbours, small docks, anchorages and probable (and improbable) landing areas were defended by a variety of weapons from 9.2-inch guns to rifles without ammunition. Even some of the remotest places had a token protection of barbed wire and sandbag emplacements.

Local invasion committees were formed in many parts of the country. Boats were removed from the anchorages, creeks and small harbours. Rumour fed on rumour. Innocent people—and some who were not—were denounced as spies. It was dangerous to have a surname that even resembled a German or Austrian one. An Order-in-Council prevented resident Germans or Austrians—many of whom had been born in Britain—from changing their names.

Flashing lights—allegedly signalling to the enemy at sea or to Zeppelins in the sky—were 'seen' in the North Sea and the English Channel. Zeppelin sightings were reported by someone almost every night. A vigilant lady in Sussex said that the West Blatchington windmill was being used by spies to signal to Zeppelins. An equally vigilant citizen of Essex reported that signals were being flashed from a 'tree house' at Frinton to offshore Zeppelins.

Behind the rumours, false accusations and reports from well-meaning busybodies the spy danger was real enough. Many spies were arrested and sentenced to be shot or to long terms of imprisonment. As with all espionage organizations the small fry were often as important as the bigger fish, and hundreds of raids and arrests were made among obscure people in obscure places. Secret wireless sets were discovered. The Germany spy network was checked but never stopped.

Germany never did have any serious intention of invading Britain, but her bluff kept a large reserve of troops at home. We shall see later how many were held back for the invasion threat and for anti-aircraft defence. Despite long-established and authoritative opinions, they did not seriously weaken the British Expeditionary Force. Except for those who were training or waiting to go overseas, the permanent reserve was made up of men who, for one reason or another, were not required in France. On the other hand, the aerial battle which was to be fought for Britain kept pilots, observers, mechanics and administrative staff from the heart of the war.

If Britain was not to be invaded, her island fortress was about to be violated. On 10 January, 1915, the Kaiser gave restricted approval for the aerial bombardment of England.

CHAPTER 4

The Trail Blazers

London was always to be the strategic objective in the aerial bombardment of England. All other targets were subordinate to it. If England itself was the crown, then London was the jewel inside it. Attacks on industrial centres, ports and railways would disrupt the war effort; but the real object was to weaken civilian resistance, which would collapse with the destruction of London.

Since the fall of Liège in August a decision to bomb the capital had been made without reference to the Kaiser. He heard about it beforehand and stopped it. He faced a painful dilemma. With millions of less exalted people, he had believed in an early end to the war. He had told his army that it would be home 'before the leaves turned'. Like all world statesmen he was concerned with his place in history. An embargo on the bombing of England would save him from the fearful responsibility of having been the first man to allow the deliberate bombing of civilians.

For five months he stubbornly resisted the pressures from his war lords and a bloodthirsty public which demanded the conquest of England by the vaunted Zeppelins.

He became the victim and not the controller of policy. The failure of the army to exploit the retreat from Mons, the missed opportunity to capture the Channel ports, defeat at the Battle of the Marne, and the certainty of a war of attrition crushed those expectations of early victory. Even a successful U-boat campaign against British shipping would be one of attrition. There was no possibility of defeating the Royal Navy. The still-distant threat of a blockade of Germany could become a frightening reality.

The once unthinkable prospect of the German people being the victims of indiscriminate bombing—implicit in the Düsseldorf, Cologne and Friedrichshafen attacks—became explicit after a raid on Freiburg by French aeroplanes in December. There were several dead among the civilian casualties.

That raid moved the Kaiser nearer to an inevitable decision about England. Those civilian casualties would strengthen him against any outraged neutral opinion. Moral condemnation by itself would not deter him. But accusations of 'barbarity'—especially in Belgium at the beginning of the war—had become a propaganda gift to the Allies, with imponderable effects on American neutrality and, even in 1914, the very distant but feared prospects of intervention.

A quick victory through the Zeppelins could end the war, and an all-conquering Germany could ignore the accusations. On 9 January, 1915, the Kaiser gave the qualified permission for the bombardment of England. Targets must be restricted to docks, arsenals and 'other military establishments in the lower Thames and on the English coast'. Royal palaces and monuments were also excluded from this fatuous order.

The Kaiser became the first in a long gallery of international hypocrites who claimed that 'military targets' could exclude death and destruction to civilians and their homes as well. In 1915, and in all the years since, the two were inseparable.

The commander of the Naval Airship Division, Peter Strasser, had anticipated the change of mind. On the same day that the decision was announced he submitted ambitious plans for his historic campaign. The projected targets were the North-East and East coasts and the Thames Estuary, all strictly within the Kaiser's orders.

For professional as well as patriotic reasons Strasser was anxious for immediate success. He had dreams of glory which went beyond the prestigious command of the Naval Airship Division. Opposition in the Imperial Navy to the use of Zeppelins for strategic operations had to be overcome. There was the threat of more attacks by the Royal Naval Air Service.

This was the moment to deal the first crushing blow against England. The Naval Airship Division had a seemingly powerful strength of six Zeppelins: L 3, L 4, L 5, L 6, L 7, and the most recently commissioned ship, L 8. Captains and crews were at their peak. The aeroplane raids in the Thames area between 21 December and 25 December, and especially that by the Albatross on Christmas morning, had confirmed the weakness of the outer defences.

Typical of the response to those incursions were the few shells fired at the Albatross by an ancient muzzle-loading gun at Sheerness. All the other guns were either out of range or suffered from inaccurate range-finding, inadequate location and observation. A Vickers F.B. 5 aeroplane, with a forward-sited machine gun, had climbed to 15,000 feet, but the German marauder was never threatened.

Since those December forays more guns had been brought in to defend the London approaches. Aeroplanes and seaplanes were on constant patrol, optimistically to attack any enemy raiders that could be intercepted at attainable heights. But on the eve of the Zeppelins' first attempt to bombard England, the air defences concentrated in and around London were useless.

The efficient German spy network reported every detail of these defences. Long before the war it had provided first-hand information for future Zeppelin raids. In his boastful and not always reliable book, *The Dark Invader*, Captain von Rintelen, the German naval intelligence officer and spy, claimed that he and another spy had mapped the streets in cities such as London and Liverpool. And after the war began 'Large-scale maps were printed for us on the Admiralty's own presses . . . and our immediate business was to mark on them with very large red circles so-called "vulnerable spots".'

Bad weather would surely be the only enemy on that first Zeppelin raid. It could not only prevent airships from reaching England but could also force them within range of enemy counterattacks. The best bombing period was then reckoned to be eight days before full moon until eight days after it.

The conditions, the weather and the forecast seemed to be favourable for 13 January. This historic date was a critical one too. The results of initial failure were obvious. And the eagerly-sought success could be double-edged. It could bring an antagonistic reaction from the most influential sources outside Germany. Accusations of 'barbarism' and 'Hun frightfulness' would have more substance than the bizarre and general charges made in Belgium earlier in the war. Strasser knew that there were faint hearts in his own country who worried about criticism from neutral countries and, of course, especially the United States of America.

He had no illusions about the effects of bombing. There could be no distinction between civilian and military targets. A disciple of the Prussian philosophy of total war, he had no patience with hypocritical pretence. Moreover, he did not deceive himself that it was physically possible to make such a distinction.

The entire river route from the Estuary to the tidal limit at Teddington was a genuine military target. There were batteries at Shoeburyness; naval dockyards at Sheerness and Chatham; aeroplane and seaplane bases on the Isle of Sheppey; oil storage tanks at Thameshaven; the arsenal at Woolwich; an explosives factory at Silvertown and the lifeline of Britain's seaborne trade—the docks of Tilbury, East India, Royal Victoria and Albert, King George V, West India, Surrey Commercial, London and St Katharine's.

In the context of total war it was unfortunate that thousands of civilians lived there as well. The working-class houses, cottages and tenements in the narrow streets, alleys and passages of Wapping, Shadwell, Limehouse, Poplar, Millwall, and Rotherhithe were so close they might have been knitted together.

Although they were temporarily outside the Kaiser's 'permitted areas' some of the suburbs were in potential peril too. Within the briefest flying distance of Tower Bridge, Sopwith was manufacturing aeroplanes at Kingston-upon-Thames. At Cricklewood, north of the river, Handley Page was constructing bombers. At nearby Hendon there was an operational aerodrome. And there were small engineering firms which had turned to making components for munitions.

Although Strasser knew that the Naval Airship Division could bomb the approaches to London before the Army airships were ready, his first raid was planned for the more accessible ports of Lowestoft, Great Yarmouth and Harwich. Three Zeppelins were ordered to take part in this momentous sortie: L 3 (*Kapitänleutnant* Hans Fritz), L 4 (*Kapitänleutnant* Count von Platen), and L 5 (*Kapitänleutnant* Heinrich Mathy). Strasser was unable to lead the raid, and the coveted command went to Mathy, who was his deputy.

As the shed doors opened on the morning of 13 January, at Fuhlsbüttel for L 3 and L 4, and at Nordholz for L 5, the crews who were tensed to deliver the first of the death blows against England would have remembered the current patriotic song:

Fly, Zeppelin
Help us win the war,
England shall be destroyed by fire,
Zeppelin, fly!

Mathy was to become the greatest of all the Zeppelin captains, but that first attempt ended in a humiliating anti-climax. Despite the favourable weather forecast, heavy mid-afternoon rain forced him to abandon the raid when the airships were over the sea.

Naval Airship crews had long experience of the unpredictable and often hazardous North Sea conditions; but training and scouting sorties and the Christmas Day action were no substitute for the reality of crossing the German Ocean on an operational mission. With an unreliable wireless link to the homeland and without escort vessels, those early raids were in effect journeys into the unknown.

Heavy rain was only one of those unpredictable hazards. Snow, ice, thunder, lightning, fog, gale-force winds and sub-standard temperatures affected and often defeated projected attacks. Engine and other mechanical failures could leave airships at the mercy of the elements.

The isolation of each airship exceeded even that of the submarine. Comradeship and discipline intensified the intimacy of dangers which were shared and exclusive. The discipline itself, although strict and willingly accepted by people who were all volunteers, was less rigid than that in a warship. Commissioned and non-commissioned officers were closer to one another—and not just because of the physical limitations.

But this self-contained community had its own isolations. Although all the crews were so physically close, different duties and operational stations segregated some of them into groups of comparative loneliness.

Generally a Zeppelin crew consisted of eighteen or nineteen: captain, executive officer, two warrant officers, about six petty officers and nine or ten machinists. Operational requirements could reduce the size of a ship's company, as on the second raid of the campaign, when a Zeppelin was manned by only eleven, to allow for a greater bomb load.

Command and control were in the forward gondola, where the captain, executive officer, warrant officer navigator—with his instruments and chart table—and two petty officers, in charge of rudder and elevation control, were cramped in the enclosed car and its observation windows. Two petty officer wireless operators were also in the forward gondola but separated in a small sound-proofed compartment from the roar of the four Maybach engines and other distracting noises.

The warrant officer engineer and his eight or nine machinists were situated aft in the engine gondola with easy access to the engine casing attached to the hull. Below the keel was the petty officer responsible for the maintenance and repair of gas cells and outer cover—the sailmaker. On some raids the sailmaker's skill was to make the difference between death and survival.

There were two nominal on- and off-duty watches. On many sorties crews were seldom off watch; and never, of course, during a raid or when there was the remotest chance of enemy action, or when the weather called for maximum alertness. It was seldom possible for a complete watch to sling their hammocks in the keel. Coffee, strictly-rationed cognac, and the simplest of hot food such as ham and eggs sustained the crew during the long flight.

Navigation was elementary. There was a magnetic compass, which could freeze in sub-zero temperatures. Dead reckoning was used over the sea, and physical recognition over land. But on bad-weather nights (and on many good-weather nights too) matching physical features to maps proved to be unexpectedly difficult.

Navigation errors, high winds, fog and other kinds of bad visibility could take a Zeppelin many miles off course. For the first three months of the campaign parachute flares were the only means with which to verify or establish a position. Because there were no radio direction finding stations then in service, captains could not call for a 'fix'. And when the stations were ready, in April, 1915, they were not only unreliable but were also monitored by Britain.

By definition, Zeppelin crews were brave men but there was always the suppressed dread of the holocaust which had destroyed LZ4 in 1908 and the sudden, almost mysterious, hurricane-like gale which had sent L 1 crashing helplessly into the sea in 1913. Except for a brief period during the war, parachutes were not carried in combat airships.

In 1915 armament consisted of eight or nine 9-mm Maxim machine guns. As a rule, two were carried in the control car, two in the after-engine car, two or three on the top platform, one on the tail platform, and one in each wing gondola. The top platform was literally on top of the envelope; the tail platform was astern near the apex of the tail. Both platforms were totally exposed and protected only by a light railing.

Six days after that abortive first attempt, conditions were reckoned to be suitable for a second raid. On 19 January three Navy Zeppelins took off to try to redeem that embarrassing failure. L 3 (*Kapitänleutnant* Fritz), L 4 (*Kapitänleutnant* von Platen) left from Fuhlsbüttel, and L 6 (*Kapitänleutnant* Horst von Buttlar) from Nordholz.

The River Humber on the North-East coast was the objective for L 3 and L 4. The main target, the lower Thames on the threshold of the forbidden city, was von Buttlar's prvileged objective. Peter Strasser flew with him. The commander of the Naval Airship Division intended to make regular flights to share the dangers and maintain the hubris of his élite force. Frequent trips with different captains would also give him the chance to see how they reacted to active service situations and give him an experienced understanding of their raid reports; he was to make very good use of it.

L3 and L4 each had a crew of sixteen, fuel for a 30 hour round trip from Fuhlsbüttel to the Humber, carried eight 110-lb explosive bombs and a dozen incendiaries. L 6, whose objective was at least psychologically more important than that of the other Zeppelins, carried ten explosive bombs and some twelve incendiaries. Because the flight to the Lower Thames from Nordholz and back was estimated to be three hours longer, she had fuel for 33 hours and a reduced crew of 11. Each Zeppelin was armed with three Maxim machine guns which were fitted in the gondola.

The weather was fine when the three Zeppelins left, but the struggle against the elements began even before a landfall was made. Rain, snow showers and bad visibility made England a featureless landscape. The attempts by L 3 and L 4 to make an accurate landfall emphasize the navigation hazards. Fritz, in L 3, was the first to reach the English coast. He thus had the envied distinction among his peers of commanding the first combat Zeppelin to fly over England and of dropping the first bombs.

A change of wind caused him to miss his Humber objective by some 80 miles. He made for the Norfolk coast, which he reached at about 8.30 pm. He reported by wireless that he had identified the village of Happisburgh, the Happisburgh Light, and the Winterton lighthouse; he then flew on to Great Yarmouth.

The weight of rainwater forced L 3 down to 5,000 feet, but accurate orientation was still impossible until Fritz dropped parachute flares as he made a landfall. Having missed his original target by some 80 miles, this pinpoint identification over a coast with few conspicuous physical features was a tribute to Fritz and his navigator. All the same, he had missed his target by many miles; it proved to be an ominous warning of coming events.

Fritz dropped six explosive bombs and nine incendiaries on Great Yarmouth. Two people were killed and three injured. The town itself, the harbour, and the racecourse were hit in a raid which lasted about ten minutes. The damage, estimated to be about £7,500, was severe by contemporary money standards.

L 3's return flight was hampered by even worse weather but she arrived safely at Fuhlsbüttel at 9.40 am.

Fritz's decision to avoid the Humber was a deliberate one, caused by the unexpected weather change. Von Platen, however, decided to try to stay on course but he never quite knew where he was. Eventually he, too, crossed the coast at Norfolk, over Bacton, but thought he was at the mouth of the Humber. Even when he flew as low as 800 feet it took him some time to realize that he was also about 80 miles from his objective. When he dropped the first of his explosive bombs he still believed he was in the Humber area. It fell on Snettisham village, near Hunstanton, and inland from the Wash.

Still ignorant of his position he released his seven remaining bombs over King's Lynn, where two people were killed and 13 injured. The incompetency of von Platen's expedition is confirmed by his wireless message to base, reporting that he had successfully bombed 'fortified places between the Tyne and Humber'.

Strasser met an even worse fate. L 6 never reached the mouth of the Thames. When she was over the North Sea one of her engines failed, and she was back at Nordholz nearly two and a half hours before L 3 made her landfall over the Norfolk coast.

Although the island fortress had been breached the raid was a failure. The British people had accepted this unique experience calmly and, outside East Anglia, with only a passing interest, even indifference. No significant military or industrial targets had been hit. But the first incursion by Zeppelins was enough for newspapers and some very vocal critics to repeat their warnings and try to rouse the nation from that apparent indifference.

The East Anglians, however, were not to be persuaded into hysteria or panic. After the immediate fear of imminent death had gone, they were puzzled rather than angry at the lack of retaliation. What had happened to the warplanes? This was a particularly pertinent question in Great Yarmouth, where the population did not understand why its own seaplane station, in the very eye of the bombing, had allowed L 3 to escape, or why two Zeppelins had been left unmolested to maraud over a wide area.

No one was sure how many seaplanes did go up; at the most there would have been no more than six. They had never even sighted the two airships. Much was made of the heavy rain and thick cloud which had, apparently, hampered the RNAS pilots, but poor visibility was not an acceptable excuse in Norfolk. People had actually seen a Zeppelin flying beneath the clouds. L 3 had flown over the town-centre at Great Yarmouth, had been seen there and as she made her way to the racecourse. At King's Lynn L 4 was seen as she circled twice round the town.

The Admiralty was cautious, tight-lipped even, after the raid. It did not know of the Zeppelins' navigation and location difficulties. It is supposed to have been disappointed that the London and Estuary fixed defences had not been challenged. In reality, their Lordships must have been very relieved that the poverty of their resources remained unexposed.

Next day, the German Naval Staff was almost as cautious. A restrained communiqué, dated 20 January, stated:

> On the night of January 19–20 naval airships undertook an attack on several fortified places on the English East coast. Numerous bombs were dropped successfully in misty weather and rain. Two ships were fired on, but returned undamaged.

The caution and formality were unavoidable. The Naval Staff did not then know the true results of the raid. Experience would soon show the unreliability of all bombing reports. Von Platen's claim, for example, that he had been fired on and caught in searchlight beams was a lie, almost certainly invented to cover his failure.

But the communiqué's plain words needed no embellishment for a jubilant Germany. It was enough that the Zeppelin campaign had begun, that the first bombs had been dropped. Officially-inspired propaganda stories were exaggerated and enlarged in the newspapers. They endorsed public conviction that the Zeppelin was a weapon of victory. The *Kolnische Zeitung* reflected and encouraged public opinion when it wrote, 'This is the best way to shorten the war.' There were eagerly-read reports of wide-spread panic in Great Yarmouth, of carnage and burning buildings.

The Naval High Command knew that the raid had failed. On their first operational flights across the North Sea the Zeppelins had been victims of the weather. Although he was many miles off his target, Fritz had made an accurate landfall, but von Platen had come on his by chance. Already there were excuses for these early failures: January weather was always bad; the radio direction finding stations would reduce or correct navigation and identification errors; there were certain to be unsolved problems on the first flights; the engine failure in L 6 could be put down to sheer misfortune.

If it had occurred to anyone that any of these difficulties might be major handicaps they were put aside in the fervour of the freedom to attack, restricted though that was. The fervour was still there; but six Zeppelins in all had set out to begin the aerial destruction of England. Only two had crossed the coast, and only one captain had responded positively in a crisis.

There were protests about the raid from neutral Switzerland, Holland, Norway, Sweden, Denmark and Spain. Since none of them would join the war they could be ignored, and in any event not all of the protests were sincerely inspired. Germany recognized the expediency of a public outcry, but she had influential diplomatic links in well-disposed diplomatic quarters.

Condemnation from the United States of America could not be ignored. She was committed to isolation by the Monroe Doctrine. The chances that she might ever become a belligerent on the Allies' side were extremely remote; but there was a latent fear that events could change an apparently inflexible policy. Protests about that first raid were handled with consummate skill by an astute German ambassador in Washington. Later,

when the bombing of British civilians was to have an embarra-
singly hostile reaction in America, he manipulated the United
States Government and the pro-German and commercial interests with equal skill and shrewdness.

In any event, there could be no going back. Germany was
committed to the airship, strategically, tactically and material-
ly. The first of the million-cubic-feet ships for the Navy and the
Army were already building at Friedrichshafen. Beyond that,
Strasser and others were thinking ahead to the projected 'super
Zeppelins'.

German agents in Britain and neutral sources soon showed
the captains' reports to have been inaccurate. The inspired
propaganda stories had no substance either. There had been no
panic. People caught by surprise, out of doors, had sensibly run
for cover. Almost everyone was very frightened indeed by this
first experience of being under fire, with the deafening explosions, the sound, sight and smell of burning, the night sky
brightened by leaping flames. But there were others who went
into the streets to catch a moment in history.

The indignation was loudest among politicians, newspapers,
other scaremongers and self-interested parties. In both Houses
of Parliament there were 'grave situation' comments and demands for immediate action.

Once the loud fears of the night had gone there was a less
frenzied response in East Anglia. There were, to be sure,
worries in Yarmouth about the failure of the RNAS seaplanes
which were 'just down the street'. It seemed strange, too, that
so important a place should not have been defended by anti-
aircraft guns. But to most people, if this was the long-
threatened 'Zeppelin menace', then it was a good deal less
frightening than the prospect of further seaborne attacks. They
had been fleet assaults in which big ships had taken part.

In Norfolk, on the other hand, two isolated raiders had
dropped about 23 bombs in scattered attacks, killed 4 people
and injured 16; there had, admittedly, been severe damage.
There was tragedy for the families of the dead and disturbing
emotions for everyone else. But the raid had not brought the
terrible havoc which the Germans, and some forecasters in
Britain, had promised. Although some of the damage was
heavy it did not suggest that the war would be brought to the
streets of Britain.

Now, people looked at that damage with curiosity and were

surprised that it was not more severe: there was the roof which had collapsed into an almost perfect V-shape; the bed which was suspended between a hole in its own ceiling and the ground floor; the outside wall which seemed to have decided not to fall but to shore up its sagging building.

To meet the call for better protection, and to give a spurious confidence to Eastern England, an anti-aircraft unit was cobbled together. Pom-poms, Vickers and Maxim machine guns, and searchlights on motor chassis made up the grandly-named Eastern Mobile Force, whose very limited mobility was its only asset.

Three months passed before the Zeppelins came again.

The Naval Airship Division was determined that its next raid would have important and spectacular results. To bring about the surrender of England, to sustain the faith and jubilation of the German people, and to silence critics in the Imperial Navy, there must be devastation of the great docks on Humberside and Merseyside, and famous industrial areas such as Birmingham, Sheffield and Manchester. All this would lead to the final hammer blows against London. The German public was avid for news of places of which they had at least heard and not of obscure or unknown names like Great Yarmouth, King's Lynn, Bury St Edmunds, Sheringham, Snettisham or Cromer.

The Naval High Command put forward a plan which was calculated to end the Kaiser's vacillation: an unrestricted assault against London. The Emperor pretended to reject it, but on 12 February his Imperial Order authorized attacks on 'war material of every kind, military establishments, barracks and also oil and petroleum tanks and the London docks'.

The hypocrisy is underlined by his insistence that residential areas should be excluded. But to the Navy and the Army the Imperial Order left them free to bomb the capital. Who could decide where a restricted area began and ended? St Katharine's Dock, for example, was immediately below, and inseparable from, Tower Bridge and the Tower of London itself. Not even the sophisticated bomb-aiming devices of some thirty years or more later could have been as selective as this farcical instruction demanded.

The two services were now ready to outrival each other. The Army had four ships, SL 2, Z X, LZ 35, and ZX 11 to compete with the Navy. But the fortunes of war were to deal both services even-handed blows.

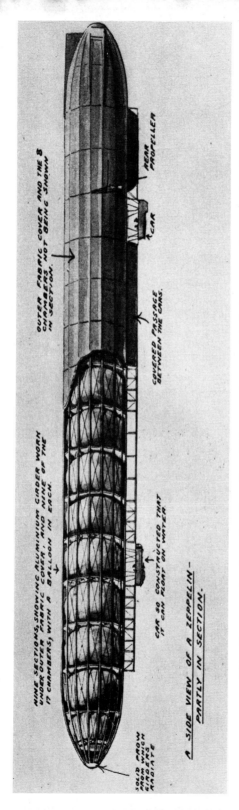

NINE SECTIONS, SHOWING ALUMINIUM GIRDER WORK
UNDER OUTER FABRIC COVER, AND NINE OF THE
17 CHAMBERS, WITH A BALLOON IN EACH.

OUTER FABRIC COVER AND THE 8
CHAMBERS, NOT BEING SHOWN
IN SECTION.

REAR PROPELLER

CAR

COVERED PASSAGE BETWEEN THE CARS.

CAR, SO CONSTRUCTED THAT
IT CAN FLOAT ON WATER.

A SIDE VIEW OF A ZEPPELIN—
PARTLY IN SECTION.

SOLID PROW
FROM WHICH
GIRDERS
RADIATE.

This diagrammatic view of a Zeppelin which came into service during 1915, shows the interior construction of the hull, buoyancy methods, and the outer covering—partly stripped—to reveal the lattice-girder framework and gas-bag balloons. Although there were many changes and refinements throughout the 18-years of Zeppelin development, the principle of the original design remained unchanged.

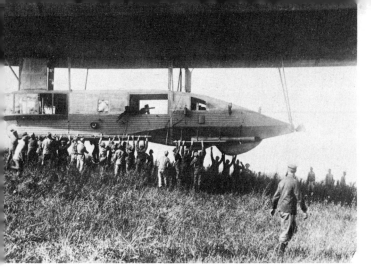

Three basic features of a Zeppelin. (*Above*): the forward control gondola which carried the captain, executive officer, navigator, and two petty officers in charge of rudder and elevation control. There were also two wireless operators in the car but they were enclosed in a sound-proofed compartment. (*Centre*): the electric bomb-release switch—in foreground of panel—was part of the forward gondola equipment. (*Below*): machine-gun and look-out position on the outer envelope.

With the growth in the Army's airship power, Strasser had lost the initiative. His anxiety to regain it reduced his Zeppelin strength and was a betrayal of his own tactical principles.

On 26 February he sent one Zeppelin, L 8 (*Kapitänleutnant* Helmut Beelitz) to raid London. A strong wind forced Beelitz to turn back and he landed at the Army's base at Gontrode, near Ghent, where he was an unwelcome guest. Five days later the Army sent him on his way to Düsseldorf. He decided to make another attempt to reach England before he returned. L 8 was hit by small arms fire from Belgian troops and was destroyed in a forced landing.

Beelitz could not be blamed for his second bid for honour and glory, since Strasser had already committed him to a foolhardy solo attack on England. The decision was all the more inexplicable because two more Zeppelins had been lost two days earlier.

Strasser never ceased to oppose the tactical misuse of his Zeppelins. He accepted the necessity of patrolling and scouting duties (throughout the war there were always to be more more scouting and reconnaissance sorties than raids); but he feared that the navy's demands would emasculate his bombardment force. In his opinion, co-operation with the fleet was a sideshow, a weakening of one of the tactical military principles—concentration of effort. The answer to conflicting requirements was an even greater Zeppelin building programme.

Co-operation with the fleet had not, so far, been very successful. The results obtained by the Zeppelins on the Christmas Day engagement had not justified the dangers to which they were exposed. The failure of L 5 to support the Imperial Navy at the Battle of the Dogger Bank in January had strenghtened his conviction. And there was a disastrous endorsement of it on 16 February.

Two airships, L 3 (Hans Fritz) and L 4 (von Platen) were sent on a scouting mission to the Skagerrak, between Norway and Jutland. L 3 was wrecked on the Danish island of Fano; Fritz and his crew were interned. L 4 broke up in the North Sea with the loss of four men—the first Zeppelin casualties of the war. Von Platen and the survivors were interned.

The embarrassment of learning that the Army was, after all, to make the first attack on London amounted almost to shame; but for the immediate future, at any rate, it was short-lived. On 17 March all four of the Army's ships were ordered to attack

England, with London as the objective. They lost their way in thick fog, and ZX 11 was damaged on landing, after having dropped bombs on Calais. Three days later LZ 35, Z X, and the old Schutte-Lanz, SL 2, raided Paris. Z X, having been hit by ground fire, was destroyed on the return flight. In mid-April LZ 35 was irretrievably damaged when she made a forced landing on the Western Front. SL 2 was taken out of service but a rebuilt version was to be the first airship to bomb the City area of London.

Heinrich Mathy took an early opportunity to exploit the Army's temporary lack of airships. On 14 April, the day after LZ 35 was lost, he took off from Hage, near Norden, in L 9, to scout over the southern part of the North Sea. By temperament Mathy was a man of action but he carried out his scouting duties punctiliously in spite of their extreme monotony; but after the failure of that first attack on England, he still had to justify his place as Strasser's second-in-command.

He found nothing during his reconnaissance and was, surprisingly, given permission by wireless to drop his bombs on England before he returned to Hage. But this was clearly Mathy's intention before he took off; a Zeppelin on a routine scouting operation would be unlikely to carry some 30 explosive bombs and about 40 incendiaries.

Early in the evening he crossed the English coast at a point he believed was Tynemouth. It was in fact at Blyth, in Northumberland, although he did find his way to Tynemouth. Throughout the raid he dropped 31 explosive bombs and most of his incendiaries. Nearly all of them fell in fields and outlying villages. Damage was slight and a woman and a child were injured. The only opposition came from a Cyclists' Battalion at Cambois, one of the nearby villages. Two aeroplanes failed to find him.

This attack was a further example of the unreliability of raid reports. Mathy claimed to have bombed industrial targets including those at Newcastle-upon-Tyne, Jarrow and Hebburn. It would be generous to believe that he had been genuinely misled; but open country could not in any conditions be mistaken for 'industrial areas' where undimmed yards and factories were a beckoning welcome to a raider. Whether Strasser believed him or not, he ordered another attack on the following night.

Strasser himself flew in L 7 (*Oberleutnant* Werner Peterson). L

5 (*Kapitänleutnant* Alois Bocker) and L 6 (*Kapitänleutnant* von Buttlar) completed the fleet. Their objective was the Humber.

The raid was a chaotic failure. Navigation errors were worse than those on the first attack. All three airships missed their landfall. Two of them lost their way over England and dropped bombs on places whose names they could only guess at. The third returned with a full bomb load and never reported that she had even crossed the coast.

The raid reports of all three captains differed from those which were more accurately prepared in Britain. It is hard to escape the conclusion that, from the outset of the campaign, there was a conspiracy among captains and crews to hide incompetency and failure, and to claim credit for having overcome counterattacks which were either non-existent or, at best, feeble.

Bocker, in L 5, and von Buttlar, in L 6, made their landfall over Suffolk and Essex respectively. L 5 bombed Lowestoft and Southwold. L 6 dropped bombs on Maldon and the village of Heybridge.

The worst embarrassment was again reserved for Strasser, in L 7. In his report, obviously approved by Strasser himself, Peterson hid his failure with a flagrant lie: that strong head-winds made L 7 turn for home when she was 'forty nautical miles south-east of the mouth of the Humber'.

In fact L 7 crossed into England over the Wash and Burnham Flats, where she was sighted at approximately 2.40 am. Peterson, however, reported that he began his return at 2.30 am; but the British plotted his course to Cromer and Great Yarmouth, where L 7 flew out to sea at 3.35 am, carrying all her bombs with her. It is impossible to accept that such experienced men as Peterson and Strasser could have been so incompetent not to have realized that they had crossed the coast. Although emergency lighting restrictions were imposed, they were not so efficient as to cause a total blackout of the landscape. Moreover, the captains are unlikely to have made such a gross time miscalculation. There is no reason to doubt the well-prepared British records. Even with poor visibility L 7 could have dropped to a lower altitude or used parachute flares for identification. The conclusion is inescapable that Peterson, aided and abetted by Strasser, flinched in weather conditions which had literally blown them off their original course.

Peterson further embellished his report by claiming that he

had been attacked five times by anti-aircraft fire from ships at sea. Von Buttlar reported having been caught in searchlight beams and hit several times by artillery and machine guns. Bocker, too, claimed to have been exposed by searchlights and attacked by gunfire.

British records, however, show that there were no Royal Navy ships in that area; no searchlights were used anywhere during the night; the only anti-aircraft fire as such was from three pom-pom shells; and the only attempt at interception was an unsuccessful one by a seaplane from Great Yarmouth.

L 6 was hit, not by artillery as von Buttlar reported, but by rifle fire from the 6th Battalion, Sussex Cyclists at Easton Bavents, in the Suffolk countryside.

Strasser's failures came at an appropriate time for the Army. In April it received the first million-cubic-feet Zeppelin, LZ 38. The Navy was to take delivery of its counterpart the following month.

These million-cubic-feet ships were almost replicas of each other, and a brief description of LZ 38 will show the power of this new strain in the breed. She had a capacity of 1,126,700 cubic feet, a length of 536 feet and a diameter of 61 feet. She was driven by four 210 h.p. Maybach engines, had a maximum speed of about 55 miles per hour, but could climb away from an attacking aircraft at 1,000 feet a minute. Her armament consisted of six Maxim guns, four in her gondolas and two on the top platform.

London was the objective for this aerial arsenal. Unlike the Naval Airship Division, the Army believed in the principle of a concentration of effort. London was the exclusive objective, with no diversions to far-away targets, except for three reconnaissance sorties.

Anticipating the open secret that the Kaiser was about to authorize the virtual unrestricted bombing of London, LZ 38 (*Hauptmann* Erich Linnartz) made three raids on England, which were a reconnaissance of the route to London and a probe of the defences. He made the first of these sorties on 29/30 April, dropped ten explosive bombs and all his incendiaries in Suffolk; most of them struck Bury St Edmunds before he flew out to sea over Aldeburgh. There were no casualties, the damage was negligible, and air and ground opposition was minimal.

Early in May the Kaiser made his long-expected decision

about London: bombing could not take place 'east of the longitude of the Tower'. Despite the familiar warnings about civilians and royal palaces, the Emperor himself and the airship crews knew that the capital was an open city. Although 'everyone' knew that the decision had been made, the order was not released until the end of May, when only the Army was able to take advantage of it.

In Britain, the failure of the Zeppelin offensive had, inevitable, brought complacency. The voices of doom which warned that the campaign had not even begun were lost among more dramatic and traumatic events.

As usual, the sharp edge of the warnings was blunted by overstatement. Early in 1915, the First Sea Lord, Admiral of the Fleet Lord Fisher—the great 'Jackie' Fisher, maker of the modern Navy and a rumbustious, popular figure—gave a highly imaginative forecast, which exceeded even the direst of warnings from Germany. In a memorandum he wrote of:

> A Zeppelin holocaust from a ton of explosives dropped from the clouds on to Horse Guards Parade, destroying in one shattering explosion all the historic buildings surrounding that square with Admirals, Generals, Statesmen and Civil Servants under the ruins in one red burial tent.

Admiral Fisher's forecast never did live up to the melodrama. But there were hammer blows to come. The 'red burial tent' of his imagination had its counterpart in the streets and homes of more humble people than 'Admirals, Generals, Statesmen and Civil Servants'.

CHAPTER 5

The First of the Hammer Blows

Scarcely anyone gave a thought of LZ 38's probing towards London. Linnartz's forays and the fear of the Zeppelins were now only a pale backdrop against the more garish setting of the war at home, at sea and on the Western Front.

At 2.45 am on 10 May LZ 38 dropped an incendiary bomb alongside the hulk, *Royal Edward*, which was moored off Southend and in which there were some German prisoners of war. Over Canvey Island the Zeppelin was fired on by guns at Cliffe, and then dropped four explosive bombs and about 120 incendiaries on Southend itself. Two people were killed and one injured. Eleven aircraft pursued her but she was always out of their reach. Having been fired on again by the guardship in the Downs, LZ 38 had a narrow escape from disaster when she was over Armentières, in France. Flight Sub-Lieutenant Mullock, of the Royal Naval Air Service, in an Avro 504, attacked her when she was at 2,000 feet. A jammed Lewis gun deprived him of the honour of being the first British pilot to destroy a German airship.

A week later, on 17 May, Linnartz raided Southend and Ramsgate; two people were killed and one injured. His final probe took place on 26 May with another raid on Southend, when three people were killed and three injured. Once again, LZ 38 easily avoided all anti-aircraft fire and the five RNAS aircraft which searched for her in vain.

On that morning of 26 May the British people were more concerned with some of the surprises and shocks in Asquith's new coalition Government than the activities of one Zeppelin over Southend. Winston Churchill had been sacked from the

Admiralty and relegated to the modest post of Chancellor of the Duchy of Lancaster. The Lord Chancellor, Viscount Haldane, had suffered an even worse fate. Like Prince Louis Battenberg (who had been forced to resign as First Sea Lord in October, 1914), he was the victim of the same scurrilous political and press accusations that he was (to say the least) pro-German. The brutal allegations and, in more respectable quarters, the collective gossip and innuendo, made his departure inevitable.

Both men had served Britain well. Prince Louis had been chiefly responsible for the high state of efficiency of the Royal Navy on the outbreak of war. Haldane, as Secretary for War from 1905 until Kitchener took over in 1914, had radically reformed the Army. When he left the War Office to become Lord Chancellor he left, also, the legacy of the British Expeditionary Force. Never before had the British Army been ready for war.

Only two weeks previously there had been another shock when Fisher had resigned as First Sea Lord because of disagreements with Winston Churchill over the Dardanelles campaign.

Any shocks and surprises were acceptable if they produced unity in government and could break the stalemate of the war. Few people were in the mood to criticize some of the notoriously weak appointments or to notice that there was still no minister responsible for co-ordinating the air services. But there was a feeling that the war would now be waged more aggressively with David Lloyd George in the newly-created post of Minister of Munitions. Even his numerous enemies and opponents conceded that he might be the new saviour.

One was certainly needed as the nation braced itself for the second year of the war. If anyone thought about the Zeppelin threat it was merely to be thankful for its absence.

Casualties on the Western Front had been grotesquely large. More than 60,000 officers and other ranks had been lost at the second Battle of Ypres, where the Germans had used poison gas against unprepared Allied troops. At home, crowds of spectators, held back by a rope barrier, watched the daily and nightly arrival of ambulance trains at main line railway stations. Military hospitals throughout the country—most of them converted schools, mansions and large houses—were overcrowded. The less seriously wounded or convalescent non-commissioned men, in their hideous 'hospital blue', were a familiar sight in every town and village. Mourning dress, black

ties and arm-bands were silent testimonies to private tragedies.
The names of the dead were being printed in ever-increasing
numbers in small-type columns in the newspapers.

On 7 May, 1915, the 30,000 ton Cunard liner *Lusitania* was
torpedoed by the German submarine U 20. She sank off the
Irish coast in about 20 minutes, and 1,198 men, women and
children—128 of them American—went down with her. Public
fury was expressed in the mob-wrecking of shops or businesses
owned by long-resident or second-generation Germans and
Austrians, or, once again, those with Germanic names who had
not been interned. Police and soldiers broke up fierce, often
savage, outbreaks of violence.

Lord Northcliffe exploited popular discontent with thunder-
ingly successful attacks in his newspapers on the shell shortage,
but his attempts to denigrate the seemingly impregnable Kitchener were singularly unsuccessful. The euphoria of the war's
opening weeks had given way to stubborn determination.
There were nagging doubts, discontents and some bitterness.
No one now believed in a quick or even an early victory. But
scarcely anyone doubted that it would come.

Germany was certainly looking for a quick victory. If the
'Zeppelin menace' was all but forgotten in England, *Hauptmann*
Linnartz, again in LZ 38, now brought it out of the backdrop to
the very centre of the stage.

On the morning of 31 May, LZ 37 (*Oberleutnant* Ernst
Lehmann) and LZ 38 (Erich Linnartz) were under orders to
bomb London. The weather was fine and so was the forecast.
There was a light wind—described by Linnartz as 'gentle
breezes'—thin cloud cover and the prospect of a clear sky
throughout the night.

The two ships took off at dusk: LZ 37 from Namur and LZ 38
from Brussels-Evere, but LZ 37's envelope was damaged and
she turned back. Everything was in Linnartz's favour as he
crossed the North Sea: the weather, tactical surprise perhaps, a
load of thirty-five explosive bombs and about ninety incendiaries, and contemptible enemy opposition. Because the
centre of London was still theoretically forbidden territory,
the docks were the target for the night.

His course took him to the edge of the seaside town of
Margate, at an altitude of 10,000 feet. He made his landfall near
Shoeburyness and flew over Southend. By about 10.40 pm he
was cruising over the capital's north-eastern suburbs.

Even before the war most suburban residents spent weekday evenings at home. Without the radio and television of later years, they went to bed early, having spent their time reading, playing the piano, playing card games, doing dressmaking and sewing, carpentry and fretwork and, in the spring and summer, working in the garden. They visited families and friends at weekends and on Bank Holidays' and made occasional trips 'up West' to a theatre or a musical hall, with perhaps a meal at one of the popular restaurants or a dinner for a few shillings a head in Soho.

Although the fear of a Zeppelin onslaught had receded in the early months of 1915, most suburban people were anxious to be home before dark. The dimmed street lighting created a feeling of isolation; and the suburbs, at any rate, were tightly buttoned-up places.

Only a few minutes' flight away, but a world away in style, parts of the East End bustled with activity every evening and late into the night. And on the evening of 31 May people were on their way home from the picture palaces, the second house of variety theatres and the public houses. The residential roads and streets may have been effectively dimmed, but well-lighted landmarks guided LZ 38 as she steered for the docks. The main East End thoroughfares such as Commercial Road, and London's pleasure ground, the West End, were easily identified. 'There seemed,' Linnartz wrote later, 'to have been little effort to dim the city.'

By 10.50 pm he was inside the target area and, if not precisely over the docks, near enough to drop the first bomb.

With brutal suddenness some of those buttoned-up places and the East End were shocked and shattered by a unique horror—the crashing of explosive bombs and fires from incendiaries. Linnartz's attack brought death, injury and a new kind of fear to the people of Stoke Newington, Dalston, Hoxton, Shoreditch, Whitechapel, Stepney, West Ham and Leytonstone.

Linnartz and his crew knew at once that the first of the hammer blows had struck with deadly effect; below, there were great spurts of fire from the explosive bombs and enveloping blazes from the incendiaries. As LZ 38 left on her exit course to the coast her crew looked down on that landscape of flames and swirling smoke; not surprisingly, they believed that their attack had been devastating.

His report, and his descriptions to American newspapermen, embellished his success. Anti-aircraft guns, he said, had 'spat viciously' as LZ 38 crossed the coast. He and his crew 'could hear the shells scream past us'. And over London:

> Shells screamed past us. There were glowing tracer shells which we had never seen before, but had heard all about— slim projectiles that tore a hole in the ship's fabric and then burst into flames.

He claimed to have been attacked by more anti-aircraft fire as he left England: 'Shell after shell whizzed past, some of them the dreaded incendiary type. Some burst dangerously near.'

He exaggerated his achievement even more by his fanciful description of aeroplane attacks:

> Now a new menace threatened us—aeroplanes. Pilots had orders that if they failed to reach us with machine-gun fire they were to climb above us and ram our gasbags with their machines.
>
> Evidently the supreme sacrifice meant nothing to these brave men. One by one they came from their airfields that had been established round the coast.

The reality was different. LZ 38 was seen, although not identified, only once from the ground when she crossed the Thames Estuary. The observation was passed on to the Admiralty, but more than one airship was reported to be approaching London. The only anti-aircraft fire came from totally ineffective attempts by coastal guns. Nine RNAS machines failed to find her, although one did claim to have seen her as she made for the capital. Another aircraft which sought her, a Sopwith biplane from Hendon, crashed at Hatfield, in Hertfordshire. The pilot, Flight Lieutenant D. M. Baines, was killed, but his observer, Flight Sub-Lieutenant B. Travers (later the famous playwright Ben Travers), had a remarkable escape.

The first bomb ever to fall on London, an incendiary, struck 16 Alkham Road, Stoke Newington. The occupants rushed out of the burning house to safety; but the attack brought a fatal experience to a family in neighbouring Cowper Road, where a house was also set on fire. A baby was burned to death and her sister died in hospital later. In Ball's Pond Road, Dalston, a man and his wife were burned to death.

The main attack hit the East End. The narrow alleys, courtyards, and streets off Whitechapel High Street, Whitechapel Road, Commercial Road, Shoreditch High Street and Hoxton Street made the crashing of bombs sound even more terrifying than it was; they also made the frantic search for safety more difficult. But there were few hiding places. The horror and bewilderment of the night were increased by the flames which flared into the sky, the clanging of fire engine and ambulance bells, the shrieks and cries for help, and the stridency of police whistles.

Today there are few traces of that historic event. The house in Alkham Road was outwardly unchanged in 1979. Cowper Street, too, remains much as it was, one of the few Victorian oases in a vast and encroaching council housing estate. These streets are still relatively quiet places, and to visit them, 64 years on, it is not difficult to visualize the impact of an unimagined horror.

An office block stands on the site of the house in Ball's Pond Road, where a Mr and Mrs Good died. It was the source of an inquest which, briefly, became infamous throughout the world.

The East End of 1915 disappeared in the Second World War air raids and the subsequent rebuilding. Social conditions which were a disgrace to London disappeared with it; and so did a seemingly unbreakable community bond which had been forged in distress and deprivation.

That vanished East End has been described by romantic nostalgics as a collection of villages. More accurately, it was a settlement of tribal areas, with the rough, protective loyalty of more primitive tribes. Each district had its own character; yet each shared the common identity of East Enders, different in attitudes and living conditions from those in any other part of London.

Not all of east London was the East End of fact and fiction. The East End itself was not a precise geographical area marked by defined boundaries. Some adjacent areas were part of it; some were not. In general, it was made up of Bethnal Green, Spitalfields, Bow, Shoreditch, Whitechapel, Stepney, Mile End, Hoxton, Poplar, Shadwell and Limehouse.

It is a common mistake of some latter-day social historians to assume that the entire East End was one vast slum. There were many enclaves of working-class houses whose regularly holy-stoned doorsteps were an outward sign of the cleanliness and respectability behind lace-curtained windows.

For most of its inhabitants, however, the East End meant a life of squalor, extreme poverty, constant unemployment, slum dwellings, disease, a high death rate, a struggle to avoid the dreaded workhouse, and a determination not to be buried in a pauper's grave.

Devoted social workers fought a losing battle against too-frequent pregnancies, violent fighting, the beating of wives and children, and the amount in a small wage that went on heavy drinking; many wives had as little as £1.00 a week with which to keep a large family. The pub and the pawnshop were indispensable institutions. But nothing and no one could destroy the people's cocky pride in being East Enders.

Generations of immigrants had been accepted in the East End with guarded tolerance. There were Germans, Austrians, Hungarians, Poles and Lithuanians. Many of them were Jews, fugitives from persecution and pogrom. The Chinese were there, too, in their private, exclusive community of Limehouse; but they were not East Enders—only foreigners who forever remained strangers.

After the raid some of these foreigners were the victims of the East Enders' fury. Although that guarded tolerance had been built over many years, it proved to be fragile. Once again Germans and Austrians who had not been interned, or people with Germanic names, were accused of signalling by lights to guide the Zeppelin, of having secret wireless transmitting sets. Innocent people were violently attacked. Shopkeepers had their windows smashed; some had their entire premises wrecked. The harassed Metropolitan Police were accused of 'taking sides' against the foreigners and, equally, of indifference to the violence.

Revenge was not confined to the East End. At Edmonton, in North London, which had heard the explosions but not experienced the raid, an innocent, long-resident German baker had his shop wrecked early the next morning, before he could serve his customers. All the local people had bought his freshly-baked bread for many years. Those who broke down his shop and hurled bread and flour on the pavement were among his oldest customers. He was rescued from his bakery at the back of the shop—and from serious injury—by the police.

The East Enders' anger was increased by the lack of retaliation, the first official communiqué, and then the sightseers, many of whom saw the district for the first time. It was no secret that there were anti-aircraft guns and searchlights in a six-mile radius of Charing Cross; but not a single gun had been heard in London. No searchlights were seen either, and the people of East London would have been amazed to read that LZ 38 had moved through 'an endless sea of dazzling light'.

The first communiqué was issued from the Admiralty shortly after midnight. The fires were still burning and people were stunned with distress and shock. The announcement was bleak and, to the thousands who had endured the raid, blatantly inaccurate:

> Zeppelins are reported to have been seen near Ramsgate and Margate and in certain parts of London. Many fires are reported, but these cannot absolutely be connected with the visit of airships. Further particulars will be issued as soon as they can be collected and collated.

With the bulletin, the Admiralty imposed an even more severe censorship:

> The press are especially reminded that no statement whatever must be published dealing with the places in the neighbourhood of London reached by aircraft, or the course proposed to be taken by them, or any statement or diagram which might indicate the ground covered by them.
>
> The Admiralty communiqué is all the news which can properly be published.

Written in haste and under unexpected pressure, the communiqué was a clumsy misjudgment. Time, however, was not on the Admiralty's side. People elsewhere in the capital did not know that there had been a raid. The bombs were not heard in Central London or anywhere south of the Thames. Many police stations did not know of the raid either. On the other hand, residents in the East End and the north-eastern suburbs believed that the entire city had been savagely attacked.

The Admiralty's immediate concern was to minimize the

rumours and prevent the Germans from knowing where the bombs had fallen and details of the damage.

But Linnartz had known precisely where he was. Helped by his previous sorties, ideal weather conditions and easy identification, his navigation was perfect. Part of the East End was dockland and justified his claim to have bombed the docks themselves. If Stoke Newington and Dalston were not in that area, they were, in flying terms, near enough to be included as a target.

That he had missed the docks, even so narrowly, did perhaps justify the Admiralty's early news embargo; but it did nothing to stem the rumours or satisfy a restless Fleet Street and the foreign correspondents.

Neither the Admiralty, the War Office nor the Press Bureau had any experience of the consequences of censorship. No thought was given to its effect on the morale of the people. From the beginning of the war there was undisguised hostility to the newspapers. The Army in particular had not forgotten its disastrous relations with war correspondents in South Africa. All wartime censorship must be a conflict of interests; but co-operation and compromise would have prevented most of the scandalous and often dangerous exploits of reporters at the front. By 1914 nothing had been learned from that painful experience. Matters were not improved when three newspapers had evaded the censorship to print part of the truth about the retreat from Mons, and showed that it was indeed a retreat and not a glorious feat of arms. Almost invariably, however, newspaper proprietors and editors were very conscious of the severe penalties for rule-breaking.

At home the reporting of raids was restricted to an official estimate of casualties with only a passing reference to damage. Locations were indicated by general references to 'parts of London', or 'the coast', or 'the Home Counties', or 'in north-western areas of England'.

A second communiqué was issued at 5 pm:

> In amplification of the information which appeared in this morning's papers, the following particulars of last night's Zeppelin raid are now available for publication. Late last night about ninety bombs, mostly of an incendiary character, were dropped from hostile aircraft in various localities not far distant from each other. A number of fires (of which

only three were large enough to require the services of fire-engines) broke out. The fires were all caused by the incendiary bombs. All fires were promptly and effectively dealt with, and only one of these fires necessitated a district call. No public building was injured, but a number of private premises were damaged by fire and water.

The number of casualties is small. So far as at present ascertained, one infant, one boy, one man and one woman were killed, and another woman is so seriously injured that her life is despaired of. A few other private citizens were seriously injured.

A 17-hour delay, however, allowed rumour to flourish as never before. There was speculation and suspicion, a universal conviction that something was being 'hushed up'. Those newspaper stories of the retreat from Mons had planted seeds of doubt. The communiqués and evasions after the seaborne attacks on Hartlepool, Scarborough and Whitby had made them grow. London's first raid had brought them to full bloom.

Sightseeing visits to the East End began early the following morning. All London, it seemed, knew exactly where the bombs had fallen. German spies in the crowds, and journalists from neutral countries, reported the facts as they saw them or as they wanted to see them. Details of casualties and damage may have been an official secret but some highly coloured reports appeared in overseas newspapers and in spies' messages back to Germany.

It was easy enough for foreign correspondents to outwit the censor. Once their stories were smuggled out of Britain, nothing could prevent their publication. American reporters, in particular, created some very imaginative descriptions. They were based only partly on what they saw but were enlivened by that generally unreliable source, the on-the-spot 'eyewitness'.

Exaggerated stories of casualties, damage and personal experiences were to become inseparable from all air raids. The first raid on London set the pattern. Even in their misery people were flattered by reporters' questions and suggestions. A pint of porter stout, or even the manna of a golden sovereign, inspired imaginations. There were suddenly-remembered stories of sensational escapes from death. One ambulance or one fire engine became several. The tales of bodies dug from wreckage would have been more appropriate to the Blitzkrieg of the Second World War.

The eager reporters converged on the worst-damaged areas and saw the interiors of rooms without a wall, the shorn-off sides of buildings, the crumbling and collapsed roofs, the wreckage spilling haphazardly on to pavements and roads. And when someone in the crowd said he had just heard that 'they copped it something 'orrible over Camberwell' or that the Strand had been closed, those first stories in overseas newspapers gave a firm impression of London on the edge of collapse. The reporting was highly selective. The good news about the rest of London was no news at all to correspondents whose editors demanded high drama.

There was some hostility to the sightseeing crowds, and bitterness as well. Society women in smart, chauffeur-driven limousines, people in hired taxi-cabs, and passengers on open-topped omnibuses made a gala expedition to the East End. To many of them it was their first sight of a slum district, of bare-footed, pallid children who were louse-ridden and bandy with rickets, whose ragged breeches were often cut-down men's trousers. Dormant class hostility exploded into a few ugly scenes.

The worst of the bombing was at Hoxton, especially in the narrow alleys off Hoxton Street, where still smouldering buildings were a vivid witness of the cruel night.

Despite the numbing shock of that first raid, the human and material results were disproportionate to the sound and fury. Only seven people, including four children, were killed, and thirty-five injured. Structural damage was later estimated to have been £18,500: in all, a poor return for thirty explosive and some ninety incendiary bombs.

The British people were unable to see the sensational reports in foreign newspapers or read any details in their own. The impact of the raid would have decreased almost immediately except for the inescapable public inquest on those who had died. A secret inquest was unacceptable and would have imposed equally unacceptable restrictions on the freedom of an increasingly frustrated press.

The inquest on two of the victims, Mr and Mrs Good, of Ball's Pond Road, Dalston, has become a legend in the records of the aerial bombardment of England. The macabre circumstances of their deaths, together with the coroner's comments, fed the hungry newspapers, whose sensational reporting of the inquest strengthened the suspicion that censorship hid untold horrors and disasters.

The middle-aged Henry and Caroline Good had been burned to death by an incendiary bomb. Their bodies were almost naked; the man's arm had been round his wife's waist, and they were assumed to have died as they knelt by their bed and prayed. The phrase 'in an attitude of prayer' became an emotional flashpoint. For a few hours the names of Henry and Caroline Good—who had lived uneventfully in that modest Victorian house in Ball's Pond Road—shared the attention of the press with the dead children, 'innocent victims of the baby killers'.

This emotional accusation, and the morbid fascination of the deaths of Henry and Caroline Good, held the brief attention of the international press. Had the raid not been on London, the international coverage would have been small. Neither would the sense of outrage have been as widespread.

The provincial cities and towns may have been jealous of the metropolis, thought it gave itself airs and graces, and was seemingly well defended at their expense. Nevertheless, it was the capital not only of Britain but also of the Empire. It was the centre of government and authority. If a lone Zeppelin could cruise unmolested over London and drop about 120 bombs, then the undefended industrial centres and docks in the provinces were naked to further raids. But the continuing shortages of artillery left the Admiralty with no choice. The lean resources had to be concentrated on the hub of the war effort and Germany's final objective. Three naval 3-inch guns were brought in to reinforce the capital's defences but they were only piecemeal additions to a piecemeal scheme.

The German people gave an hysterical reception to reports of the London raid. It had, apparently, exceeded all expectations. Huge fires were burning. Communications were destroyed. Hundreds of people were dead. The Zeppelin had proved itself to be the war winner.

By contrast, the Army High Command was disappointed with the results. It had taken very little time to sort out fact from fiction. Always more realistic than the Naval Airship Division and its supporters in the Admiralty, the High Command had doubts about the strategy. The effort had produced only one positive result: a blow to British morale. The initial enthusiasm had gone as quickly as a sunset in the tropics. The taste for jousting with the Navy was going too. A concentration of effort with a squadron raid might bring significant success. But there were a lot of second thoughts in the High Command.

Nevertheless, the need for a quick success with the Zeppelins was now more urgent. The 'baby killer' raid became yet another 'atrocity' accusation. There was public condemnation in the well-disposed neutral countries. And in isolationist America the anger, and even the rage, could not be ignored. If the Zeppelins were not being attacked on their raids over England, Germany herself was under attack because of them.

The United States' attitude to the war was a critical factor in Germany's political and, consequently, military strategy; and not the least of the things inside the kernel of that strategy was the swift killing power of the Zeppelins. A quick success was the only course open. A fatal bombardment of England would leave Germany the unchallenged victor in Europe, when accusations and even remote fears of intervention could be forgotten.

Four days after the London raid, Peter Strasser sent L 10 (*Kapitänleutnant* Klaus Hirsch) and one of the disliked SL type, SL 3 (*Kapitänleutnant* Fritz Boemack) to attack London and the Humber respectively. The attacks turned out to be a setback for Strasser's leadership and a personal humiliation for Klaus Hirsch, who was taking L 10 on her maiden raid.

Like most of his predecessors Hirsch was never sure of his position. He reached the Thames Estuary soon after 10 pm, but thought he was near Lowestoft. A wind change made him decide to bomb the Harwich naval base. He recognized it, or so he believed, and dropped nine explosive missiles and eleven incendiaries; but they fell, instead, much farther away at Gravesend. Six people were injured, and fire caused serious damage to the military hospital in the Yacht Club. The lights he had identified as those of Harwich and Ipswich were in fact those of Gravesend, Chatham and other places along the Thames and Medway—all on the outskirts of London, from which he flew away in ignorance.

Boemack, in SL 3, make his landfall at 12.30 am near Flamborough Head, in Yorkshire. He, too, cruised aimlessly, missed his Humber objective, and dropped three bombs in a field and a garden. Although Boemack reported having been over the north-east coast for about two and a half hours, nine British aircraft failed to find him.

In the continually fascinating study of German aerial tactics, nothing is more intriguing than the failure to make the best use of the Zeppelin. The persistence in a 'penny packet' policy in preference to a consistent one of concentration of effort was to be a constant flaw in the campaign.

In the Second World War the British people showed an almost unflinching resistance to bombing on a more massive scale. In the First World War they showed fortitude and resistance too, but in conditions not previously experienced by anyone. In 1915 especially, the German commands, and particularly that of the Navy, missed an opportunity to exploit this unique situation. In the unimagined nightmare of aerial bombardment, a concentration of effort on one target by several airships on successive nights would have taken civilian morale well beyond the frontiers of human experience, with, perhaps, incalculable results. It does not require any historical hindsight to point out what the airship tactics should have been. Concentration of effort is one of the immutable principles of strategy and tactics. It can be applied at sea, on land and in the air. It is as old as warfare itself.

Before 1939 Britain was psychologically and physically prepared for aerial bombardment. Lingering memories and a residual experience of First World War attacks, the remarkable improvement in aircraft development and, perhaps most of all, the Spanish Civil War bombing had prepared the nation for an all-out assault. Whatever its imperfections the Air Raid Precautions plan and policy was one of the outstanding achievements of 1939–45 and the years that preceded it.

In 1915 there were no public air raid shelters or Anderson shelters for individual family protection. It was with a spurious confidence that people sought protection under kitchen tables, in cupboards under the stairs, behind mattresses and pulled-together furniture. In some small houses floor boards were removed so that very young children (and some small adults too) could be squeezed into the space below.

On the night after the Naval Airship Division's failure to bomb London and the Humber, the Army attempted a limited application of the concentration of effort principle. It was to be the crucial test of future participation. A much more devastating hammer blow was planned for the night of 6/7 June. It was to have a permanent place in the history of aerial bombardment.

CHAPTER 6

Attack and Counter Attack

With its short summer nights, and only some four or five hours of real darkness, June was not the best raiding period. The Army High Command, however, needed to test its policy in greater strength as soon as possible.

On the night of 6/7 June three Zeppelins were ordered to bomb London: LZ 37 (*Oberleutnant* von der Haegen), LZ 38 (*Hauptmann* Linnartz) and LZ 39 (*Hauptmann* Masius). The captains and crews were determined to make this a decisive mission. They knew that the Army was now less enthusiastic about strategic bombing. And their pride was spurred by the Navy's failure of the previous night.

The Navy also set up a raid that same night, a solo attempt by Mathy in L 9. His main objective was London as well. If the Army and the Navy knew of each other's plans, there was a studied lack of co-operation or co-ordination.

When the three Army Zeppelins took off to make a rendezvous near Bruges, the weather conditions and the forecast were good. But there was a warning that the mist already lying over the German-occupied Belgian coast and extending out to sea, might turn to fog. Even to have attempted the raid was foolhardy, and it depended on the gamble that the fog might have cleared when the English coast was reached.

Linnartz's second bid for glory ended abruptly. Engine trouble forced LZ 38 back to her base at Brussels-Evere. It was a bad omen. When von der Haegen and Masius were over the North Sea a wireless message ordered them to abandon the raid because a thick fog had, after all, blanketed the North Sea.

The order to return was picked up by a British listening post at the Hunstanton coastguard station on the Norfolk coast. The information was relayed to the Admiralty, which in turn sent it to Wing-Commander Arthur Longmore (later Air Chief Marshal Sir Arthur Longmore), the new commander of the Royal Naval Air Service at Dunkirk.

Longmore recieved the message just before 12.30 am. He ordered Squadron-Commander Spenser Grey's flight, at Furnes, to try to destroy the returning Zeppelins or to bomb them in their sheds after they had landed at Brussels-Evere. Flight Sub-Lieutenant R. A. J. Warneford and Flight Sub-Lieutenant Rose were to attack the Zeppelins. In the very likely event that they failed to do so, Flight-Lieutenant J. P. Wilson (who became a distinguished National Hunt jockey and won the Grand National in 1925) and Flight Sub-Lieutenant J. S. Mills were to bomb the sheds.

Warneford and Mills were each flying a two-seat Morane-Saulnier monoplane which had an 80 h.p. Le Rhône engine and a maximum speed of about 76 miles per hour. But speed by itself was no match for Zeppelins. The Morane's slow rate of climb and maximum altitude of some 11,000 feet could not put it on equal combat terms. Each Morane carried a Vickers gun mounted forward and six 20-lb bombs which were strapped under the fuselage.

The first part of Longmore's twin plan began badly when Rose made a forced landing in a field. Although the aeroplane turned upside down he was not seriously injured. That he was now on his own, with the odds heavily against him attacking one of the returning Zeppelins, did not deter Warneford.

He was a dangerously reckless, undisciplined aviator with a greater obsession than most of his contemporaries to destroy German aircraft, especially airships. His fellow pilots and observers at Dunkirk were no less determined, but Warneford's cocky aggression and supreme confidence were unpopular even with the uninhibited flyers of the Royal Naval Air Service. It was barely three months since he had gained his wings, and his self-opinionated approach was resented by some of the more experienced pilots and observers.

'He would never have got his wings later in the war', said one of his contemporaries. 'It was easier in 1915 when you only had to fly without crashing.' Although it was a biased, jaundiced view, no one in the RNAS would have given Warneford high marks for conventional skills. He may have been below the standards which were later demanded of pilots or even of his comrades at Dunkirk, but his cool judgment in action was that of a veteran.

The statement that 'you only had to fly without crashing' was certainly not true when Warneford sighted LZ 37 at about 1 am on 6 June. With his one Vickers as his only armament apart from the six bombs, he would be out-gunned by the Zeppelin which, on this sortie, carried four Maxims in the gondolas and cars, and one forward on top of the envelope. And he would need more luck than skill to hit LZ 37 with any of his bombs. But he knew it could be done. On 17 May he and his observer, Leading Mechanic Meddis, had been one of three flyers who had attacked LZ 39. Warneford and Spenser Grey broke off the pursuit when she climbed out of range. But Flight-Lieutenant A. W. Bigsworth, in an Avro 504, found her over Ostend. He reached a height of more than 10,000 feet. The Zeppelin was below him, and he hit her with four 20-lb bombs. Smoke curled from her stern but she returned to Brussels-Evere without mishap, although at least one officer was dead and some of the crew were wounded. Like Flight-Lieutenant Mullock before him, Bigsworth was unfortunate not to have been the first pilot to destroy a Zeppelin in mid air.

Napoleon is said to have asked for lucky generals, by which he meant those who took their opportunities. It was Warneford's luck that he sighted LZ 37 when she was descending en route to Gontrode. He, too, seized his opportunity. He tracked the Zeppelin for 45 minutes. Over Bruges, when he was about half a mile astern of her, and closing on her all the time, she opened fire with her Maxim guns. Warneford knew that a gun fight would end in failure and probably death. His only chance of success was to climb above the airship before she could outclimb him. He turned to give himself more room to make his ascent. Von der Haegen followed him and Warneford continued to be under heavy fire. Nevertheless, he climbed slowly above the Zeppelin.

Von der Haegen then made a sudden descent for Gontrode, leaving Warneford to be dealt with by anti-aircraft guns. But when he reached an altitude between 10,000 and 11,000 feet he dived, releasing his six bombs when he was no more than 150 feet above her. The last of his bombs scored a direct hit. LZ 37 exploded, broke up in the air, and the blazing wreckage fell on a convent, where one person was killed and several others were injured. Coxswain Alfred Muhler had an astonishing escape. He was the only survivor. His forward gondola crashed through the convent roof and he landed on a nun's bed.

The force of the mid-air explosion momentarily threw Warneford's Morane out of control. With a skill which would have surprised his critics and instructors he quickly regained control. But the effect of the explosion had damaged his petrol supply. He was forced to land in an open field about 35 miles behind the German lines.

Like all pilots he had orders to set fire to his aeroplane rather than abandon it to the Germans. Warneford, however, was not the man to burn an aeroplane unless he was almost face to face with the enemy. To do so now would almost certainly mean his being captured. No one, apparently, had seen or heard his forced landing. Half an hour later he had repaired the damaged joint in the petrol pipe. With considerable skill he swung the propeller himself and started the rotary engine. While it was running he scrambled into the cockpit and took off for Dunkirk; but he lost his bearings and landed at Cap Grisnez.

Von der Haegen has been maligned for having broken off the flight, for having in effect run away. But this overlooks the order that an airship captain had to save his ship and crew, and not engage in dog fights. Decisions taken in the burden of action are often based on instant judgments, which are seen differently in cool staff college solutions of later years. Von der Haegen might have made a fatal error by counterattacking Warneford at all. He might have left his descent to Gontrode too late. But once the Morane was well placed, von der Haegen knew that, even with its bomb load, it could outspeed him. Then he had no choice but to counterattack as a defensive rather than an offensive move.

During those early morning hours the other British pilots, Wilson and Mills, each flying a Henry Farman biplane, made daring attacks on the Brussels-Evere sheds. Wilson was the first to reach them. He dropped three bombs on one shed. It was still ablaze, and first light was only a glimpse away, when Mills followed him. He was driven off by anti-aircraft fire but returned to drop four bombs on the same target.

The shed was destroyed. And London's first raider, LZ 38, was destroyed with it.

The stories of Warneford, Wilson and Mills are not retold just because they showed supreme courage, coolness and devo-

tion to duty. They have a place in a history of aerial bombardment because their actions had a decisive effect on the course of
that history.

While the Army airship strength was being bled almost to
death, Heinrich Mathy, in L 9, was making his solo raid on
England. A strong headwind and bad ground visibility meant
that an attack on London could not be completed during the
few hours of darkness. He decided to raid Hull.

Because of thick fog beyond the Wash he missed the Humber
estuary. Even with good visibility this was a difficult coastline
for air-to-ground observation at night, and Mathy flew offshore
of the long line of Holderness cliffs for thirty miles before he
dropped parachute flares. He identified Flamborough Head and
the town of Bridlington, from which he turned south to Hull.

By the time he reached Humberside the fog had changed to a
drifting mist. Just before 1 am he released more flares for a
precise target identification. Once again a city was blasted out
of its sleep by the noise and shock of a new experience. Mathy
descended to heights which varied between 6,000 and 8,000
feet. He dropped thirteen explosive bombs and more than forty
incendiaries. Twenty-four people were killed and forty were
reported to have been injured. Gunfire from the light cruiser,
Adventure—in dry dock for repairs—did no more than make
Mathy take leisurely avoiding action.

He dropped the rest of his incendiaries on the sister port of
Grimsby where there was only minor damage. Some of the
useless pom-poms fired at him before he left.

There was pandemonium and some panic in Hull. The
heaviest damage was suffered by the terraced, undetached
houses, shops and warehouses which stood shoulder to shoulder in the narrow streets by the docks and on the quayside.
Between forty and fifty houses and shops were said to have been
'demolished'. Like so much raid damage, most of them were
eventually, and surprisingly, repaired. But there were many
families that night whose wrecked homes seemed gone for ever.
The total damage was estimated to have been £44,795, and was
almost certainly an underestimate.

People ran everywhere, except into the Humber, to escape.
As in London, there were no real hiding places. Chance was the
only factor. Some of the casualties were caused in the streets;
others were trapped in the wreckage. A man, his wife and their
five children crouched against a scullery wall. When the raid

was over and he saw the extent of the neighbouring damage, he realized the futility of that pathetic grasp for safety.

The reaction of Hull's citizens to the raid has been described as one of 'indignation'. It was, in fact, one of unabated fury. Inevitably, some of that fury was directed to long-resident Germans and people, many of them small shopkeepers, who were suddenly accused of being Germans because they had 'funny' names. Crowds damaged and wrecked their premises until soldiers helped the police to break up what can accurately be described as riots.

Although most of the nation knew that Hull had endured the worst raid of the war, the official communiqué merely stated that it had occurred in the north-east area. The Admiralty's typically arid announcement increased the people's anger by its understatement that there had been 'fires in a drapery establishment, a timber yard and a terrace of small houses'.

The raid was not to be Hull's only ordeal. The national shortage of anti-aircraft guns left it vulnerable and exposed. Before the next attack, many people left the city each night to seek safety in nearby woods, fields and farm buildings.

The almost simultaneous news of Warneford's triumph and the bombing of the Zeppelin sheds by Wilson and Mills was a timely stroke of fortune which saved the Admiralty and the Government from even worse criticism. Warneford became the new national hero, perhaps the first 'people's hero' of the war. There was no shortage of heroes but Warneford had destroyed a direct menace to the homeland, the reality of which had been so tragically apparent that same night.

He was awarded an immediate Victoria Cross. Whether, as some snide critics suggested, he did not strictly meet the stringent qualifications of that exclusive decoration, the public would have accepted nothing less. Popular feeling was endorsed by King George's personal telegram to him:

> I most heartily congratulate you upon your splendid achievement of yesterday, in which you singlehanded destroyed an enemy Zeppelin. I have much pleasure in conferring upon you the Victoria Cross for this splendid act. George RI.

On 17 June Warneford took off for Paris in a Henry Farman biplane, with an American journalist as a passenger. When he was about 700 feet from the ground, the Farman's tail broke. Warneford and his passenger were killed.

The loss of the two Zeppelins signalled the end of the Army's strategic policy for airships. The appreciation of the situation was starkly realistic.

Linnartz's raid on London had brought prestige to the German people and a temporary blow to British morale. None of it had justified the effort. Furthermore, it was unlikely that other raids would have so much in their favour. There were no plans for a fleet of Zeppelins which might have brought decisive results with squadron attacks. The drop-out losses en route, the long distances between base and target, unpredictable weather, unreliable navigation, and now the vulnerability of the sheds, were unacceptable risks.

Even if a fleet of new airships was built for strategic bombing, control and co-operation were virtually impossible. And it seemed to the Army that when Britain had a powerful defence, Zeppelins as individual raiders were fatally vulnerable.

There were to be more Army airship raids on England, one of which was to have a special place in the story of aerial bombardment; but the Army's Zeppelin resources were to be concentrated on tactical support, and the forward bases in Belgium were abandoned.

But the conquest of England by air was not abandoned. Squadrons of powerfully-armed bomber aeroplanes, flying in mutually-supporting tactical formations, could succeed where airships had, so far, failed; and, in the Army's appreciation, were doomed to fail.

Nearly two years were to pass before the Gothas and the Giants began a new phase in the aerial bombardment of England.

Peter Strasser did not share the Army's gloomy appreciation, and he was to have a production line of new airships to support him: the six-engined 'super-Zeppelins'. He would have to wait a year before the first of them, L 30, was ready. Meanwhile, he was unimpressed by the loss of LZ 37. He reckoned that Warneford had been exceptionally lucky to have caught her at so low a height. There were, of course, lessons to be learned from that loss, and in a similar situation his Zeppelins faced the same danger. At operational heights, however, they were safe from attack by British aeroplanes with their slow climbing speeds, inadequate armament and lack of tactics.

But the wait for the 'super-Zeppelins' posed dangers of a different kind. Although the Navy was irrevocably committed to the 'big airship' policy, Strasser knew that the possibilities of a change of plan were undiminished. Failure to achieve a strategic success, or heavy losses, could mean that even the 'super-Zeppelins' would have a restricted rôle and thus dilute his strength against England.

Strasser was acutely aware that the High Seas Fleet Command believed that the Battle of the Dogger Bank, on 24 January, 1915, might have been a victory instead of a defeat if there had been better scouting by the Zeppelins. As it was, only one airship, L 5, had accompanied the Fleet. Driven off by Admiral Beatty's light cruisers, she was unable to track the British force. It is, in fact, unlikely that more scouting Zeppelins could have overcome the faulty tactics of the High Seas Fleet Commander-in-Chief, Admiral von Ingenohl, but additional airships would at least have kept the Royal Navy under constant observation.

Von Ingenohl lost his command after the Dogger Bank defeat. His successor, Admiral von Pohl, was determined never to be caught without the protection of scouting Zeppelins. Strasser was equally determined to have at least a fair share of the resources; but he would have to fight for it until he had proved beyond argument that the airship was a strategic necessity. During the wait for his 'super-Zeppelins' he would make the maximum use of his fleet.

A week after the raid on Hull he planned an attack on Tyneside. On the afternoon of 15 June L 10 (*Kapitänleutnant* Hirsch) and L 11 (*Oberleutnant* von Buttlar) took off from Nordholz. Over the North Sea L 11 turned back, having broken a crankshaft. Hirsch miscalculated the time of his landfall. He reached the north-east coast some 20 minutes after sunset and lay out to sea until shortly after midnight when he made the landfall at Blyth.

He turned south for Tyneside. No one saw L 10 as she glided to her target, and there was no warning of the raid. Almost as soon as she had crossed the coast, L 10 flew near the naval air station at Whitley Bay; but the only action from there came after the raid when two aircraft failed to catch her as she left the coast at South Shields.

Hirsch needed no flares to find suitable targets. Tyneside was working a wartime night shift. Lights from the yards, workshops and blast furnaces gave a vivid panorama. No target could have been more brilliantly displayed. In it was a great prize ready for the taking: the Dreadnought *Resolution*, which was building at Palmer's Jarrow yard.

Hirsch dropped about 60 explosive and incendiary bombs on Wallsend, Jarrow, Hebburn and South Shields. Eighteen people were killed and seventy-two injured. All of the injured, and seventeen of the dead, were casualties at Palmer's, where the engine shop was severely damaged. *Resolution* escaped. There was serious damage elsewhere on Tyneside but none of it was as bad as that at Palmer's.

Although all but one of the casualties had occurred in Palmer's engine shop, the shock and distress were seen and felt in the labyrinth of working-class streets. Some were mean slums. There was a similar outburst of anger and resentment as there had been in London and Hull. Tynesiders were mystified as to why such a truly vital area was not protected by search-lights, guns and aeroplanes. There was a cynical response to the news that aircraft had searched for L 10 and that she had also been fired on by a guardship in the Tyne.

The long-established claim that the Germans did not know until after the war where the bombs fell is insupportable. Hirsch may not have known exactly where he was—in his report he assumed that he had attacked Sunderland or Blyth—but it is inconceivable that the German Admiralty was ignorant. The censorship notwithstanding, most of Britain knew that Tyneside had been raided, and, of course, rumour had it that the damage was even more severe than it was. Foreign correspondents of newspapers in the neutral countries knew just as easily. And neutral ships put in at the north-eastern ports. Secret agents had no difficulty in identifying the location.

Whatever its deficiences in materials, administration or purpose, the Government had to be seen to be doing something in the face of press, public and political demands; and not only for the north-east. Additional aerodromes were planned. The Royal Flying Corps at home was to be more readily available, but this was scarcely a reinforcement. For the most part, the flying strength of the RFC consisted of instructors, who were hard-pressed to train the maximum number of pilots in the minimum amount of time, and qualified pilots who were waiting to go on active service.

These additions were only a gesture. They did not solve

fundamental problems. Zeppelins had to be attacked at night, but night flying was elementary, chancy and dangerous. What instruments there were in the cockpit lacked sophisticated lighting. Crude flarepaths were the only guides to take-off and landing. There were no purpose-built, night-fighter aircraft. Even if the available aeroplanes could match the height of the raiders, they took too long to do so. Even the B.E. 2c—which was to become the most successful of the Zeppelin hunters— took fifteen minutes to reach 3,500 feet.

Nearly two months passed before the Naval Airship Division made another raid. Although Hirsch had been virtually un-opposed, he realized that the short summer nights were danger-ous. While he had waited offshore for full darkness, he had hovered as low as 1,200 feet, and his bombing height had been down to 6,000 feet.

The delay of nearly two months was a prelude to some even heavier hammer blows.

CHAPTER 7

New Tactics

The German Navy used the lull to improve its plans for the destruction of London and the demoralization of the provinces. Military establishments, docks and communications were always important targets, but the most important of all was the will of the British people.

In July the Kaiser finally surrendered the pretence that central London should be saved from bombing. He made his routine order that historic buildings and statues were to be avoided, and expected people to believe that if an airship captain dropped a missile on Victoria Station he could avoid Buckingham Palace half a mile away.

An unrealistic and grandiose combined operations idea, to include aeroplanes as well as Army and Navy airships, was rejected. The Naval Airship Division was strong enough to be completely independent. By August it had L 10, L 11, L 12, L 13 and L 14, supported by SL 3 and SL 4.

With this apparently formidable fleet, and more ships on the way, there was renewed optimism. The view that Zeppelins would be more effective in a scouting rôle was muted but not silenced. The England offensive was planned and timed to coincide with the best of the late summer and early autumn weather.

The offensive opened on 9 August when L 10 (*Oberleutnant* Friedrich Wenke), L 11 (von Buttlar), L 12 (Werner Peterson), and L 13 (Heinrich Mathy) were ordered to attack London, while L 9 (*Kapitänleutnant* Odo Loewe) was to raid the Humber area. Strasser, with Wenke in L 10, was to control the London operation.

Shortly before 3 pm the five Zeppelins had made a rendez-vous and were on their way across the North Sea, but L 9 left the others about an hour later for her Humber objective. Mathy was forced to turn back when L 13 developed engine trouble over the Thames Estuary. Wenke, under the critical eye of Strasser, claimed to have bombed London, but the missiles fell on the RNAS station at Eastchurch. Von Buttlar, in L 11, dropped about twelve bombs on Lowestoft when he thought he was at Harwich; one woman was killed and seven people injured.

Loewe waited offshore for nightfall and then made a landfall at Atwick, between Bridlington and the Humber. To his surprise two RNAS aircraft from a new station drove him out to sea. He tried to come in nearer to Bridlington itself, but again found himself near Atwick, where another RNAS machine forced him to change direction. When he did arrive over England a ground mist made him unsure of his bearings, until he believed he had identified Hull. In fact he was some twenty miles away at Goole, where he dropped his bombs and killed sixteen people before he left the coast at Hornsea.

Peterson, in L 12, made an altogether different contribution to a night of almost unmitigated failure. He bombed Dover in the belief that he, too, was at Harwich. He dropped two 220-lb and twenty 110-lb explosive bombs as well as about seventy incendiaries. Most of them fell immediately offshore. There was very little damage—except to L 12 herself.

She was counterattacked by the most accurate anti-aircraft fire met by an airship to date. She was hit aft and, losing gas rapidly, she made for an emergency landing in Belgium. But time as well as gas ran out on her. Shortly after 3.30 am she landed gently on the sea, a few miles from Dunkirk, where she was towed into Ostend. The tow was made in daylight and RNAS pilots from the Dunkirk Squadron tried to attack her while she was at sea and when she was moored at Ostend. One pilot was killed and none of the others could be credited with her destruction. She was dead already, with a broken back.

Two nights later four more naval Zeppelins set out for London. Two never reached England; von Buttlar may have edged over the North Foreland and then retired; the fourth dropped bombs on Suffolk, where six people were killed and twenty four injured.

It was the persistent and skilful Wenke who saved the

beginning of the great offensive from complete failure. His L 10 was one of the four Zeppelins which Strasser sent to London on 17/18 August. Once again, two ships did not cross the coast. Von Buttlar, in L 11, made a characteristically untrue claim to have bombed the capital, but his attack was on Ashford and Faversham, in Kent, where his eighteen explosives and some forty incendiaries caused no casualties and only slight damage.

Wenke made a planned landfall on the Suffolk coast and was over the London area soon after 11.30 pm, at an altitude of about 10,000 feet. Accurate though his navigation had been, and despite the easily-seen lights of the metropolis, as well as a fine, clear night, he missed the prime target, the City of London itself, and bombed its eastern suburbs at Leytonstone, Leyton and Wanstead Flats.

In his raid report he stated that he had bombed the City 'between Blackfriars and London bridges'. Various explanations have been offered for Wenke's supposed error and, perhaps, his self-deception, one being that he had mistaken ponds and reservoirs for the Thames. This does not stand up to even a superficial consideration.

At 10,000 feet on a clear, starry night, the Thames, with at least six bridges in sharp focus, prominent landmarks such as the Houses of Parliament, St Thomas's Hospital, St Paul's Cathedral, and the especially well-lighted north bank, was unmistakable. Unlike von Buttlar, for example, Wenke was not a captain whose resolution was suspect. He was troubled by searchlights but they did no more than push him to a higher altitude. On such a fine night he could not have failed to see London spread out below him, and he must have believed that there were more important targets in the eastern area. His claim to have bombed between Blackfriars and London Bridges was another example of facts which were invented to fit a report.

Despite that lost opportunity, Wenke had made a welcome entry on the credit side of the campaign. His raid had killed ten people and injured forty-eight. Many houses were severely damaged, and some were destroyed, by the twenty explosive bombs and forty incendiaries. There were the inevitable protests, criticisms and outbursts of anger; but except, for the people in the raid, the attack did not have the same impact as that of Linnartz's pioneer assault. More sporadic, it did not concentrate on a comparatively small area of tight-packed

The first bomb to be dropped on England by a German airship fell at Great Yarmouth, Norfolk, on 19 January 1915. Two people were killed and three injured. Although the damage was severe and unique, like that at St. Peter's House (*above*), the raid caused no more than mild curiosity; only a few 'scaremongers' forecast future events. During the next three years, attacks—reinforced by Gotha and Giant aeroplanes—brought heavy casualties, extensive damage, fear, and a demand for reprisals.

Typical of the damage was that caused by a 660-lb missile dropped outside Odhams Printing Works in London on 28-29 January 1918, by a lone Giant bomber. More than 500 men, women, and children, trapped in the basement, fought to escape from the explosion and the horror of fire, a collapsed wall, and water. Thirty-eight people were killed and 85 injured.

The Zeppelin L 12 mortal[ly] stricken with a broken ba[ck] after she had been hit by an[ti-]aircraft guns over England d[ur]ing a raid in August 1915. H[er] attempt to make a safe landf[all] ended when she alighted [on] the sea near Dunkirk (*abov[e]*).

This dramatic photogra[ph] (*left*) of the first German airsh[ip] to be brought down over En[g]land was taken by an amate[ur] photographer, Mr. M. A. E[d]wards. SL II fell in flames [at] Cuffley, Hertfordshire, on [3] September 1916. She had be[en] attacked by Second Lieutena[nt] W. Leefe Robinson, RFC, w[ho] was awarded an immediate Vi[c]toria Cross.

streets. That first raid on the Empire's capital had had an unrepeatable emotional effect.

L 10 was never to make another operational raid. Three weeks later, commanded by Klaus Hirsch, she was struck by lightning while on patrol over the North Sea. Hirsch and his crew of nineteen were killed.

On 7/8 September the Army was back in action in an attempt to raid London. LZ 74 (*Hauptmann* George), LZ 77 (*Hauptmann* Horn), and the re-built SL 2 (*Hauptmann* von Wobeser) reached England, but Horn lost his way over Hertfordshire and took no part in the operation.

George's excitement, inexperience and indiscretion made him miss a prize that was there for the taking. LZ 74 had ground identification troubles before she reached the London area and George dropped all but one of his bombs on Cheshunt, in Hertfordshire. He flew on to the inner part of the capital, where the inefficiently-dimmed streets made it a target that no one could miss, except the unhappy George. His extravagance over Cheshunt had left him with one incendiary bomb, which he dropped on Fenchurch Street.

If the raid was a failure for the Zeppelins, it was a triumph for their poor relation, the rebuilt SL 2. *Hauptmann* von Wobeser made his landfall over the River Crouch, in Essex. Welcoming lights on the ground eased his route to the dockland area, where he bombed Millwall, Deptford, Greenwich, Woolwich and houses in adjacent suburbs. Damage to the docks was severe but not crippling. Eighteen explosives and thirty-eight incendiaries killed eighteen people, including three children, and injured thirty-eight.

The immediate public dismay and virulent criticisms of a seemingly abject Admiralty and Government were still loud and clear when Strasser sent four Zeppelins to England on the very next day. L 11 (von Buttlar) and L 14 (Bocker) took off from Nordholz between 1 pm and 1.20 pm, and L 9 (Loewe) and L 13 (Mathy) left Hage shortly after 2 pm. The weather prediction for a fine, clear night with light, fluky winds and some ground mist, proved to be accurate; conditions were exactly right.

Mathy, von Buttlar and Bocker were under orders to attack London. Loewe, with Strasser on board, had a different objective: the benzol works at Skinningrove, on the cliffs between Saltburn and Whitby.

The almost inevitable engine trouble forced von Buttlar to return only an hour after take off. L 14 was reported to have had similar difficulties, and Bocker dropped his bombs without effect over Norfolk before he returned to base.

After some difficulty, Loewe found the Skinningrove plant. His bombs scored direct hits on it but, remarkably, the damage was negligible. The extent of that escape from destruction was summed-up by H. A. Jones, in the official history, *The War in the Air*:

> One incendiary bomb made a direct hit on the benzol house, but it failed to penetrate the concrete. Another, a high-explosive bomb, fell within ten feet of it, and although the bomb broke the water-main and the electric light cables, and did other minor damage, it failed to damage the benzol house. Had the bomb hit this or the tanks, which held 45,000 gallons of benzine, not much of the works could have survived. The works had one other extraordinary escape, as a bomb which made a direct hit on a T.N.T. store failed to explode.

Nearly 300 miles away, Heinrich Mathy was the hero of the night. Having waited off the English coast for complete darkness, he set his course for London. His route took him over what was in general a well-illuminated landscape. Places which were efficiently dimmed were in sharp contrast to those which were not. Ahead of him was the distant glare of a virtually undimmed capital; and there the lights were bright enough for Mathy to recognize and identify individual areas and features.

Flying in from the north-west, he dropped five bombs on Golders Green; and then, at an altitude of between 8,000 and 10,000 feet, he released fifteen explosive bombs and more than fifty incendiaries on Bloomsbury, the Holborn district and the City of London itself. Liverpool Street station was damaged. Office buildings and close-together textile warehouses in the lanes and streets between London Wall and Cheapside erupted into soaring flames. Although it showed that unfaltering courage and determination which never deserts the fire services, the London Fire Brigade could do no more than contain the blaze, and the damage and destruction were heavy.

Mathy ended his raid by dropping the last of his bombs on Liverpool Street station, where seven people were killed and two motor omnibuses were hit.

Wood Street, which linked Cheapside and London Wall, was said to have had the greatest single damage; but the greatest single impact was on Bartholomew Close, just north of Newgate Street, where Mathy dropped his heaviest bomb. The effect was devastating. Of all the bombs which he dropped that night, this one was the most important to him. It weighed 660 lbs and was the largest missile yet dropped on Britain. He mentioned it particularly in his report: 'The explosive effect of the 300-kg bomb must be very great, since a whole cluster of lights vanished in its crater.'

The total casualties in London were twenty-two killed and eighty-seven injured. Damage was estimated to have been more than £530,000—serious by any air-raid standards but sensationally so in 1915.

As the City's fires blazed, all London's anti-aircraft defences tried to trap and shoot down L 13. More than a score of searchlights probed the sky, while about thirty guns 'thundered away'. They were unsuccessful but a shell from one of them, stationed on Parliament Hill, Hampstead, was close enough to force Mathy to climb from 8,500 feet to between 11,000 and 12,000 feet. He found refuge in the clouds away from the gunfire and the searchlight beams.

The whole of Britain was angrily astonished by this third proof of the capital's vulnerability. Londoners in their thousands had watched L 13 in a clear, starlit sky. She was so low, some said, that details of the Zeppelin could be picked out. There were others who were certain they had actually seen the crew. An eye-witness on the roof of the *Morning Post* building, in Wellington Street, Strand, captured a brief but vivid impression:

> For a few minutes the Zepp seemed to float above us, as still as a becalmed yacht. It moved its way in and out of the searchlights as if they and the Zepp were playing a game. When the beams lit up the long, slender cigar shape, the scene might have been a set-piece in a Crystal Palace fireworks display, with the guns as theatrical noises off. It was all spectacularly beautiful, and then, like some silver ghost, she glided away northwards. Next morning I could hardly believe that it had been a murderer in the sky.

Experts, self-styled experts, the newspapers, politicians and a largely uninformed public demanded immediate action and straight answers to some awkward questions. Linnartz's raid had not been widely seen or heard. But the attack by L 13 had brought tragic reality to thousands. It was a miracle, they said, that there were not even greater casualties. Three hospitals, for example—St Bartholomew's, in West Smithfield, and two in Queen Square—had been precisely in the bombing area.

The questions were not merely awkward but embarrassing as well. If the Zeppelin had been seen by thousands over London on a fine, clear night, why was she not seen and reported en route *to* the capital? Why had the Eastern Mobile Section—set up especially to cover Zeppelin incursions over East Anglia—failed to fire at L 13 when she made her landfall at Wells-next-the-Sea and crossed above King's Lynn? Why had aircraft from Hendon, Hounslow, Northolt, Eastchurch, Grain, Westgate and elsewhere failed to intercept her? Why had machines from Redcar and Whitley Bay allowed L 9 to make her leisurely way to Skinningrove? Why was there no anti-aircraft fire from Tees and Humber?

People in the inner circles of the Admiralty and the War Office knew the answers. Apart from the shortage of guns and aircraft there was a lack of alertness at some observation posts and warning stations; there were local allegations that posts had been unmanned when the Zeppelins had crossed the coast. Undoubtedly, the reporting chain from coast to Admiralty had been inefficient.

Seven aircraft were known to have tried to find the airships that night. Three from Great Yarmouth had seen nothing of Bocker and Mathy. Three from Redcar had missed Loewe. A seaplane took off from a trawler in the North Sea in a fruitless search. One RNAS pilot had been killed when his aeroplane had crashed on landing, in the darkness, at Bacton, Norfolk. It was blown to pieces by its own bombs.

Public reaction to anti-aircraft fire depended on where people were. To those who had personally endured the London raid, the sound of the guns was muted if not lost in the crescendo of crashing bombs and collapsing buildings. Only those who were near to the gun sites felt that a real attempt was being made. Elsewhere, the gunfire was reported to have been 'intermittent'; an impression caused by the twenty-six guns which fired, if not separately, at least not collectively. A South African war veteran, who watched L 13 from the Thames Embankment, said he could hear only the 1 pounder pom-poms which were, he said, 'no better than a child's pop-gun'.

There was a swift response from a discomfited Admiralty. Three days after Mathy's raid the 62-year-old Admiral Sir Percy Scott—who had retired in 1913—was recalled to take charge of the air defences of London and its approaches. But the appointment of this brilliant, self-opinionated officer was stamped with failure from the outset.

A famous and admired public figure, popularly known as the 'father of naval gunnery', Scott was anything but a complacent cipher willing to keep within the ring fence of naval convention. He was a radical, in the mould of his previous chief, 'Jackie' Fisher. On the eve of the war he had made a sensational statement that submarines would be paramount and that the big warships would be destroyed by them. A man who had spent almost all his service with battleships, he was dogmatic in his opinion that Britain should stop building them and concentrate on submarines and light surface craft.

In the event his gloomy forecast was wrong, but only, perhaps, because the battleships seldom put themselves at risk. No British or German battleship was sunk by submarines, but at the beginning of the war the Royal Navy's other losses from U-boats were enough to justify his prediction. In the first three months of the war five British cruisers were German submarine victims. Three of them, *Aboukir*, *Hogue* and *Cressy*, each of 12,000 tons, were sunk on the same day by U.9, with a total loss of sixty-five officers and 1,400 petty officers and ratings. And Scott's forecast about the power of the submarine was to be grimly endorsed when the Merchant Service struggled for survival.

He had been responsible for putting 'big guns in big ships' and had also devised various improvements to enable naval guns to be used in the South African War. Progressive, inventive, and open-minded to new ideas, Scott nevertheless had little faith in the aeroplane as a Zeppelin killer; not, at any rate, until there were specially-built night fighters with specially-trained pilots and improved take-off and landing strips. The aeroplane and even the seaplane—in which he had even less faith—were, of course, to be part of his new defence scheme. But to the man to whom gunnery was a creed, aeroplanes would always be the handmaidens of the guns. 'The defence of London by aircraft', he said, 'begins over the Zeppelin sheds and the defence by gunfire begins at the coast.'

His request for 120 additional guns—suitable for anti-aircraft defence—and fifty searchlights was the first of his setbacks. The Admiralty could not supply him immediately with any more guns because, among other things, there were no appropriate time fuses for high-explosive shells. Nevertheless, Scott wasted no time. He begged, borrowed and otherwise acquired a variety of guns from Woolwich and the Royal Navy. But, most of all, he wanted one of the French 75-mm mobile guns—the 'auto cannon'—which had been used for the anti-aircraft defence of Paris. It fired a high-explosive shell with a time fuse and was credited with an effective range of 21,000 feet. By itself it could be a realistic reinforcement for immediate use and could be copied for multi-manufacture.

Admiral Scott asked Arthur Balfour—Churchill's successor as First Lord—for authority to send his newly-appointed assistant, Commander Rawlinson, to Paris and bring back the 75-mm gun.* The amiable Balfour showed his customary dilatoriness; he neither approved nor arranged the visit. Scott took direct action and Rawlinson was back with the 'auto-cannon' while the First Lord was still in a cocoon of remoteness which shut off uncomfortable thoughts about aerial bombardment. On its own this incident is unimportant, but it emphasizes the extraordinary indifference at the highest levels to aerial bombardment. Throughout his brief service as London's master gunner, Scott was frustrated by the 'usual channels' and the Admiralty's ponderous response to his urgency.

The 'auto-cannon' was a significantly different weapon in his hurriedly-formed defence plan. In addition to static weapons, he had six 13-pounder mobile guns from an Anti-Aircraft Section which was mobilizing at Woolwich, and some 3-pounder high-velocity Vickers mounted on lorry chassis. The 1-pounder pom-pom, that useless left-over from the Boer War, was official discarded.

Scott's first attempt at planned, co-ordinated protection was based on defence in depth. The greatest striking power of the guns was concentrated on the coast; the other back-up guns were sited along the routes to London. In and immediately around the capital itself the last defence link would deal with those raiders which had avoided the aerial blockade. Search-

---

* Rawlinson was a Lieutenant-Colonel, Royal Garrison Artillery, but while he was under Admiralty orders he assumed the rank of Commander, RN.

lights were integral with all the guns. On paper, at any rate, aeroplanes were in a relatively minor supporting rôle.

In just under a month Admiral Scott had given London its first anti-aircraft defence organization. Gunners, searchlight crews and ground observers were trained as well as possible in the short time available. But the plan was scarcely stitched together when airships struck once more at the heart of the capital, to begin the first phase of a great offensive.

CHAPTER 8

The Great Offensive

The first challenge to Sir Percy Scott's defences came on the night of 13/14 October. Three previous attempts had failed; one of them, on 13/14 September, forced Mathy, in L 13, to make a hurried exit from the East Coast when two of the gasbags were hit by a 6-pounder at Felixstowe. The defenders did not know of the hit, or that Mathy's ship was damaged on landing.

L 13, however, was ready for the next raid a month later. The planned objective was Liverpool, but because bad weather prevented the long flight to the north-west, a raid on London was ordered instead.

L 11 (von Buttlar), L 14 (Bocker) and L 15 (*Kapitänleutnant* Joachim Breithaupt) left Nordholz soon after midday and made a rendezvous with L 13 (Mathy) and L 16 (Peterson) from Hage. All five ships, with Mathy in operational command, began the crossing in formation; but L 11 lost touch and the four other Zeppelins crossed the coast at Bacton within half an hour of each other. L 11 arrived about an hour later.

This time the four airships, and, later, L 11, were observed and reported to the Admiralty, together with the positive information that the four (L 13, L 14, L 15 and L 16) were making for London. Scott's defence system was facing the test of a co-ordinated raid. It was to be a severe baptism for Scott's co-ordination as well. Even the Royal Flying Corps aeroplanes from airfields at Suttons Farm, Joyce Green and Hainault Farm, in Essex, were sent up to search and destroy.

While Mathy led the three Zeppelins to London, von Buttlar was attacked almost as soon as he made his landfall. Machine guns from the Eastern Mobile Section drove him off. He dropped his bombs on neighbouring villages and then retreated out to sea. There were no casualties and only minor damage. He reported that he had bombed West Ham and Woolwich— which were more than 130 miles away.

People in London and on its outskirts could not complain about the lack of gunfire on the night of 13 October. The guns thundered into action and gave the confident impression that Zeppelins no longer had the freedom of the skies. Many residents were more frightened by this new sound and the danger of falling shrapnel than they were of the bombs. Conversely, the shuddering, shaking noise convinced people that if a Zeppelin survived the barrage it would be driven away from the capital.

This experience was so new that the number of weapons and their locations were deceptive. Guns were said to have been in the most unlikely places. A man walking along Grosvenor Place from Victoria Station said: 'I was almost blown off my feet by the gun which fired from just over the wall in the garden of Buckingham Palace.' Someone else was certain that one was placed below Nelson's column in Trafalgar Square.

The absolute secrecy about the number of guns and their locations was perhaps the strongest justification of a rigid censorship. The conflicting and often confusing reports were encouraged. The defences in the outer ring, along the Thames and in the centre of London, put up a barrage of fire which surprised the Zeppelins and heartened the citizens.

There was astonishment when L 15 was seen to glide over the capital in a clear, starlit sky. Breithaupt, on his first mission to England, was the only captain to reach inner London. The reflected glow of lights, which he saw some forty miles away, helped him check his course. He dropped his first bombs at Broxbourne, in Hertfordshire—about twenty miles from his objective—to silence a 13-pounder mobile gun. He reached the centre of London at about 10 pm.

Despite warnings to 'take cover' and the experience of previous raids, crowds in the streets watched L 15 in awed wonder as she cruised overhead. Searchlight beams exposed her even more clearly. Nearly everyone was sure that she would bomb the capital; but, with an illogical optimism, few of the sky-watchers believed they were in danger. L 15 was a world away from reality. Later, a member of the Lyceum Theatre staff said: 'She was as pretty as a picture up there, and even afterwards, when I saw the dead bodies and the terrible injuries and helped with the wounded, I could not believe somehow that she had done it.'

There were cheers from the crowds as the Green Park gun forced L 15 to climb out of range. Breithaupt's main targets were said to have been the Admiralty, the War Office and the Bank of England. The scene below him was so brightly-etched that he was able to recognize famous buildings, landmarks and the great parks. He knew, however, that it would be impossible to pinpoint one particular target; he would be lucky if he hit any of those three objectives.

All the same, his first attack was only a few rooftops away, about 600 yards east, on the streets which ran north from the Strand and on parts of the Strand itself. Some of his nineteen explosive bombs and many incendiaries fell on Aldwych, Wellington Street, Carey Street, the Royal Courts of Justice, Chancery Lane, Gray's Inn, Lincoln's Inn, Hatton Garden, Holborn and Farringdon Road.

Almost every theatre was full. As the first bombs fell the laughter and enjoyment of audiences for *The Scarlet Pimpernel* at the Strand, *The Prodigal Son* at the Aldwych, *Between Two Women* at the Lyceum, and *To Night's the Night* at the Gaiety turned to screams and a minor panic in a rush for the exits. The front of the Strand Theatre was severely damaged. A dozen people were killed outside the Lyceum. An omnibus was blown to pieces in Aldwych itself.

There were dead, dying and injured in the crowded streets, some of which were as narrow as lanes, and into which ambulances and fire engines forced their way. There was pandemonium. But there was coolness and some quiet bravery as well, and not least in the theatres. The hoary tradition that 'the show must go on' was upheld by, among others, Julia Nielson and Fred Terry, who tried to calm the Strand audience and keep people in their seats, and by Leslie Henson, who said he never worked so hard to raise laughs out of the Gaiety patrons.

Fragments and shrapnel from bombs, anti-aircraft shells and splinters of flying glass caused death and terrible injuries. There were mutilations which resembled those in a Casualty Clearing Station in France; except for those who had seen active service, no one had ever experienced anything like this. There were corpses which were unmarked, victims of blasts, a phenomenon not then understood.

Breithaupt turned east over London, seeking perhaps the Bank of England. If he was complacent after his first scatter of bombs, he was alarmingly disturbed by the French 'auto-cannon'. It had been taken to the Honourable Artillery Company's headquarters at Finsbury. Commander Rawlinson saw that the Zeppelin, flying at an estimated 11,000 feet, was well within range. There was a brief, tense wait for the first 'kill' of an airship over Britain. The shell exploded at 7,200 feet. Before a second round could have any effect L 15 had climbed high enough to avoid the gun's maximum elevation of 83 degrees. But the threat was enough for Breithaupt. L 15 left hurriedly for home and safety.

Mathy, Bocker, and Peterson had mixed fortunes. Mathy, in L 13, had the heaviest bomb load, of 4,370 lbs; it included another of the 660-lb missiles, one of which had shattered St Bartholomew Close on 9 September. Now, because he was so heavily loaded, he planned to attack a secondary but important target and thus be free to bomb London at the most effective height. He chose the Hampton waterworks and reservoirs on the Middlesex bank of the Thames.

But this was not Mathy's lucky night. He dropped his first bombs, four 110-lb explosives, to distract a 13-pounder mobile gun between Hertford and Hatfield. He found the upper Thames with some difficulty. A failure to recognize the difference between the Thames itself and the River Wey made him miss the Hampton objective, and his attack caused only minor damage to the nearby village of Shalford.

He dropped the rest of his bombs at Woolwich, which had a remarkable escape. The vital arsenal, the barracks and hundreds of homes were untouched by the bombs, which included the 660-lb missile. There was one fatal casualty and only minor damage.

Instead of following Breithaupt's route to the northern approaches, Bocker, in L 14, steered south-east to the Isle of Sheppey and then to Hythe, where he released nine explosive bombs. Fifteen soldiers were killed and eleven injured. Bocker turned for London but reached Croydon, twelve miles or so from the city centre. His arrival was officially logged at just before 12.30 am, although some local records put it as much as an hour and a half earlier. He unloaded the remainder of his bombs on a sleeping, unsuspecting population.

Bocker's attack on a relatively unimportant objective suggests that, because of the junction of railway tracks, he mistook Croydon for one of the approaches to a main line London terminus. His eighteen bombs killed nine people. Three of these were brothers, aged 10, 14 and 15: one was killed instantly; another was dead on arrival at hospital; the third died later from shock.

Peterson, in L 16, did follow much the same route to London as that taken by Breithaupt, but he never reached the capital. He dropped sixteen explosive bombs and thirty incendiaries on Hertford, twenty-five miles away. Nine people were killed and fifteen were reported to have been injured.

Five RFC aeroplanes took off from three airfields: Hainault Farm, Joyce Green and Suttons Farm. Only one of them even saw a Zeppelin, a B.E. 2c, piloted by an 18-year-old Second-Lieutenant, J. C. Slessor, who became the distinguished Marshal of the Royal Air Force and Chief of Air Staff, Sir John Slessor.

He had no difficulty in spotting L 16, but when he was 1,000 feet below her she escaped. In his book, *The Central Blue*, Sir John wrote: 'The great bulk swung round—the most extraordinary sight—cocked its nose up at an incredible angle and climbed away from me.'

The casualties for the raid were seventy-one killed and 128 reported injured. Damage was estimated at some £80,000 (of which more than £50,000 occurred in London). Official records of bombs dropped are never unarguably accurate, but the night's total was stated to have been 189 explosive and incendiaries; about eighty of them fell on London. In terms of casualties, damage and a further blow to the nation's morale, the raid had been a success by any standards—except one: the maximum force of a consolidated raid on London had not been achieved.

Sir Percy Scott's object had failed too, but his guns had diverted the Zeppelins and saved London from more serious damage. Four of the five airship captains were impressed and surprised by the fire power. Scott cannot be blamed if none of it was a serious threat. His dispositions were too scattered to bring a concentration of effort anywhere; but he had made the best use of modest resources.

Given more time and freedom of action, he might have improved even those modest resources. But circumstances had forced him to make hurried dispositions and put together a co-ordination system which, at best, was an enthusiastically-trained compromise. He had to carry the responsibility of apparent failure. The frustrations of what he described as 'red-tapism' were such that four days after the raid he threatened to resign. On 18 October he sent a typically pugnacious Minute to the First Lord:

> If I am to be responsible for the gunnery defences of London, I must be allowed to do things my way, and not be interfered with by the Admiralty. If the Admiralty are to settle what guns are to be used in the defence of London and how they are to be obtained, then they become responsible for the defence of London and I resign . . . I must have a free hand to procure what is wanted, and how best I can, and not be handicapped by Admiralty red-tapism.

Admiral Scott remained in charge, but his eventual departure was inevitable.

For Germany, too, the raid left unsolved problems. There had been twenty attacks since the campaign had begun on 20 January. Two hundred and seven people had been killed, and official figures gave 543 as having been injured. But the citadel was still intact. There had not been one strategic result.

A greater concentration of Zeppelins was essential to achieve the object, and yet the commitment to the destruction of London was still marred by indecision and uncertainty. The use of a larger fleet was questioned; and if performance on this last raid was a yardstick, there was good reason for questions and, perhaps, critical examination.

Control and communications during the operation had posed more serious problems than those of Admiral Scott's unexpected fire power. Mathy had been in wireless touch with his five ships over the North Sea, but when the coast was crossed, inter-communication between four of the five Zeppelins was soon lost. It is true that L 16's transmitter broke down, but the lack of overall control emphasizes the unreliability of a scarcely-developed system.

Although Mathy and Bocker had navigation difficulties, they ended up only a short flight away from the centre of London. It is hard to understand how Peterson could have mistaken the small country town of Hertford, some twenty miles away, for

Stratford, East Ham and West Ham, which were the targets he reported.

For whatever reason, Mathy and Bocker had been diverted by secondary targets. If the 660-lb bomb had hit Woolwich Arsenal the results would have been sensational, and it is possible that Bocker believed he had wrecked a main line junction. It is impossible to accept Peterson's claim that he was ever over London. The fascinating question remains unanswered: why did none of the captains—and especially Mathy and Bocker—reinforce Breithaupt's success? The flashes of gunfire, the flames from burning buildings, and the clear sight of L 16 illuminated by the probing criss-cross of searchlight beams were—or should have been—a beckoning beacon to all three captains.

Superficially, at any rate, there was some encouragement to Germany's strategic thinking that attacks on the capital would affect the rest of the country. There was alarm and despondency among night-shift workers. In the North and Midlands there were places where production was suspended during an air raid or when there was word-of-mouth news, or rumour, that 'Zepps' had been sighted or reported. In the mornings after an attack people were late for work—in an era when hardly any employee was ever late. There was an unprecedented amount of time lost because of illness; only some of it, and some of the night-shift interruptions, justified the accusations of more safely-placed critics that all munitions workers were 'shirkers in a cushy job'.

There were the natural malingerers who made the most of a novel situation, but for everyone in an undefended factory, shipyard or blast furnace a raid, or even the prospect of one that did not take place, was a new and very frightening experience.

Throughout the country there was a loud demand for revenge—more politely called reprisals—against the German people. It was well nurtured by some Members of Parliament and by newspapers which reflected their readers' emotional opinions.

There was no serious intention to bomb Germany strategically, although it was politically expedient to create a public impression that reprisal raids were only a matter of time. Britain had no suitable aeroplanes for the task. Handley Page was still working on his 0/100, but its completion, and that of its successors, was too far off to be included in any short-term strategic policy. In any event, there was a consensus in the War Office (and in a Government that did not know what to do for the best), and among the knowledgeable commentators and students of war, that victory against the Zeppelins would be won only by destroying them in the air. And a diversion of effort to satisfy what was certainly a serious public clamour could be made only at the expense of night-fighter aircraft and pilots, genuine anti-aircraft guns and the British Expeditionary Force's desperate need for day fighters.

During the three months' lull before the next raid many people who could afford to do so closed their houses in vulnerable or potentially vulnerable areas. Brighton, for example, had a large influx of fugitives, who could use the hour-long rail link with London and sleep safely and peacefully at night.

Even some of those people, however, might have slept less peacefully if they had known that more powerful Zeppelins were being built, designed and tested. Two ships in the L 20 class were already in service. Much more threatening were the 'super-Zeppelins'—the 6-engined 'big thirties' class—to be ready for operations by mid-year. Allied agents had confirmed that airships even more powerful than the L 20 class were under construction at Friedrichshafen and Lowenthal. Details were secret; but the agents learned enough for Britain to realize that the 'super-Zeppelins' would be a formidable reinforcement for the aerial battleships.

Peter Strasser was staking his reputation on the 'big thirties'. Although his superior officers' faith in him was apparently undiminished, he had not won a quick victory or, indeed, shown that the Zeppelin could bring it about. Time was beginning to evaporate for him. The London defences were still weak, and the rest of England was still virtually unguarded. But he knew that the British were trying to improve their night-flying and that they must soon have an array of purpose-built anti-aircraft guns. His critics would become more impatient and therefore more vocal. He needed his 'super-Zeppelins' to fight enemies on two fronts.

But the first of the 'big thirties' did not fly on her first operational mission until July, 1916. Meanwhile he had to make the best use of his present fleet, and especially his new L 20 ships. Each of these had a capacity of 1,264,100 cubic feet, a length of 585 feet 5 inches, a diameter of 61 feet 4 inches, four

Maybach HSLu engines with a total horsepower of 960, and a speed of 55–60 miles per hour.

The L 20 ships and the others would keep the assault going until the 'super-Zeppelins' were ready. Significantly, however, Strasser was now thinking ahead. His hopes for a quick knock-out blow had gone. More time as well as more ships would be needed. But the 'big thirties', the pride of his fleet, would lead the decisive armada. Although their design and construction details were unknown to the British, Germany made no secret of the existence of the 'super-Zeppelins'. They were well publicized as a propaganda weapon as well as a combat one.

Britain, however, was developing a new weapon, too. And that was very secret indeed.

CHAPTER 9

Chaos and Confusion

On 8 January, 1916, Vice-Admiral Reinhard Scheer succeeded Admiral von Pohl as Commander-in-Chief, High Seas Fleet. He had very decided views about the use of Zeppelins.

London was still to be the primary target but not to the exclusion of other objectives. The Admiral shared the conviction that the aerial bombardment of the capital would be decisive, but he had an equally firm conviction that surrender would come more quickly with stronger attacks on a broader front. He was not alone in this view, of course, but his plan was one of indiscriminate bombing which would strike most of England and leave it waiting abjectly for submission after the fall of London.

Munitions production would be seriously and, finally, fatally disrupted. Railway and telephone communications would be destroyed. The immobilization of ports would dangerously reduce food and material supplies. As the entry haven for large cargoes from America, Liverpool was now a specially important, and immediate, target.

Despite the urgent necessity to reduce England to submission by aerial bombardment, Admiral Scheer did not believe that the Zeppelin alone should, or indeed could, achieve it. He was a modern, progressive officer without the closed mind of his peers. He had always recognized the potential raiding power of the Zeppelin, but he was a blue-water man. Every separate unit in the Imperial Navy, from battle-cruisers to U-boats, was part of the High Seas Fleet. And so was the Zeppelin.

Admiral Scheer saw the assault on England in wider terms than those of airship raids or isolated seaborne attacks.

Airships could become part of combined naval operations, to cause confusion, chaos and heavy casualties in the country and on the coast; all of it part of the great assault on London.

Strasser and Admiral Scheer quickly developed a close and lasting mutual understanding. The Commander-in-Chief was to support him against strong opposition and criticism. All the same, Strasser's power and influence were now restricted. As commander of the Naval Airship Division he had operational independence and responsibility; but policy decisions and control rested firmly with the Admiral. Strasser was never allowed to forget that scouting and fleet protection were no less important than the aerial bombardment of England; and he never ceased to resent it.

There was nothing contradictory, nor any confusion of priorities, in the Commander-in-Chief's policy. He was confident that he would have enough Zeppelins for the grand design of his combined operations, for separate raids on England, and for scouting and fleet protection.

By the time the Naval Airship Division began the second phase of the great offensive, on 31 January, 1916, Britain had endured other setbacks and shocks. Field-Marshal Sir John French had been replaced as Commander-in-Chief of the British Expeditionary Force by General Sir Douglas Haig. The Gallipoli offensive had ended in a humiliating defeat, and the peninsula had been evacuated on 8 January. The Battle of Loos, in September, 1915, had cost Britain some 50,000 casualties in nine or ten days.

In January the Military Service Bill brought an end to voluntary recruitment and brought conscription to unmarried men and widowers without children between the ages of 18 and 41. The Home Secretary, Sir John Simon, resigned in protest. Although there had been only minor opposition to the Bill in its stages in the House of Commons, and although the nation recognized the necessity of it, the Bill and the subsequent Act caused resentment and suspicion, especially among the workers; industrial disputes and unofficial strikes were to follow. They were to increase the public dislike of munitions workers, who were accused of being overpaid and underworked.

The early administration of conscription did nothing to stop resentment. Men in genuine 'reserved occupations' or on 'work of national importance' were conscripted while men in jobs which the public reckoned were 'cushy' rather than essential were excluded. Too many 'shirkers', it was said, were finding that munitions work had, apparently, an ever-increasing army of its own, and always with room for recruits.

There were other discontents as well. A policy of fair shares all round was, of course, a failure. Better-off people were not experiencing the effects of increasing food shortages. Business 'profiteers' became the new bogeymen but, as with munitions workers, it was a general rather than a particular expression of contempt. Many of the discontents were real enough but were rooted in jealousy and spitefulness rather than idealistic indignation.

Sir John Simon's resignation had strengthened rumours of disagreements in Government. The *Globe* newspaper had been suppressed for two weeks in Novemeber, 1915, for a revelation that the nation's hero, Lord Kitchener, was about to resign. As the price of its re-appearance the newspaper was compelled to deny the rumour, but the story was near enough to the truth to make the Government act so drastically.

Kitchener's influence had certainly gone, and the Government wanted to be rid of him, but dare not face the public anger if he went. To the politicians he was a spent force. To the people he never ceased to be a great man. The *Globe's* story was prompted by a devious plan which had been devised to push the Secretary for War sideways. The idea was to send him to Gallipoli to make on-the-spot assessments and decisions. Meanwhile Prime Minister Asquith would take over the War Office 'temporarily', and changes which Kitchener could not accept would be made. But he stayed as Secretary for War until he was drowned seven months later.

The patriotic fervour of the war's opening months had been replaced by ironclad determination. The absence of official good news was taken as a sign that things were not going well, or were probably going badly.

The silence about casualty figures, some hidden naval losses, the euphemisms about Gallipoli and the Dardanelles, the natural glorification of minor successes inside major failures, deceived hardly anyone. Even the highly-publicized heroism at the Gallipoli landings in April, 1915, did not hide the disaster of that fatal expedition.

At home those human symbols of war on a unique scale were now commonplace: the growing casualty lists in the newspapers were being set in even smaller type; there were many more women in mourning clothes and men in black suits with black ties and armbands; the blinded and limbless soldiers, whose active service was over, were still the objects of sympathy but no longer caused surprise or curiosity.

All this, then, was a tempting situation for the German High Seas Fleet Command and its Naval Airship Division. But this was also the point at which, perhaps, a serious miscalculation was made. A nation of grumblers, accustomed to expressing itself without restraint, was taken for a nation in despair.

Admiral Scheer and Peter Strasser had agreed on a plan for the comprehensive bombing of England. There were to be three separate raiding areas: Northern, Midlands and Southern. The North's principal objectives were to be those of the Forth and Clydeside. The Midland's main targets were designated as Liverpool, the Humber and its hinterland, Birmingham and Sheffield. The Southern zone had London, of course, as its main objective, with East Anglia as a secondary one.

On 31 January, 1916, nine Zeppelins left Germany to begin the second phase of the great offensive. Although seventy-one people were killed and 113 injured, the raid was a serious setback for Strasser and revealed, once again, familiar flaws which threatened the strategic concept. The weather was an almost insurmountable barrier to the nine Zeppelins which took off. Freezing rain, snow and thick ground mist over England made visibility and accurate navigation impossible. The radio-direction-finding stations at Nordholz and Bruges were unreliable and, at times, useless.

The plan to make squadron attacks on England 'middle and south' began and ended in almost total confusion. That confusion was shared by the British ground observers. The Zeppelins' courses were so haphazard that the observers lost track of them and were unable to allocate to particular airships many of the 379 bombs which were reported to have been dropped. Complete allocation-accuracy was seldom possible when several Zeppelins were attacking; but the raid of 31 January/1 February was the only one by airships when allocation and movement-tracking were so unreliable.

Burton upon Trent, for example, was bombed three times that night but there is no reliable record to confirm which ships were responsible. Von Buttlar, in L 11, and *Kapitänleutnant* Franz Stabbert, in L 20, are generally credited with having made two of the attacks, and the third was indisputably carried out by Mathy in L 13. All of the ships except L 11 (von Buttlar, with Strasser on board) made bombing attacks, but to say that their captains' reports differed from what was eventually confirmed in Britain is a monumental understatement.

Mathy and Max Dietrich (L 21) crossed the coast together. Mathy's first bombs fell harmlessly on Stoke-on-Trent Parachute flares and the radio-direction-finding stations were no help even to that resourceful captain. We know he may have attacked Burton upon Trent, and he certainly bombed Scunthorpe—which he mistook for Goole—where three people were killed and seven injured.

Dietrich claimed to have bombed Liverpool and Birkenhead. In his report he was sure he had identified both places:

> Steered out to sea north of Liverpool, then attacked both cities . . . Docks, harbour works and factories of both cities were attacked with thirty-five 50 kg and twenty incendiary bombs. Explosions of all bombs and good results were clearly seen from on board.

The bombs were dropped on Birmingham, sixty-five miles away. The claim to have 'steered out to sea' and to have identified 'docks and harbour works', in the middle of England emphasizes the conspiracy of deceit among the Zeppelin crews and captains. In Birmingham thirty-three people were killed and twenty were known to have been injured; almost all the casualties occurred in the suburbs.

If there had been a prize for the greatest exaggeration of the night it would surely have been won by Joachim Breithaupt in L 15. He probably had the most serious engine trouble of all the similarly affected ships. Despite two of his four engines having failed before he reached the English coast, Breithaupt flew on with determination.

No one knows exactly where he went or how far he penetrated the country beyond the East Coast. There were unconfirmed reports that he dropped bombs near Cambridge, that L 15 was one of the untraced ships which attacked Burton upon Trent. One thing we do know: he was never, as he stated, near Sheffield; and least of all was he anywhere near Liverpool, which he reported as having bombed at 9.30 pm.

He excelled Dietrich in his detailed description of a target area he could not possibly have reached. A 'large city complex, divided in two parts by a broad sheet of water, running north and south, joined by a lighted bridge,' was identified as Liverpool and Birkenhead, although they were not linked by a bridge. He embroidered his claim to have made a successful attack: 'A huge glow of fire was seen to cover the city from a great distance.'

In the unlikely event that L 15 did bomb Burton upon Trent, no one could have mistaken that town on the comparatively small River Trent, and on the Trent and Mersey Canal, for 'a large city complex divided into two parts by a broad sheet of water'.

The Mersey docks system was on either side of that river. On the Liverpool bank it ran from Bootle to Dingle and covered about six and a half miles. The area enclosed by the docks and basins was about 470 acres. The Gladstone Graving Dock was then the largest dry dock in Europe. On the Cheshire side of the Mersey, at Birkenhead, the area enclosed by the docks was about 160 acres, and there were over nine miles of quays. On the famous Liverpool skyline there were three unmistakable buildings: the seventeen-storey Royal Liver Friendly Society, the Cunard Steamship Line and the Mersey Docks and Harbour Board. Burton upon Trent, by contrast, was a modest-sized town with an area of some 4,000 acres and a population of fewer than 50,000. The combined population of Liverpool and Birkenhead was about 950,000.

Bocker, in L 14, made no extravagant claims. He flew as far west as Shrewsbury, but then lost his way to Liverpool. His report states that he bombed Nottingham; understandably he mistook this for Derby, only 16 miles distant. His nine explosive missiles hit the Midland Railway Company's maintenance works where three men were killed and two injured.

Peterson, in L 16, had engine trouble. He spent a fruitless three hours above the East Coast and reported that he had dropped all his bombs on Great Yarmouth; but he is believed to have released only two bombs over England, at Swaffham, more than forty miles away.

Kapitänleutnant Herbert Ehrlich, in L 17, was another captain whose ship had engine trouble. She is known to have flown in over Sheringham. Searchlights picked her up at nearby Holt, where Ehrlich dropped his bombs in some fields. Incredibly, he believed, or so he claimed in his report, that he had bombed Immingham, more than 100 miles away. If an airship captain could recognize anything that night, Immingham, or at least its immediate setting, would have been easily identified. The Humberside port was only a short distance upstream from Grimsby, which itself was prominent not only for its 140-acre, deep-water docks system but also for the most famous Humber landmark, the 306-feet high Hydraulic Tower.

In the best of conditions it would have been difficult to identify Immingham separately from Grimsby; but the pinpoint precision of the claim suggests another strand in the conspiracy of deceit, and an attempt by Ehrlich and his crew to credit themselves with an important success to hide their failure.

Franz Stabbert, in L 20, was also handicapped by engine trouble. He could have been genuinely mistaken in his belief that he had bombed Sheffield, which he decided to attack because he was unable to fly as far as Liverpool. He certainly dropped bombs on Loughborough, in Leicestershire, where ten people were killed and twelve injured; and he probably bombed Burton upon Trent as well.

Peter Strasser, with von Buttlar in L 11, had another humiliating night. L 11 was believed to have been over England for some five hours. There were reports that she had bombed the iron works at Redbourne, in Lincolnshire, in an attempt to attack the iron and steel works at Frodingham, near Scunthorpe. Von Buttlar, however, never mastered the fog and never knew where he was. At one period he believed he was near the main objective of Liverpool, but soon after 11 pm he and Strasser, having failed to identify anything, accepted failure and returned with a full bomb load.

Although von Buttlar commanded L 11, he must have been influenced by the presence of Strasser. We do not know who took the decision not to release the bombs. It seems uncharacteristic of Strasser not to have tried to bomb something. All the same, the official historian, H. A. Jones, wrote in *The War in the Air*:

> It is pleasant to pay tribute to *Korvettenkapitän* Strasser for his high concept of his duty. He had been over British soil for four hours or more and had sighted a number of possible targets, but as he recognized no objective of definite military importance he was content to take his bombs back as he had brought them.

All of Strasser's ships returned safely, but with difficulty, to Nordholz and Hage—except L 19. Her captain, Odo Loewe, came in over Sheringham at about 7.20 pm, and tried to set course for Liverpool. He attacked Burton upon Trent at 10.45 pm. The town was reported to have been well lighted, but Loewe was able to identify it more easily because of fires started by the two previous raiders. He is believed to have followed L 21's route and example by dropping the rest of his bombs harmlessly on the suburbs of Birmingham. Loewe must have been even more confused than the other captains. He left the Norfolk coast at Winterton at 6.25 am, having spent some nine hours over England.

When Strasser returned to Nordholz shortly before 11 am, his personal humiliation was partly alleviated by reports of apparently successful raids on Liverpool, Birkenhead, Manchester, Sheffield, Nottingham, Birmingham, Goole, Immingham and Great Yarmouth. But the good news was soon overshadowed by the bad news that Loewe was overdue. Nothing had been heard from L 19 since her last wireless call, timed by the British at 6.41 am, when she asked for a position. She was then just off the English coast.

Strasser had good cause to be uneasy. He had, rightly, every confidence in Loewe and the crew. L 19, however, was a brand new airship, but her engines had not been properly run in and there had been no time for a series of familiarization flights.

Naval vessels searched for her. All German ships in the North Sea were ordered to keep a look-out. The most effective of all the seekers, the Zeppelins, were grounded by high winds.

We know now that L 19 was in trouble with her engines during her attempt to return to base. She gradually lost height and in the late afternoon was damaged by Dutch gunfire over Ameland. She sank on to the North Sea, doomed unless help arrived quickly.

The story of L 19's fatal loss is among the best-known controversies of the First World War, but it merits a brief recapitulation because it recalls a recognized code of chivalry which has declined, often disappeared, as warfare has become more brutal and degrading.

The British trawler *King Stephen* found L 19 at 7.00 am, but the master refused to take the Zeppelin crew on board, although they were certain to be drowned if abandoned. He has been accused of callousness and of having broken the Geneva

Convention; but he probably did his duty as he saw it, in protecting his ship. He believed, not unreasonably, that Loewe and his fifteen companions might have overpowered him and his crew of nine, and he maintained that he searched in vain for a British warship which might have gone to the rescue.

Weeks and months later bottles containing messages from L 19 were found in Swedish waters. The last of the messages, dated 7 February, gave a different, accusatory version of the incident. It gave, too, a propaganda opportunity which Germany was quick to exploit.

Those who have known later wars, in Korea or Vietnam, may find it hard to appreciate the long-held bitterness over the loss of L 19. The Germans were genuinely shocked, and their propaganda was based on a true sense of outrage. But in the First World War—and to a lesser degree in the Second—there was a mutually-accepted, unstated understanding, a code of conduct between the British and German armed forces, which often went beyond the requirements of the Geneva Convention. A battle might have been bitterly fought; a U-boat or British submarine might have sunk several ships with heavy loss of life; a Zeppelin might have killed a score or more of civilians, but if any survivors surrendered, or were otherwise captured, or were wounded, they were not left to die or be executed. Although there were some well-publicized exceptions, this code between the two armed forces survived through the four years of war.

Britain's defence of the incident was weakened by the Bishop of London, who praised the skipper's behaviour in abandoning L 19's crew and denounced them as 'baby killers'. This further offended Germany, but the bishop had judged the civilian mood correctly.

That mood became aggressively sharper after the raid. It was particularly ugly in the Midlands and one of the main causes was resentment that London's nest was being feathered at the expense of the provinces. But even in the capital the defences had been a failure in the October raid.

The public had no faith in the aeroplane. Although Warneford had destroyed a Zeppelin, his victory had occurred outside Britain, and the euphoria of it had gone. There were dramatic accounts of RFC successes in France, but they were too remote to give any confidence at home.

Routine statements about attempts by aeroplanes to attack raiding airships were received with indifference or disbelief.

Outside the RNAS and the RFC no one had any idea of the difficulties of night interception, take-off and landing. On this last raid, the weather, of course, had been bad, but not everywhere and not all the time. No aircraft had attacked the airships at well-lighted Burton upon Trent, which had been made even brighter because of the fires.

Sixteen aeroplanes had taken off that night, but thick ground fog and the crudely-inefficient take-off and landing arrangements hampered the pilots, whose courage and determination were never in doubt. Two of the most experienced died from injuries after they had crashed into a fog-hidden tree. One of them, Captain Penn-Gaskell, commanded the Northolt Training Squadron.

Press and political criticism continued to reflect and exploit public anxiety. But it was all un-cordinated until, quite suddenly, there was a collective voice of the people, with some very influential spokesmen.

CHAPTER 10

A Blanket of Bombs

Under the chairmanship of the Lord Mayor of Birmingham (and future Prime Minister of Britain), Mr Neville Chamberlain, a committee of public authorities in the Midlands told the Government what it should do. Unlike many of the critics, the committee knew that there were not enough resources to carry out its proposals. It believed, too, that priority was given to Sir Douglas Haig in France, and that the air defence of Britain was neglected because of it. Powerful voices at home might do something to redress the balance and put an uncertain Government on a more positive, decisive course.

Although the Midlands had suffered below a defenceless sky, the proposals—some of which amounted almost to demands—were intended to create an interlocking national defence scheme. Lighting restrictions should be enforced and standardized. Public air-raid warnings must be made as soon as German airships reached the coast. The entire nation could then be in darkness or, in industrial areas, the night-shift factories, blast furnaces and shipyards could at least be dimmed. Anti-aircraft guns must be available for places outside London, especially for the vulnerable industrial areas. Everything—guns, searchlights, aircraft—should be co-ordinated.

It so happened that the Government was trying to allay public discontent with short-term and long-term plans. But there were discordant and entrenched opinions. A proposed new defence organization made a bad beginning.

Field-Marshal Sir John French, having been recalled from his command of the British Expeditionary Force, had been created a viscount and appointed Commander-in-Chief, Home

Forces. His new responsibilities included the air defence of
Britain. Despite some gestures to quieten the clamour from the
provinces, the revised defence plan was still forced to concentrate on London and its approaches. Its first and most obvious
need was that of single-minded co-ordination.

Lord French was the least qualified of men to set it up. He
was 63 years old, deflated by his painful experience in France,
and a cavalryman whose career—despite subsequent distinguished appointments—probably reached its zenith in the South
African War. He knew a good deal about conventional gunnery
in a conventional war setting, nothing about the use of aircraft—except for the brave but slapdash work of the RFC in
France—and by temperament and training lacked the vision to
see that one particular kind of officer of General rank should
have a free hand while nominally under his command.

The situation demanded a man of Admiral Scott's ability
who would be supported with an independence that Lord
French lacked. The anti-aircraft gun defence of London was
put in charge of an able Royal Engineer officer, Lieutenant
Colonel M. St.L. Simon.

Meanwhile public confidence and sympathy were not gained
by one monumentally inept official statement and a brutally
honest speech by Lord Kitchener. Almost immediately after
the last raid, the Press Bureau issued a statement which was a
feeble and astonishingly insensitive attempt to mollify public
opinion. The statement compared air raid casualties with those
of the *Lusitania* disaster. The Press Bureau said—wrongly—
that 133 men, ninety women and forty-three children had been
killed in air raids since the war began. In the *Lusitania*, on the
other hand, 1,198 'innocent civilians had been murdered'.

Although the Government and its satellites did not know
about 'public relations' in 1916, it is hard, more than sixty-five
years later, to imagine the kind of men who could make such a
clumsy and inopportune comparison.

Lord Kitchener had never flinched from telling the truth. His
bluntness had endeared him to an adoring public. But a
negative statement during a House of Lords debate was an
ill-timed shock:

> It is beyond our power to guarantee these shores from a
> repetition of incursions. But although we have only one
> example of a Zeppelin being destroyed by aeroplane

attack—I allude to Lieutenant Warneford's gallant action—there have been several cases in which we have so disabled the enemy's aircraft as to bring them eventually to the ground, or render them useless. During the last raid, while we are sure that one airship was lost at sea, we have very good reason to believe that a second was placed out of action.

From the soldier who had defeated the dervishes at the Atbara, won a famous victory at Omdurmann, ruthlessly avenged the death of General Gordon, and finally defeated the Boers, this was almost a confession of despair. The characteristic challenge to the enemy was missing.

The Government acted in the wake of events rather than in the van. The Germans gave it some breathing space before they made their next attack at the beginning of March.

For long-term planning Prime Minister Herbert Asquith organized a Joint War Air Committee, with Lord Derby as president, to co-ordinate supplies and designs 'for the material of the Naval and Military Air Services, upon such points as will be referred to it by the War Committee, the Admiralty, the War Office, or any other Department of State'.

Although he had his critics in Government and in the Army, the seventeenth Earl of Derby—an intimate friend of King George V—was a highly respected public figure, and apparently, an impeccable choice as president of the Joint War Air Committee. Before he succeeded to the earldom, he had been a Conservative Member of Parliament from 1892–1906, Lord of the Treasury, Financial Secretary to the War Office and Postmaster General. His famous 'Derby Scheme' had recruited some two and a half million men.

The long-term plan became a very short one indeed. Internecine jealousies and power struggles were to kill the committee within two months. Neither the Royal Naval Air Service nor the Royal Flying Corps wanted an impingement on its freedom and independence. Each of them saw co-ordination as the first step to incorporation. The idea of incorporation, however, was not to die, although the birth of a combined air force did not take place for two years.

German agents in Britain and even more reliable neutral sources soon showed that the raid reports for the first attack of 1916 were, to say the least, exaggerated. All the same, Admiral

Scheer and Peter Strasser were satisfied with the operation. Some 379 bombs had killed seventy-one people, injured 113 and caused extensive damage (later estimated at £520,000) in a raid carried out in snow showers, severe icing on the Zeppelins, dense fog and thick ground mist. Weather conditions would not always be so bad and on the night of 31 January they might have been exceptional. They would certainly be better in spring and summer. The increasingly strident protests in Britain were presented to the Kaiser and the German people as the cry of a nation in despair.

Through the intelligence service, Scheer and Strasser knew of the revised defence plan. They knew, too, that when it was ready it would add little except quantity. Without effective fire support, both from the ground and in the air, it was like a tiger without claws. Only a few of the additional guns and none of the extra aeroplanes—mostly B.E. 2cs with 90 h.p. engines—could attack an airship at its operational altitude. Nevertheless, the forthcoming raids would not be without danger to the Zeppelins. The immediate hope was to trap them within range of the guns or force them up to ineffective bombing heights.

For Britain it was the first attempt, if an elementary one, at national co-ordination. England, Scotland, and Wales were divided into eight 'vulnerable areas' between the Firth of Forth and Portsmouth.

Two hundred and ninety-five guns are reported to have been available, but an analysis shows that some of them were taken on the strength merely to make up the numbers. The discarded pom-pom was brought back. The patchwork artillery included 1- and 2-pounder pom-poms; 3- and 6-pounder Hotchkiss; 4.7-inch naval guns—some of which had 'auto-cannon' mountings; 6-inch mobile guns on railway wagons; additional French 75-mm 'auto cannons' as well as other 75-mm guns with high-angle mountings. These had been designed for the Russian Navy but twelve had been acquired by the Royal Navy.

There was to be an urgent expansion of the Royal Flying Corps. Eleven night-fighter squadrons were to augment the one already in existence. The training squadrons could concentrate almost exclusively on producing more pilots and observers. The demands from the British Expeditionary Force for night-fighter pilots was insatiable. Thirty-three new aerodromes were to be prepared, all equipped with what were still elementary flare-paths.

As a result of the Birmingham committee's request, an early-warning system was set up. The first warnings were to be sent through the public telephone system to each of the Warning Controllers in the eight vulnerable areas. The Controller would pass the information to his own telephone exchange which in turn would pass it to the police, other authorities, local controllers and factories and the like. A central control room at Home Forces Headquarters, Horse Guards, in Whitehall, was to record and co-ordinate individual raid information—both for early warnings, subsequent incursions and for attacks themselves—on a transparent map illuminated by coloured lights. Public warnings, by hooter, were left to the discretion of each local authority.

Even with urgent application this defence plan would need time to make it cohesive. But any sense of urgency was dissipated by unclear military and political objectives, lack of leadership and central command.

The unhappy Lord French was boxed in. He asked for extra and more suitable guns. Sir Douglas Haig and the British Expeditionary Force, however, were the first priority not only for guns but also for aeroplanes. The Admiralty broke what was assumed to be a promise to supply eighty-six guns because they were needed for merchant-ship defence against U-boats. Britain's secret weapon, for which there were some very high hopes indeed, was not ready either. There is no reliable evidence to show that Germany was even remotely aware of it.

Scarcely any of the plan was ready when the Naval Airship Division resumed the offensive on 5/6 March. Strasser was poorly equipped for it. With only three Zeppelins available, the frustration of delay and the need to keep his crews in action against England could have been the only reasons which made him order the raid. Five ships were grounded while their unreliable HSLu engines were being modified at the Maybach factory. This left him with L 11 (*Korvettenkapitän* Viktor Schütze), L 13 (Heinrich Mathy), and L 14 (Alois Bocker).

The target for 5/6 March was 'England North' with the Firth of Forth and the Rosyth naval base as the main objectives. But the weather over the North Sea on the afternoon of 5 March was bad. A north-westerly wind was increasing to gale force. This, together with hail, snow, icing and heavy rain made it impossible to reach Scotland. That seemingly intractable problem, engine trouble, added to the hazards of the night.

But there was no attempt to abandon the mission. As alternative targets, Mathy and Bocker were to attack Tyneside, and Schütze was to raid Middlesbrough. Mathy had every excuse to turn back. A burnt-out crankshaft crippled one of his engines while he was over the North Sea. The weight of the snow on the envelope was dangerously heavy; to reduce it, he released some of his fuel. Finally, having groped his way through a long stretch of impenetrable weather, he made a landfall at the mouth of the Humber, where he had further engine trouble. To lighten L 13 still more, he dropped fifteen explosive bombs and thirty incendiaries without serious results.

As further proof that a raid over England could still be a journey into a vacuum, he was then blown across to the Midlands, down to the Kent coast and the Thames Estuary. He still believed he was near the Humber. Unable to reach a safe altitude, he escaped being hit by guns at Shoeburyness and Sheerness, and avoided a Royal Naval Air Service aircraft from Eastchurch.

Mathy decided to make for the nearest haven at Namur, in Belgium. He had to nurse L 13 all the way back and re-fuelled at Namur, then took off for Hage; but another breakdown forced him to return on only one effective engine.

Meanwhile, Bocker and Schütze made heavy attacks on Hull. Almost exactly nine months had passed since sixty-four people had been killed and injured in the city's first raid. But Hull was still totally undefended. Snow and ice were an almost constant danger; yet, paradoxically, it was snow on the ground which helped the Zeppelins and made Hull so fully-exposed a target, although it was a comparatively well-darkened city.

Bocker was the first to arrive, at about 1 am. He, too, had been blown south by the gale, but he had recognized the Humber estuary. Having dropped six bombs on Beverley, nine miles from Hull, he then released eight explosive and thirteen incendiary bombs on the city.

The driving wind had blown Schütze, in L 11, away from Middlesbrough, and he, too, was on an unintended course for Hull. Snow on the ground helped him identify details. He had already seen the explosions from L 14's bombs, and the fires from those and the incendiaries were as bright as an open furnace. To help him further, there was better visibility below 10,000 feet.

Despite the wind, Schütze and his crew 'held' L 11 over the city until Bocker had finished. The second attack followed almost immediately. Schütze dropped more than twenty explosive and incendiary bombs. Eighteen people were killed and fifty-two injured. As in the previous raid, the residential areas near the docks suffered most of the casualties and damage. One feature helped to increase the fury of the people of Hull. A week after the first attack, nine months earlier, the Lord Mayor of the city had made some proposals to the Admiralty for its protection. The official reply was blandly reassuring: 'In respect to the near future,' the Admiralty stated, 'we intend to make the air service on the East Coast efficient. We intend to provide your large towns and cities with aircraft guns.'

This statement was encouragingly endorsed when some mobile guns were trundled through the streets of Hull. No more was seen of them, but everyone assumed that they were in readiness nearby. In addition, a gun was mounted on the roof of an engineering works. It was always guarded by sentries.

On the night of 6 March not a single gun was heard. The mobile weapons had been a cruel gesture of deceit. The gun on the roof of the engineering works proved to be a dummy.

Nearly three weeks later Strasser opened a concentrated attack, spread over four successive nights. The intention was to drop a blanket of bombs on the vulnerable areas, which were all covered by the German designation of 'England South, Midlands, and the North'.

At about noon on 31 March, seven Zeppelins set out for a southern area raid, with London as the first objective. Two of them, L 9 and L 11, failed to reach England. The other five were L 13 (Heinrich Mathy), L 14 (Alois Bocker), L 15 (Joachim Breithaupt), L 16 (Werner Peterson) and L 22 (Max Dietrich).

Some accounts of the raid suggest that Dietrich was ordered to make a diversionary attack on 'England North', but Strasser's order to 'attack in the south, main target London', was explicit. Moreover he knew that the Zeppelins' flights could be observed and monitored, not only by direct observation but also from his own ships' wireless messages. Although he now ordered wireless silence on operations, he would have realized that the British could no longer be deceived by a diversionary attack by one airship.

The mistake over Dietrich's intention almost certainly arose because he could not keep up with the rest of the fleet and sought an objective elsewhere. Dietrich, in fact, was the victim of a still unlearned lesson. Like the lost L 19, his newly-commissioned L 22 was not fully run in. He decided to raid the Humber district instead of risking the longer flight to London. Hull was spared a third raid when Dietrich dropped six bombs on Cleethorpes, some twenty-four miles away on the Lincolnshire bank of the Humber. They struck a Baptist chapel, in which soldiers of the Manchester Regiment were billeted; twenty-nine were killed and fifty-three injured.

Mathy again found that L 13 was too heavily loaded for him to set course for London, and he tried to attack a munitions factory at Stowmarket in Suffolk. His bombs fell near an anti-aircraft battery, which fired back at him. He was also caught by searchlight beams. The gunfire damaged two of the gas cells. The battery's success was a minor one in that L 13 escaped; but it was an indication that there was growing danger from anti-aircraft fire. And that danger was enough to make the intrepid Mathy break off the raid.

The gunners' hits were not confirmed until the following day, and then by extraordinary chance. A German naval signal form from L 13 was found near Stowmarket after it had been blown overboard. Addressed to Chief-of-Staff, High Seas Fleet, it reported that L 13 had bombed a battery at Stowmarket 'with success' and added that she had been hit and was returning to base.

Bocker, in L 14, with Strasser on board, had wandered over Lincolnshire, Suffolk and Essex. He claimed, falsely, to have dropped bombs on London, as did Peterson in L 16. He dropped his missiles in Suffolk, where nineteen people were killed and eleven injured at Sudbury. The nearest he went to London was Thameshaven, where his incendiaries hit two empty oil tanks.

Breithaupt, in L 15, also reported that he had bombed London, but he could not avoid the much-improved outer defences. He had altitude difficulties from the time he arrived over the English coast. Here, too, he encountered anti-aircraft fire. He shed nearly all his ballast but could not fly above 8,000 feet. Trapped in searchlight beams, he became an inescapable target for the Thames Estuary guns, which, with those in and around London itself, provided the inhabitants with a welcome chorus of noise.

A gun from Purfleet scored a direct hit. At least four of the

Zeppelin's cells were damaged. In a bid to gain height, Breithaupt released fifteen explosive bombs, which fell in a field. Seventeen aircraft—eight from the RNAS and nine from the RFC—tried to intercept. One of them, a B.E. 2c, piloted by Lieutenant A. de Brandon, had been tracking the hard-pressed raider.

Brandon was carrying a supply of Ranken darts, named after Commander Ranken, who had developed them. By themselves they were never an airship deterrent, but Brandon flew near enough to hope that they might ignite the gas cells. In the face of heavy machine gun fire from L 15 he climbed above her, fired the darts, and attacked with incendiary bombs as well. He did not, apparently, score a direct hit and so missed being the first pilot to shoot down an enemy airship over Britain.

At 12.15 am, about two and a half hours after she had been hit, L 15 did come down—not precisely on British soil but in British waters, near the Kentish Knock Light Vessel.

Breithaupt and his crew fought to the end to save their ship. She was stripped of almost everything to keep her flying. Enough fuel was retained to reach the nearest base. The rest of the fuel, the remainder of the bomb load, the machine guns, unwanted gear and the ship's secret papers were all jettisoned. The last item to go was the wireless set, after Breithaupt had asked for 'immediate assistance'.

L 15 then broke her back and fell into the sea. One of the seventeen-man crew was drowned; the others were rescued and interned. An attempt to tow the Zeppelin to port failed when she disintegrated off Westgate.

The passing years have dimmed the glory of the Purfleet gunners. At the time, they themselves believed that they were deprived of the credit for an historic feat. But many of the gun crews which had fired that night believed their shells had hit the Zeppelin first. The commander of the Purfleet gun requested that his men should receive the prize of £500 which the Lord Mayor of London had offered for the first airship to be brought down in Britain. There was a hotly-contested argument. Did a hit on a Zeppelin while she was over the land, but which fell in the sea, meet the condition that an airship was brought down on 'British soil'?

The distinction may now seem to have been a quibble, but with so many claims—including that by Lieutenant Brandon who was certain he had been the first to strike the fatal blow (over Britain)—precision was essential. In the confusion of the night could anyone be sure who had scored a direct and decisive hit?

History has given the Purfleet gun the credit but, in 1916, there was general agreement with the Lord Mayor that the prize should be shared among all of the crews whose guns *might* have made the decisive hit. When it was realized that each man would receive less than £1.10s (£1.50), a commemorative medal was awarded instead. The unlucky Brandon never ceased to believe that he alone was the hero of the night.

While Britain was celebrating the destruction of L 15, Strasser continued to attack. On the following night L 11 and L 17 took off for London. Because of a change of wind, they received wireless orders to switch to alternative targets in the North and Midlands. L 17 is believed to have dropped bombs in the sea off Flamborough Head.

Schütze, in L 11, made his main attack on Sunderland. His fourteen explosive bombs and several incendiaries killed twenty-three people and injured about 120. Four RNAS machines failed to find L 11 or L 17, although the latter was believed to have been off the Yorkshire coast for more than an hour. One gun near Sunderland fired without effect at L 11, as did some other guns from trawlers in the North Sea.

At noon on 2 April, L 13 (Mathy), L 14 (Bocker), L 16 (Peterson) and L 22 (Dietrich) left Hage and Nordholz to make another attack on Scotland. The main objectives were again the dockyard and naval base at Rosyth, the Forth Bridge and the Firth of Forth. German wireless instructions had been intercepted. The navy defences at Rosyth and as far north as Scapa Flow, in the Orkney Islands, were warned of a possible raid.

None of the Zeppelins reached their objectives. Mathy had engine trouble and took no part in the projected attack. Peterson dropped bombs near Newcastle upon Tyne and caused only minor damage. Dietrich flew up the Firth of Forth, waited near Edinburgh, dropped a few harmless bombs and departed.

Bocker, in L 14, was the only successful captain. In pre-war days he had sailed in the Firth of Forth while serving in the mercantile marine with the Hamburg-Amerika company. Despite this, and because he was distracted by searchlights, he missed Rosyth and the Forth Bridge. Instead he bombed Leith and Edinburgh. In all he killed thirteen people; twenty-four were reported to have been injured. The damage in both places was extensive. Many buildings were wrecked, including three hotels and a railway station in Edinburgh.

Almost incidentally, and for no apparent reason, two Army airships set out for London that night. LZ 90 was turned back by anti-aircraft guns at Waltham Abbey, some sixteen miles from the capital. LZ 88 made a token flight over Suffolk and dropped most of her bombs, including a large number of incendiaries, all to no purpose.

Two more failures followed. On the night of 3/4 April, L 11 and L 17 were sent to bomb London. As part of a sustained offensive it was a singularly poor effort both in its planning and execution. High winds over the North Sea were too great a handicap to L 17 and she returned to Nordholz. It was the wind, too, combined with poor visibility, which made Schütze change course to attack eastern targets, and Great Yarmouth in particular. He failed to locate any of them and unloaded his bombs in the sea. On 4/5 April five Zeppelins set out to attack the Midlands, but the raid was cancelled because of bad weather.

The last of the sustained attacks took place on 5/6 April, when L 11, L 13 and L 16 took off to raid 'England North'. Mechanical trouble frustrated Mathy (L 13) again and he failed to make his landfall. Schütze, in L 11, made for the Firth of Forth and Rosyth. As on his previous sortie, he was an almost helpless victim of high winds, which diverted him to Hull, more than 230 miles from his objective. This time, however, Hull was a well-defended city, as indeed it was bound to be after the embarrassing revelations following the last raid, and heavy anti-aircraft fire drove him away, though he did drop four bombs which injured four people and caused slight damage. Schütze was a determined and resolute captain. He turned north again, to attempt another attack on the Firth of Forth, but an engine failure made him abandon the idea. When a second engine broke down, he decided to make for home. On the way he saw the brilliance of the Skinningrove works, flew over this tempting target and dropped nine explosive bombs and about twenty incendiaries. The reward was negligible. A laboratory was wrecked and two houses and a shop were damaged.

Peterson, in L 16, had a confusing visit. He made his landfall near Hartlepool—which he mistook for Scarborough—and dropped his bombs, apparently aimlessly, on working-class

cottages in the Bishop Auckland area. One child was killed and
five people were believed to have been injured.

The short, sharp blitzkrieg had failed in its strategic object
and in its tactical objectives. Inexplicably, it was misconceived.
Fewer raids would have allowed the crews some respite and
given them a greater opportunity to use their airships in a
concentration of effort. Experience since the campaign had
begun in January, 1915, had proved that a raiding force was
almost invariably weakened by ships dropping out. By the
spring of 1916 concentration on a single, important target was
the only answer to the increasingly powerful anti-aircraft defences and searchlights. At the very least they prevented accurate bombing, and a danger of direct hits was now evident.

Five raids had been made by fourteen airships during the last
blitzkrieg. More than 630 explosive and incendiary bombs had
been dropped. Eighty-five people had been killed and 217 were
known to have been injured. Material damage had been heavy
but nowhere disruptive.

Details of the casualties and damage could be exaggerated
and distorted to maintain the faith of the German people in the
Zeppelins' invincibility. But it was not only the people from
whom failure had to be hidden. It was still necessary to mislead
the Kaiser and some senior naval officers. Confirmation of the
conspiracy comes from a report which was given to the Kaiser
after the 31 March/1 April raid.

Having referred briefly to an attack on Grimsby, where 'a
battleship in the roadstead was heavily damaged by a bomb
and had to be beached' the report claimed that extensive
damage had been inflicted on London:

> At Kensington an aeroplane hangar was wrecked, near
> Tower Bridge a transport ship was damaged, in Great
> Tower Street a factory wrecked, and north of the Tower a
> bomb fell in George Street only 100 metres away from two
> anti-aircraft guns. It was reported that a large fire had
> broken out at West India Docks, and that at Tilbury
> Docks, a munition boat exploded (400 killed). Specially
> serious explosions occurred at the Surrey Commercial
> Docks and at a factory, close to the Lower Road, at which
> shells were filled with explosives. A railroad train already
> loaded with these shells was stated to be completely
> wrecked.

On the last of the raids Peterson reported that he had bombed the railway line between Leeds and York, and the city of Leeds itself; but since he had mistaken Scarborough for Hartlepool it is unlikely that this precise identification could have been made by mistake.

On the principle that the end justifies the means, Strasser could justify his part in the conspiracy. Setbacks, losses and the failure to bring about the destruction of England did not affect his fanatical belief in the power of the Zeppelins. If that belief needed reinforcement, the new 'Super-Zeppelins' would provide it. Their commissioning was long overdue, but the first of the 'big thirties', L 30, would be ready in two months. By summer's end he should have at least three.

To Strasser, the eternal optimist, there was always another tomorrow, a new dawn. But the corrosion of optimism was an unrecognized trap. There is no authentic record to show that Admiral Scheer had any doubts about the strategy, not in the early days of 1916 at any rate. But the seeds must have been there; some four months later he was to show signs of caution, if not hesitation. Meanwhile his belief in the Zeppelins was maintained, and perhaps sustained, by his own commitment, by Strasser's unwavering faith and, of course, by the prospect of the 'Super-Zeppelins'.

CHAPTER 11

A Grand Design

After the destruction of L 15 and the German failure to demoralize Britain, people began to believe that the Zeppelin might not, after all, be invincible. But complacency was shattered by a warning from Lord Montagu of Beaulieu in a sensational speech at Birmingham on 12 April, 1916, immediately after he and Lord Derby had resigned from the short-lived War Air Committee.

We have seen that Lord Beaulieu was among those who had been branded as 'scaremongers'. As far back as 1911 he had warned of the 'Zeppelin menace' and demanded an efficient flying service to fight raids which 'would be more nerve-shattering and would do more to shake the confidence of the people than a definite threat on sea or land'. As a long-time campaigner for efficient air defence, he was a natural choice to have been independent member of the Committee. But he and Lord Derby had ben swiftly disillusioned by the intractable jealousies of the two air services and by the Committee's weak terms of reference. Lord Derby, whose sense of public duty supplanted his judgment, complained of matters which he should have foreseen: the Committee's lack of executive power, which prevented it from discussing policy, and an imposed inability to decide anything unless the members were unanimous.

It was the kind of organization which governments set up as a reassurance to the public that something is being done, when in reality the intention and method are fatally infected by compromise and weakness. For the War Air Committee a quick death was certain, with the RNAS and the RFC as the chief executioners.

Within days of the Committee's collapse Lord Montagu delivered his attack at a meeting in Birmingham under the chairmanship of Neville Chamberlain. This time, however, polite requests and suggestions were replaced by what many people considered to be an unpatriotic stridency:

> Let me tell you that you live barely three hundred miles from the nearest Zeppelin shed, and are just as likely to be attacked as though you lived at Dover or Yarmouth. There is no part of industrial England to which a Zeppelin cannot fly and rain destruction. . . . In this war the power of defence has grown so largely that it has largely stopped offence. This can have only one result. On sea it will drive warfare into the sphere of the submarines, and on land it will drive it into the air . . .
>
> Then I come to our own shore. In the first months of the war, no Zeppelins came, and the whole thing was neglected. Now we have had twenty-eight raids, some of them very serious, and these raids will not only be repeated, but they will become more serious as time goes on. Yet in the twentieth month of the war we have only just begun to have a system of anti-aircraft defences in this country. I am not going to reveal secrets or talk about dummy guns, but I will say that there is hardly a town, with the possible exception of London, that can be properly defended against attacks from Zeppelins. But what can we do with guns that are too small and preparations that are inadequate? It is almost incredible to me that things should have been left so long in this direction and in others. It must have been well known to the Government that we were running this risk.
>
> Is it possible to go on running the air defence of this country, or an air defence by two departments—sometimes three—without any link between them, and with traditional jealousies?

The spring and summer did not justify his forebodings, though the aggressive Admiral Scheer tried to do so. Twelve days after Lord Montagu's warning, he launched a powerful seaborne attack on England. A task force of Dreadnoughts, battle-cruisers, destroyers and submarines sailed on the morning of 24 April. The intention was to bombard Lowestoft and

Great Yarmouth with four of the battle-cruisers. Three Zeppelins were to make reconnaissance sorties and escort the assault ships.

Although this attack was not Admiral Scheer's projected combined operation, it was part of a larger plan which involved nine other Zeppelins as well. The main strategic object was to exploit the British Government's confusion caused by the unexpected Irish rebellion on 25 April, and to bring the Grand Fleet to action.

But the operation went hopelessly wrong for both Admiral Scheer and Strasser. The Royal Navy was alerted to the task force's passage across the North Sea, though four of the battle-cruisers did shell Lowestoft and Great Yarmouth without causing serious casualties or damage.

It was an unsuccessful day for the Royal Navy as well. Commodore Tyrwhitt's Harwich Force failed to overtake or intercept the High Seas Fleet, but the scouting Zeppelin, L 9, had a remarkable escape. She was below 3,000 feet when two RNAS pilots, Flight-Commander Nichol and Flight-Lieutenant Hards, each in a B.E. 2c aeroplane, attacked her with bombs. They were counterattacked by machine guns from L 9's top platform. The two pilots continued to harass her but, without machine guns of their own, missed what was virtually a sitting target.

Peter Strasser flew in L 21 with the eight other Zeppelins. His intention was to widen the scope of the main assault by raiding 'England South', with London, of course, as the principal objective. Seven of the Zeppelins crossed the coast but were handicapped by heavy rain, thick fog, and an unfavourable wind. Unexpectedly they were attacked by intense anti-aircraft fire and dropped their bombs haphazardly in East Anglia, where a few houses were damaged and one woman was reported to have died of shock.

This failure of the Zeppelins set the pattern for a frustrating, inconclusive and—with the loss of two airships—somewhat disastrous spring and summer. There were nine raids between the end of April and the first week in September; the Army took part in four of them. No airships were destroyed on raids, but two Zeppelins were lost—one on her way back from Scotland and the other during an action with the Royal Navy.

On 2 May Franz Stabbert, in L 20, after having been totally lost over the Highlands and the Scottish coast, eventually found his way to Harsfjord, near Stavanger, in Norway, where L 20 was forced to alight on the water. A sea anchor failed to hold her. Some of the crew jumped into the fjord before she lifted off the surface. Out of control, she struck a hill, sank and was a total loss.

Fishing boats rescued six crew members who were still in the water. The Norwegian Government classified them as 'shipwrecked mariners' and repatriated them immediately. Stabbert and the others reached the shore. As they had actually landed on neutral territory (instead of neutral water) they were interned. Six months later Stabbert escaped without difficulty.

On 3/4 May the Royal Navy tried again to bomb the Zeppelin sheds, this time at Tondern. It was a ruse to draw the High Seas Fleet out of Wilhelmshaven. Eleven RNAS Sopwith 'Baby' seaplanes—transported in the carriers *Vindex*, *Engadine* and *Campania*—supported a Grand Fleet force of cruisers, destroyers and submarines.

The two fleets did not meet. Eight of the Sopwiths did not take off; one was wrecked after it had collided with the wireless antenna of a destroyer; another had engine trouble and took no part in the action; the one which did take off was unable to find the sheds. But there was, as we shall see, a minor compensation for the Royal Navy in the destruction of a Zeppelin, to make a disastrous two days for Strasser and the Naval Airship Division.

The High Seas Fleet's immediate response to the approach of the Royal Navy was to scout ahead and report enemy strength, dispositions and possible intention before committing the main body. This traditional work of cruisers was always supplemented by airships, and on 4 May L 7 and L 9 searched for the Grand Fleet. L 9 saw no sign of it and returned to Hage. *Kapitänleutnant* Hempel, in L 7, was more persistent. He saw two of the escort cruisers, HMS *Galatea* and HMS *Phaeton*. The Zeppelin met long-range fire from both ships. The third round fired by *Galatea's* 6-inch guns hit L 9's fuel tank. It was a fatal shot, which set her ablaze. She fell into the sea and seven of her crew were rescued by the submarine E 31.

Neither Strasser nor anyone else in the High Seas Fleet knew of her fate. Having waited for her scouting signal, Strasser, who had just returned from a raid, reported her missing. A search of the North Sea revealed no trace of her. There was no trace of the Grand Fleet ships either. They had waited off Horns Reef, while the High Seas Fleet in turn had waited for L 9's report. And when the Fleet did sail, without a reconnaissance sighting, the Royal Navy was on its way home.

The loss of a Zeppelin as a result of a raid on England was, of course, an accepted casualty, but Strasser resented this cruel confirmation of his conviction that his airship strength was being dissipated. The risks of scouting for the Fleet, as distinct from routine patrolling, were too great. The use of Zeppelins at the inconclusive Battle of Jutland on 31 May confirmed Strasser's conviction. Only one of them saw anything of the Royal Navy.

The first 'super-Zeppelins'—L 30, L 31 and L 32—were ready for operations against England in August and formed part of Admiral Scheer's first combined operations assault. These 'big thirties' had a huge gas capacity of 1,949,600 cubic feet, a length of 649 feet 7 inches, and a diameter of 78 feet 5 inches. They were driven by six Maybach 240 h.p. HSLu engines, had a maximum speed of about 60 miles per hour and a maximum ceiling of 17,400 feet, but the operational ceiling was between 13,000 and 14,000 feet. They could carry a bomb load of some five tons. The bombs were in two chambers forward and aft of amidships, and were secured by hooks electrically-operated from a keyboard. Ten machine-guns could be carried: three on top of the hull; two in the control car; one in each of the side gondolas; two in the after-engine car; one astern near the apex of the hull. The maximum crew strength was twenty-three.

With the blunt forward end larger in diameter than amidships and the tail tapering to a fine point astern to give an overall cigar-like shape, the 'super-Zeppelins' were the first completely streamlined airships.

Three of them joined Admiral Scheer on 18 August, when he sailed with an armada of Dreadnoughts, battle-cruisers and light cruisers. Now it was the turn of the High Seas Fleet to try to bring the Grand Fleet to action. The objective was a seaborne attack on Sunderland. Nine U-boats had put to sea on 16 August to lie in wait for Admiral Sir John Jellicoe's Fleet as it steamed from Scapa Flow. With so powerful an assault attempt by Admiral Scheer, the Royal Navy would have no choice but to commit most of its available resources.

Eight Zeppelins—the three new 'big thirties', L 30, L 31, L 32—with L 11, L 13, L 21, L 22 and L 24, took up positions in the North Sea. Four more were to patrol on 19 and 20 August to provide extra support and cover the return of the High Seas Fleet.

The scouting airships were stationed over a wide area. Strasser flew in L 32 which, with L 22, L 24 and L 30, had orders to patrol between Peterhead, on the north-east Scottish coast, and the Norwegian coast, to report the passage of the Grand Fleet.

Mathy, in L 31, was ordered to the Firth of Forth to shadow Admiral Beatty's battle-cruiser squadron from Rosyth. L 11 and L 21 took up positions between the Rivers Tyne and Humber to report the movements of Commodore Tyrwhitt's Harwich Force of light cruisers and destroyers.

Admiral Scheer's attack was planned in the greatest secrecy. When the High Seas Fleet sailed on the evening of 18 August its destination was known to only a few senior officers. The Zeppelin ground crews assumed that the airships were to make a routine raid on England.

The scene was set for a great sea battle, perhaps the ultimate naval engagement of the war. But some fourteen hours later Admiral Scheer's dream of a triumphant combined operation had gone.

The British Admiralty picked up and decoded the chattering German wireless signals. Jellicoe led the Grand Fleet out of Scapa Flow on the afternoon of 18 August. Under cover of darkness Admiral Beatty's squadron left Rosyth to meet the Grand Fleet north-east of the Firth of Forth, from where they turned south. Commodore Tyrwhitt's Harwich Force weighed anchor at 11.30 pm, to patrol the area between the East Coast and the Dutch coast.

The Zeppelins' scouting was abysmal. They did not identify the type of Royal Navy ships which were spotted and this led Admiral Scheer to make wrong deductions and decisions. At various phases in the operation he did not realize that reports from some of his U-boats and the Zeppelins L 31 and L 11 were of movements of the Grand Fleet. Typical of the errors was that of *Kapitänleutnant* Prölss, in L 11, who mistook the Harwich Force for Jellicoe's ships.

It was a frustrating experience for the Royal Navy too. Contact with the High Seas Fleet was lost or broken off: a battle which might have been more decisive than Jutland was never fought. Two Royal Navy light cruisers were torpedoed by

U-boats. Admiral Jellicoe was deprived of ten scouting aircraft when engine trouble prevented *Campania* from joining the Grand Fleet. His only air support came from three seaplanes aboard *Engadine*.

The Naval Airship Division would always spend more time on scouting than on raids, but no longer at the expense of the bombardment of England. A painful lesson had been learned in a harsh school; but only, perhaps, to the satisfaction of Strasser and his men.

It was up to them to make the most of it.

CHAPTER 12

Secret Weapon

Any other German naval or military leader with Strasser's record of failure and wrong predictions would have been relieved of his command long before the autumn of 1916. Germany had been quick to replace other leaders. General von François was sacked in August, 1914, when the Russians invaded East Prussia. The Army's Chief of General Staff, von Moltke, was superseded in September, 1914, after the Battle of the Aisne. Admiral von Ingenohl lost his command of the High Seas Fleet after the Battle of the Dogger Bank in January, 1915.

The morale of the German people was Strasser's salvation and safeguard. He was Germany's *beau idéal*, a living legend. For him to become a fallen idol would have shown the legend to be illusory and been a confession that the vaunted Zeppelin was a failure; all the good news would prove to have been untrue. The effect on civilian morale would have been incalculable.

The idolatory and the still mysterious uniqueness of the Zeppelin were a powerful antidote to questions about the failure to bomb England into submission. No one in the High Seas Fleet Command had any experience of war in the air. They relied entirely on Strasser. Events had made them accept that a period of trial and error was unavoidable. Senior officers who had doubts about the strategic use of the Zeppelin were unable to make practical criticisms. The conspiracy of deceit sustained the belief that victory was only a matter of time.

Strasser's entanglement in that conspiracy was not a reckless bluff, but an inseparable part of his passionate, fanatical optimism. The defeat of England by the Zeppelin stood out for him in bold relief against the setbacks and losses. A single raid, or an unbroken series of attacks, could bring triumphant justification. And none more so than the raid on the night of 2/3 September.

No fewer than twelve naval airships, including three 'super-Zeppelins', were to attack London. Four Army airships also set out for London on that same night. It is almost certain that the two Services did not co-ordinate their intentions, although there are claims that they did so. But with sixteen airships under orders for London this was the heaviest raid yet made on England.

The capital and its suburbs were uneasy after a recent surprise attack. On 24/25 August Heinrich Mathy, in L 31, had been the first to penetrate the inner defences for almost a year. He had outwitted them by following the Thames. He dropped thirty-six explosive and several incendiaries on the south-western and south-eastern outskirts. Nine people were killed and about forty were reported to have been injured. The severe damage, mostly to domestic property, was estimated at £130,000.

Mathy's attack had been swift, unexpected and audacious. He took skilful advantage of low clouds, cloud cover and mist to avoid and confuse the searchlights, which did not pick him out until the raid was over. There was no anti-aircraft fire until the raid was over either.

For the raid of 2/3 September the Navy's twelve airships were to converge on southern England from eight different bases at various take-off times during the afternoon of 2 September. Viktor Schütze (L 11), Prölss (L 13), Manger (L 14) and *Kapitänleutnant* Erich Sommerfeldt (L 16) left from Hage. Ehrlich (L 17), Martin Dietrich (L 22) and Koch (L 24) flew from Tondern. Four captains took off from Nordholz. Frankenberg (*L 21*), *Kapitänleutnant* Wilhelm Ganzel (L 23), Peterson (L 32) and *Kapitänleutnant* Guido Wolff, who commanded the only naval airship which was not a Zeppelin, SL 8.

The Army airships took off from separate bases in the Rhineland: LZ 90 from Mannheim, LZ 97 from Darmstadt, and LZ 98 from Wildeshausen. Like the Navy, the Army had a ship which was not a Zeppelin, the new SL 11, which left from Spich. She was not only newly-built but her commander, London-born *Hauptmann* Wilhelm Schramm, was making his first raid over England as a captain.

North Sea weather forced L 17 and LZ 97 to turn back before

they reached the English coast, although L 17's captain made an outrageous claim to have bombed Norwich and to have been hit by anti-aircraft fire. The entire raid was well observed and meticulously reported by the British, and there is no reason to doubt the statement that L 17 turned back about 30 miles from the East Coast. In the unlikely event that she did slip the defences, and was damaged by gunfire, Norwich was certainly not bombed that night.

Oberleutnant Ernst Lehmann, in LZ 98, was the first to reach the London area. He crossed into England between Dungeness and Littlestone-on-Sea at midnight. He met heavy fire at Gravesend, Tilbury and Dartford. Lehmann, of course, has an unassailably distinguished place in the history of the airship, but he was a comparatively inexperienced combat captain, and this was his first raid against England. Shaken and surprised by the gunfire, he did not press home an attack but jettisoned his bombs (though he reported that he had dropped them on the docks) and turned east, where he was trapped by searchlights near Woolwich. An error of judgment by a RFC pilot saved LZ 98 from being the first German airship to be destroyed over England.

The ground defences and the searchlights were reinforced by fourteen or fifteen aeroplanes, all of which except one—a Henry Farman—were B.E. 2cs. The Farman was among the four or five RNAS aircraft which joined in the counterattack, with nine or ten RFC machines. Most of the probing and searching that night was carried out by 39 Squadron, RFC, whose B.E. 2cs operated from Sutton's Farm, North Weald Bassett and Hainault Farm to cover the Zeppelin routes into London.

With so many airships crossing the coast that night there was real confidence among the pilots. Night flying was now more sophisticated, although landings and take-off on the crudely-lit aerodromes were still dangerous and occasionally fatal. Some pilots complained that the searchlights blinded them and forced the airships to use cloud cover and climb to safety, but the beacons of the sky were in general invaluable.

Nothing, however, gave the night fighters greater confidence than Britain's new secret weapon. It had already been used operationally but no pilot had been near enough to fire it successfully against a German airship. Many of the so-called 'best kept secrets of the war' were known to Germany through their agents simply because too many people in Britain knew about them as well. But the explosive bullet was unquestionably the 'best kept secret' and one of the most decisive combat inventions of the First World War.

It was not the invention of one man, although the originator was an Australian, John Pomeroy, whose idea for an explosive bullet had been rejected by the War Office in 1914. When the Ministry of Munitions was formed in 1915, under the leadership of David Lloyd George, the idea was taken out of the files to be considered with two related developments: a phosphorous bullet devised by J. F. Buckingham and an explosive bullet produced by Commander F. A. Brock, RN. The result was the Brock-Pomeroy-Buckingham combination of explosive and phosphorous bullet which would puncture the envelope and gas cells, and the released hydrogen would be ignited by the phosphorous bullet. No one had any doubt that this was a lethal answer to raiding airships.

The first pilot to use it, on 3 September, 1916, was Second-Lieutenant William Leefe Robinson of 39 Squadron, RFC. He went up from Sutton's Farm at about 11 pm on the first of his patrols. About two hours later he found LZ 98. She was some 800 feet below him, but climbed quickly to nearly 14,000 feet and disappeared into the clouds. Leefe Robinson missed an apparently inescapable target because, as he admitted, he had relied on his altitude at the expense of speed.

Some 40 minutes later he had the kind of chance against which a bookmaker would offer very long odds indeed. He met SL 11 and shot her down in flames. Wilhelm Schramm had crossed the coast at 10.40 pm and dropped his first bombs harmlessly on London Colney, about 20 miles from the centre of the capital. He dropped more bombs on his way to the objective. When he arrived over the northern suburbs he met a thundering, unceasing barrage of anti-aircraft fire and could not escape the beams of two of the many searchlights which probed the sky round London. He scattered his bombs on the Enfield, Ponders End, Tottenham, Edmonton and Finsbury Park districts. The anti-aircraft fire became more intense and concentrated. Never before had London and its suburbs heard a crescendo of so many guns. Most of the gunfire was too far away to be effective, at least while SL 11 stayed over the northern environs; but even there she could not avoid the fire trap—or so it seemed to the thousands of people who watched the drama in the sky.

In a reference to the guns, and to SL 11, the official account of the raid, in *Air Raids 1916*, says, 'They contributed to the great volume of fire . . . which compelled her to change course at Finsbury Park.'

It was a fatal change. Three pilots from 39 Squadron pursued her. Leefe Robinson reached her first. This time he made no mistake and took care not to repeat his previous error. To the hysterical joy of the thousands of spectators ten or eleven thousand feet below, SL 11 was suddenly ablaze and, like a huge burning torch, fell to the ground.

Leefe Robinson's immortal triumph has been over-written and over-dramatized. But his report—the only unembellished source—tells us all we need to know about the action in the sky on that momentous early morning of 3 September, 1916. It is a masterly example of economy and modesty by a 19-year old hero:

> To: The Officer Commanding, 39 H.D. Squadron. Report on Night Patrol. Sir, I have the honour to make the following report on a Night Patrol made by me on the night of the 2nd-3rd instant. I went up at about 11.08 pm on the night of the 2nd with instructions to patrol between Sutton's Farm and Joyce Green. I climbed to 10,000 feet in 53 minutes . . . there were a few clouds below me, but on the whole it was a beautifully clear night. I saw nothing till 1.10 am, when two searchlights picked up a Zeppelin about S.E. of Woolwich. The clouds had collected in this quarter, and the searchlights had some difficulty in keeping on the aircraft.
>
> By this time I had managed to climb to 12,000 feet, and I made in the direction of the Zeppelin, which was being fired on by a few anti-aircraft guns—hoping to cut it off on its way eastward. I very slowly gained on it for about ten minutes. I judged it to be about 800 feet below me, and I sacrificed my speed in order to keep the height. It went behind some clouds, avoided the searchlights, and I lost sight of it. After 15 minutes' fruitless search I returned to my patrol. . . . At about 1.50 am I noticed a red glow in the N.E. of London. Taking it to be an outbreak of fire, I went in that direction. At 2.05 am a Zeppelin was picked up by the searchlights over N.N.E. London (as far as I could judge).

Remembering my last failure, I sacrificed height (I was still at 12,000) for speed and made nose down in the direction of the Zeppelin. I flew about 800 feet below it from bow to stern and distributed one drum along it (alternate New Brock and Pomeroy). It seemed to have no effect; I therefore moved to one side and gave another drum distributed along its side—without apparent effect. I then got behind it (by this time I was very close—500 feet or less below) and concentrated one drum on one part (underneath rear). I was then at a height of 11,500 feet when attacking the Zeppelin. I had hardly finished the drum when I saw the part fired at glow. In a few seconds the whole rear part was blazing.

When the third drum was fired there was no searchlight on the Zeppelin, and no anti-aircraft was firing. I quickly got out of the way of the falling, blazing Zeppelin, and being very excited, fired off a few red Very lights and dropped a parachute flare. Having very little oil and petrol left, I returned to Sutton's Farm, landing at about 2.45 am.

On landing I found that I had shot away the machine gun wire guard, the rear part of the centre section, and had pierced the rear main spar several times.

Like everyone else that night Leefe Robinson had mistaken the Schütte-Lanz for a Zeppelin, a natural error when all German airships were believed to be Zeppelins.

Because the attack was seen by thousands of spectators over a wide area, there are differences and discrepancies in contemporary accounts of the 'ground-eye view'.

As a nine-year old boy, the author of this book saw the airship attacked and destroyed, and visited the wreckage the next day. The experience remains an imperishable memory. It has been unaffected by those contemporary accounts. It reflects accurately the mood of the people in one particular neighbourhood.

On a visit to North London from the safety of Brighton, he was awakened by the sound of gunfire and of bombs falling nearby. With eight people in a very small house, even token indoor protection was hard to find. Whenever there were raids in Britain there was also a constant debate and dilemma about what to do: stay indoors with the danger of having the house demolished, or go outside and risk being hit by bombs or shrapnel.

The North London suburb was a typical follow-my-neighbour one. Conformity was the guideline even in a perilous situation. In the early hours of 3 September those foolhardy people who always took to the streets in an air raid were, eventually, followed by almost everyone else, once they had guessed from the activity in the sky that this might be the most spectacular raid of all. Above us was an airship which looked to be inescapably trapped.

Despite their concern for his safety, the boy's relatives decided to follow their neighbours' example and leave the house. The small patch of garden, sodden by previous rain, became a grandstand. Elsewhere, people spilled into the street, crowded first-floor windows and even the roof tops.

The boy could not believe that his first experience of gunfire could be worse, not even at the Front. At home, on the South Coast, the faint rumble of the guns in France could be heard on a calm, clear day. It was as remote as distant thunder in the Channel.

Now, the fire seemed to him to be only a street or so away; so near that he could pick out different sounds, like a bark, a deep belch, a sharp crack or a shuddering crump. The far-off guns made a continuous booming, as if it were an echo but without the recognizable differences of the seemingly local guns.

The bursting shells in all parts of the sky surely meant that a Zeppelin would soon be visible, caught in the beams of search-lights which swept and criss-crossed the starlike canopy, their rhythm broken occasionally by banks or drifts of cloud.

And then the Zeppelin—as they all thought it to be—was there. A great roar of recognition greeted it. Bombs were heard dropping perhaps a mile or so away, their own peculiar sound breaking into the pattern of gunfire.

Even while they all watched the airship, seemingly caught now by guns and searchlights, the knowing ones forecast where the bombs were falling. Opinions about the casualties were frighteningly thrilling. Across the garden fence small bets were made as to whether the bombs had dropped this side of the local park or the other. Pre-war loyalties to the Tottenham Hotspur Football Club were revived by the prospect that the Spurs' ground at White Hart Lane had 'caught it'. And so might Alexandra Palace, the popular amusement centre which stood prominently above the park of the same name and 'Ally Pally' racecourse.

They watched the airship turn away, but the searchlights held its every movement. Shells seemed to be bursting all round it. Suddenly the searchlights left it as if one master-switch had turned them off, and those of us on the ground lost sight of it.

A few moments later they saw it again, clearly, without the searchlight beams or the shell bursts. The gunfire died away to silence except for distant thumps elsewhere. Small dribbles of flame began to run along the side of the 'Zeppelin'. It began to change colour. Some reports were to say it was red, or crimson or orange. Those of us on the ground had no time for such fine points. We watched the dribbles from the sides and the underbelly spring into a furnace. Within seconds it was a fireball.

For a while it seemed to hang in the sky; and then it fell, a streak of consuming flame. Memory does not confirm those accounts of it 'plunging headlong to the ground'. There is a clear recollection of watching that tremendous fireball all the way until it was out of their vision. They did not know, then, where it had crashed. They did know that everyone in it must have perished.

The spontaneous barrage of cheering and shouting made the roar of a hundred thousand people at a pre-war Cup Final sound like an undertone. People danced, kissed, hugged and sang. The hysteria and the abandoned emotions were not confined to one neighbourhood. The destruction of the airship was said to have been seen from the ground more than forty miles away. The crowd reaction everywhere was described as being greater than that which celebrated the relief of Mafeking in 1900. Mafeking did not significantly affect the South African War. The destruction of SL 11 proved to be of strategic importance.

Everyone believed that the guns of London had brought her down. The next day, however, all Britain hailed a new and very special hero when it learned that Leefe Robinson was the victor. Some credit must go to an unknown and unsung gun crew. Examination of the wreckage showed that SL 11 had been hit before Leefe Robinson had fired his three drums.

The airship had come down at the small village of Cuffley, in Hertfordshire, eighteen miles from the centre of London. But it was nearer to that North London suburb. The wet Sunday morning of 3 September did not stop many of its residents from joining the huge crowd which went to see the crashed 'Zeppelin'. More than 60,000 people are said to have visited Cuffley that Sunday.

A personal recollection is one of joining an endless line of slowly-moving sightseers. Some on foot, others in almost every kind of transport—some of which had to be abandoned on the way—climbed the steep, narrow, muddy and rutted hill from the village.

A great press of spectators tried to see the wreckage that lay in the meadow between St Andrew's Church and the Plough Inn; but a small boy, lifted on to someone's shoulders, had a better view than most.

There was nothing there that looked anything like a 'Zeppelin'—just a shapeless clutter of wire, metal and cinders. Like a dying bonfire, smoke was still eddying. Early visitors realized that the tarpaulins on the ground hid scorched and mostly unidentifiable bodies.

A return visit to Cuffley more than sixty years later revealed hardly a trace of that historic event. Cuffley itself, with its single steep street, still resembles a village, but the hedgerows and fields which flanked the long hill past the church and on to the Plough, are replaced by prosperous middle-class houses facing on to pavements and a made-up road.

The meadow, too, is long since buried by 'much-sought-after properties'. The Plough Inn—where the inquest on the dead Germans was held and whose yard provided another crowded viewpoint—is no longer an inn but a smart modern pub. Inside, customers play a bar game—Space Invaders—just a few hundred yards from the vanished graveyard of those earlier invaders.

Beyond Plough Lane, on the East Ridgeway, there is a small, unkempt, moss-infested obelisk, with the inscription:

> Erected by the readers of the Daily Express to the memory of Captain William Leefe Robinson, VC ... who on September 3, 1916, above this spot, brought down SL 11, the first German airship destroyed on British soil.

The obelisk stands in a minute garden, beyond a privet hedge. The weather-rotted entrance gate is hard to open and threatens to break away from its crumbling post. On the neglected ground inside the garden another post moulders and disintegrates. The obelisk's railed-off enclosure is weed-choked and the uncut grass a squalid resting-place for empty take-away food cartons.

The only other reminder is a memorial tablet in the modern St Andrew's Church which gives thanks to God for the preservation of the church and the local people when SL 11 crashed in flames a mere two hundred yards away.

Six Zeppelin captains reported that they had seen the destruction of SL 11. Three of them, in L 16, L 32 and L 21, were over Hertfordshire and close enough to experience the full horror. Even before the hydrogen was fully ignited they knew that SL 11 was mortally wounded, presumably (and surprisingly) by gunfire.

L 16 was the nearest to SL 11. Having caused serious damage to the village of Essendon, she was only four or five miles away when she saw the intense light of the burning airship. Harassed by a Royal Flying Corps B.E. 2c, Sommerfeldt turned L 16 away and fled for safety.

L 32 saw the conflagration from Tring, dropped the rest of her bombs on Ware and escaped out to sea over Lowestoft. L 21, farther north at Hitchin, left the danger area and scattered her bombs on the way to the coastal exit, including some near the royal palace at Sandringham.

Bad weather had prevented SL 8 from reaching London. She was near Huntingdon, some sixty miles from the capital, but Wolff reported that he identified the fire in the sky as being that of a burning airship. The most distant view was reported by Schültz, in L 11, off the coast near Harwich, about eighty miles from London. He was very positive that 'the enormous flame' he saw over the capital was 'a burning airship'.

There was some scepticism about these far-off sightings because of the bad weather which had scattered the aerial armada a few hours earlier. But conditions had improved after midnight. Visibility improved, and the airships, at altitudes of 8,000–10,000 feet, had a panoramic view.

The most accurate observation was that from L 14. She was at Thaxted, in Essex, more than forty miles from London. Manger's startling opinion was that, 'It is suspected that the ship was destroyed by a bomb from a plane'. His reference to 'two Very signals, green and red, resembling recognition signals' was a near match to Leefe Robinson's reference to signals in his report.

The Germans did not know about the deadly antidote. Its details were still a 'best-kept secret' and Manger's belief that SL 11 had been hit by a bomb was fostered by Britain's statement that Leefe Robinson had used an incendiary bomb.

The whole country shared the euphoria of that historic Sunday morning. When the official announcement named Leefe Robinson, the nation's joy was unbounded. There would never be another hero of the air quite like him. Three days later he was awarded the Victoria Cross. There was no wait for a formal ceremony. He was summoned to an exclusive investiture at Windsor Castle where King George V gave him the Cross.

Early in 1917 Leefe Robinson, who had been promoted to the rank of captain, was captured after being shot down over the Western Front. He died at his home in December, 1918, one of the thousands of deaths in the post-war influenza epidemic.

The Royal Flying Corps was confident now that it had the Zeppelin permanently in its sights. There had been no fluke about the devastating effect of the Brock-Pomeroy-Buckingham ammunition. Research and testing, which had involved trials with Maxim and Lewis guns, produced a counter-attack against which the Zeppelins were helpless. Soon, however, designers and engineers were to plan another type of Zeppelin which would give preference to altitude rather than speed.

Meanwhile further successes against Zeppelins depended not only on the unflinching courage and determination of the RFC pilots but also on their ability to overcome the continuing handicap of flying in aeroplanes whose ceiling at best did not exceed 13,000 feet. Leefe Robinson had set the example and taught a lesson: if he had used the same tactics with LZ 98 he could have had a dual victory on the one night.

The loss of SL 11 was only part of the complete failure of the largest raid of the war. Fourteen airships had dropped 263 explosive bombs and some 200 incendiaries; sixty of them had fallen on London without causing a single casualty. Four people had been killed and sixteen injured more than 100 miles away from the main target, at Boston in Lincolnshire, which was bombed by L 23. The most serious damage had also

occurred far from the objective, at East Retford in Nottingham-
shire, where three gasometers were destroyed by L 13.

A few scarcely-heard critics pointed out that fourteen airships
had roamed over England with considerable freedom. But the
British people, though unaware of the secret weapon, had an
intuitive, illogical conviction that the 'Zeppelin menace' had
been conquered, after the destruction of just one airship. Once
again the war in the air had given hope and inspiration when it
was sorely needed. Despite the blandness or reticence of official
bulletins and the optimism of censored newspaper stories,
everyone knew that the war was going badly.

At dawn on 1 July, 1916, thirteen British infantry divisions
had begun the Battle of the Somme. By nightfall 57,000 of them
were casualties, nearly 20,000 of whom had been killed. It was
the heaviest loss in a single day ever suffered by the Army.
Many of the casualties were volunteers who had responded to
Lord Kitchener's recruiting appeal in 1914.

When the Battle of the Somme started Kitchener himself was
dead. He had been drowned on his way to Russia when HMS
Hampshire was sunk by a mine. No other single event in the
entire war equalled the shock and distress to the nation. 'Men
and women,' wrote Lloyd George in his *War Memoirs*, 'spoke of
the event in hushed tones of horror.' Inside the Government
Kitchener's influence and authority had become negligible. As
Secretary for War he was no more than a figurehead. To the
public he was an untarnished idol.

The Dardanelles, with which Kitchener had been associated,
had ended disastrously with the final evacuation in January,
1916. To the British it was even more humiliating because the
hitherto despised Turkish Army had been the conquerors.
Some 30,000 men had lost their lives; about 8,000 were missing
and nearly 75,000 had been wounded or incapacitated by
disease. And it was the Turkish Army to which General
Townshend had surrendered at Kut, in Mesopotamia, having
been besieged there for nearly five months. Attempts were
made to present the siege as a great feat of arms, but the public
soon realized that several thousand (about 10,000 as it proved)
British troops had been abandoned to the Turks.

By September disillusion was growing about the Battle of
Jutland. Facts and figures could be censored, a great naval
victory could be conjured up in doctored newspaper reports;
but nothing could silence the Jutland survivors. Their accounts

revealed that the Royal Navy's losses were greater than those of the High Seas Fleet. Although it had withdrawn from the engagement, the German Navy had not been defeated.

At home there was growing industrial unrest. The prohibition of official strikes in industries engaged on munitions production by the Munitions of War Act of 1915 did not prevent a proliferation of unofficial strikes. The working classes, and some of the middle classes, were fed up with food shortages, with the uneven—or unfair—distribution of food and with 'profiteering' by manufacturers, wholesalers and retailers.

Although details of shipping losses from U-boats were secret, everyone knew they were heavy; but for once even rumour and speculation under-estimated the grim figures. In September 104,572 tons were lost. By December they had reached the record total of 183,000 tons.

The Western Front was a terrible, unending stalemate. The Royal Navy had not yet defeated the U-boat, nor met it on equal terms. But on 3 September a positive, buccaneering victory had actually been seen by thousands of people. Very few of them doubted that the aerial battle for Britain had been won . . . and lost.

With the confident assumption that the Zeppelin was no longer a serious threat, more attention could now be given to the bombing of German civilians. An uninhibited Cockney newspaper seller in Piccadilly Circus summed-up the popular demand: 'Now we can hit the buggers in their own bleedin' back yard.'

CHAPTER 13

Unfinished Business

After the loss of SL 11, Strasser's immediate task was to maintain, or even restore, the morale of his crews. His inspirational leadership was the cornerstone of the Naval Airship Division's revival and, possibly, its survival.

By itself the loss of SL 11 was no more than one of those inevitable casualties. The Schütte-Lanz was not part of the Naval Airship Division, but all crews were comrades in arms. The reality of seeing the holocaust, especially for those close to it, was certain to have shaken morale; and it could have even worse effects on crews who were not on the raid but who were left to think about it.

But SL 11 was one of those wooden ships for which Strasser had no use, although he had sent SL 8 on the raid. Perhaps she had been wrongly handled by her inexperienced captain. Ignorant of Britain's secret weapon, Strasser had good reason to believe that a bomb from an aeroplane which hit an airship in mid-air was a very lucky—and unlikely—event indeed.

If the weakening of morale was to be short-lived, an immediate follow-up raid was imperative. But nearly three weeks went by before Strasser could order another raid, on 23/34 September. No Army airships took part in it, and indeed they were never to raid England again.

We have seen that the Army's commitment to the strategic use of airships had already weakened. It had never been whole-hearted. Linnartz's first raid on London had brought the sweet taste of success. The loss of SL 11 had turned it sour. The Army Airship Service was abandoned in 1917, but the strategy was not. With an alternative application already being prepared in the form of bomber aeroplanes, the Army left the airship attacks to the Naval Airship Division, certain that they would fail.

On 23/24 September a dozen Zeppelins took off from Hage, Nordholz and Ahlhorn. Four of them, led by Mathy, were 'big thirties'. Mathy himself was in L 31, von Buttlar in L 30 Peterson in L 32 and Bocker in L 33.

The eight other ships, L 13, L 14, L 16, L 17, L 21, L 22, L 23 and L 24, had only a subsidiary rôle and added nothing to the history of the aerial bombardment of England. Three people were killed and seventeen injured in Nottingham from an attack by L 17.

But three of the 'super-Zeppelins' were to make this yet another memorable raid. We can ignore the fourth. Von Buttlar, in L 30, came and went and proved once more his unsuitability for long-range operations. He covered his failure with another of his notoriously unreliable reports. He claimed to have dropped bombs on London, but he never crossed the English coast; instead he apparently released the bombs into the sea off Norfolk.

Bocker, in L 33, was the first captain to arrive over London. Like Mathy and Peterson, both of whom followed his example, he avoided the northern approaches. He crossed into England at Foulness Point and set course for London via the River Crouch. Heavy anti-aircraft fire harassed him all the way from the Thames Estuary to the capital, but he confused the ground defences with parachute flares and made his main effort in the East End districts of Bow, Bromley-by-Bow and Stratford, where L 33 dropped an unconfirmed number of explosive and incendiary bombs, which included two 660-lb missiles. Ten or eleven people were killed in an attack which wrecked or seriously damaged working-class houses, factories, offices, an oil storage tank and a timber yard.

Fires caused a considerable part of that damage. The firemen were again the under-honoured, taken-for-granted heroes. They contained and localized the conflagration, but the roar and crackle of burning buildings were heard long after the raids were over, the guns silent and the searchlights switched off. The glare, seen more than thirty miles away, was mistaken for that of another Zeppelin in flames. Next morning ash was found in the Kent and Surrey suburbs.

Having completed his mission, Bocker swept south-east

across London and then turned north-east over Kent. Under
heavy anti-aircraft fire throughout the raid, constantly sought
by searchlights, he and his crew had shown characteristic
courage and persistence. He took L 33 up to 13,000 feet, but she
could not escape the gunfire and was badly damaged by a shell.
She began to lose height and, even before he was attacked by a
B.E. 2c over Chelmsford, he knew that this was his last
operational flight in L 33.

The pilot of the B.E. 2c was the same Lieutenant A. de
Brandon who had claimed—and continued to claim—that he
and not the gunners had been responsible for the destruction of
L 15. Once again he was unlucky. Having seen L 33 in the
searchlights, he attacked her for nearly half an hour. He
reported later that 'the Brock ammunition seemed to be bursting all along it, but the Zepp did not catch fire'. He had in fact
damaged L 33's fuel tanks and Bocker, now in serious trouble,
made for the sea, where he hoped to alight on the surface and
carry out standing orders to destroy her.

But it was not to be. L 33 fell in a field between Little
Wigborough and Peldon, near Mersea Island. None of the crew
was injured and when they tried to burn her with parachute
flares there was so little hydrogen left in her that she failed to
ignite. Bocker and his crew were captured as they made an
unsuccessful attempt to find a boat in which to escape. In 1918
Bocker was returned to Germany as part of a prisoner-of-war
exchange.

To the inexpert eye L 33 looked to be a complete wreck,
although she was still clearly recognizable as a Zeppelin. She
sagged amidships as if her back was broken. Her nose and
forward part were higher off the ground than her stern. She was
naked, her envelope gone in the attempt to burn her. There
were gaps between the trellis work of her girders. Nevertheless
she was basically intact and was a first prize for Britain. Her
design was copied and she became the genesis of the post-war
airships R 33 and R 34 (which made a record trip from Scotland
to the United States of America and a return flight to Pulham in
Norfolk between 2 and 13 July, 1919, a round trip of 6,644
nautical miles).

In contrast to Bocker's humiliating experience, Mathy carried out a raid on London which enhanced his reputation as the
boldest and most audacious of the Zeppelin captains. He and
Peterson crossed the coast together at Dungeness. Peterson is

assumed to have had engine trouble because he cruised there for more than an hour.

Mathy soon realized that he had too heavy a bomb load for an effective attack on London and dropped ten 120-pound missiles near Dungeness lighthouse. He then flew across Kent and Surrey. Soon after midnight he reached the outer suburbs and dropped parachute flares at Croydon. Like those released by Bocker, they confused the ground defences.

The first phase of Mathy's attack began in South London. It was so concentrated that the path of the bombs might have been hand-picked: Streatham Common, Streatham High Road and Hill, Brixton, Kennington and the neighbouring residential roads.

All London was awake and alert after Bocker's earlier raid, but most of the expectant crowds had gone when Mathy arrived. When he left, people were on the streets again, this time as the frightened, bewildered and angry victims of a short, savage attack. There were craters all along Streatham High Road. Five people were killed when a tramcar was hit on Streatham Hill. Many shops were wrecked. Traders whose only damage was shattered windows or blown-out shop fronts reckoned they were lucky.

Most of the damage, and many of the casualties, occurred in the roads on either side of the main highway. The street names were reminders that this had once been a rural area—Elm Park, Beechdale Road, Acacia Road, Oakdale Road, Groveway. These were still socially-mixed suburbs but Mathy's bombs fell without discrimination. In a few minutes shattered walls and roofs exposed the privacy of upstairs bedrooms and downstairs Sundays-only front rooms.

Leaving behind a wide area of devastation, Mathy flew north over London, unseen by the searchlights and unthreatened by gunfire; yet all the London defences knew that a second Zeppelin was near the capital after Bocker had bombed it. Furthermore, its landfall at Dungeness had not been a secret. But Mathy's flares had unsighted the gunners and taken the searchlight crews by surprise. His attack revealed gross incompetence. Even before he had released the flares over Croydon, he had dropped four bombs at Kenley in Surrey.

Although his landfall had been reported, he had outwitted the entire defence system because he chose an unexpected approach route over Kent and Surrey. Nothing had been seen or heard of him until he bombed Kenley. He had flown at altitudes of 12–13,000 feet. He had made the maximum use of cloud cover. His speed had been more than 50 miles per hour. Like a ghost in the night he came and was gone before daylight. Similarly, as he sped across the capital after his attack south of the river, he caught the defences unawares. Bocker, having chosen to fly up the strongly-defended Thames Estuary, had alerted the defences, but his speed and altitude had kept him out of trouble until he turned for home.

When he crossed London Mathy, too, was making his way home, but he left behind a ferocious scene. His second attack, on the Leyton district of the Lea Bridge Road, killed twenty-two people and injured seventy-five.

It seems to have been a purposeless attack, no more than a casual, careless dropping of the rest of his bombs. His real work of the night was already done. His objective had been Central London, which he missed, although he maintained otherwise. The last of his first-phase bombs fell at Kennington Park, near the Oval cricket ground. He was unimpeded by gunfire or searchlights and his failure to bomb prominent places such as the Houses of Parliament, Whitehall, Buckingham Palace and the bridges across the Thames is inexplicable. It is impossible to accept the explanation that his altitude of 13,000 feet caused him to mistake his first-phase targets for Central London. He mentioned having crossed the Thames. Even a captain making his first operational visit would have known that the main objective was on the north bank of the river. At a similar altitude Mathy had been able to pinpoint Clapham—less than a mile away from the South London phase—and had even mentioned it by name in his report. Yet except for the open spaces of the commons at Clapham, Wandsworth, Streatham and Tooting Bec, Clapham itself scarcely had any identifiable landmarks like those in Central London or the City.

After he had bombed the Lea Bridge Road district, and with all his missiles gone, Mathy made for the coast and went out over the North Sea at Great Yarmouth shortly before 3 am. Despite his failure to hit the main objective, his raid had been the epitome of a Zeppelin captain's skill and boldness. But the brightness of his triumph was dimmed before he and his crew left the coast. They had seen another airship ablaze in the sky. It proved to be L 32 from which there were no survivors.

Peterson had reached Dartford, on the south bank of the

Above, left) Peter Strasser, Chief of the German Airship Division and Leader of Airships. He was killed in the last Zeppelin raid of the war when L 70 was destroyed off the Norfolk coast, with the loss of all hands, on 5 August 1918.

Right) Heinrich Mathy, the most audacious and successful of the Zeppelin captains, died with all his crew when L 31 was shot down at Potters Bar, Middlesex, on 2 October 1916.

Below) W. Leefe Robinson, the Royal Flying Corps hero who was the first pilot to destroy a German airship over England. He was made a prisoner of war after having been shot down on the Western Front in 1917. Died of influenza in December 1918.

The loss of two 'super-Zeppelins'—L 32 (*above*) and L 33 (*opposite*) on the night of 23–24 September 1916 proved to be one of the decisive setbacks in the assault on England. L 32 was shot down in flames by Lieutenant F. Sowrey, RFC, at Great Burstead, Essex. He was awarded the Distinguished Service Order. The 22 crew members of L 32 died in the cauldron of fire after Sowrey had hit the Zeppelin with three drums of Brock-Pomeroy-Buckingham tracer bullets.

Thames, at 1 am. He made for London, but searchlights held the airship. They lost her temporarily in the mist and she crossed to the north bank of the river, where there was no mist. At 13,000 feet the searchlights held her again. Having previously dropped his bombs haphazardly, he now jettisoned the rest. But if he avoided the persistent guns, there was no escape from a patrolling B.E. 2c from 39 Squadron.

Second-Lieutenant F. Sowrey, who had only just failed to beat Leefe Robinson in the attack on SL 11, saw L 32 in the searchlights at 12.45 am. There was no anti-aircraft fire, just L 32 trying to escape from the beams and Sowrey bearing down on her. He reported that he fired two drums of Brock-Pomeroy-Buckingham ammunition which 'had apparently no effect, but the third one caused the envelope to catch fire in several places . . . I watched the burning airship strike the ground.'

Before she was hit multitudes of people had turned out to watch a spectacle that was even more thrilling than the destruction of SL 11. People who claimed to have seen Leefe Robinson's B.E. 2c were examples of the 'I Was There' vanity which made so many 'Zepp watchers' wise after the event. But on this night crowds over a wide area were rewarded with a duel in the sky. Although no one saw Sowrey's aircraft, there was the drama of the Zeppelin's attempts to escape from the beams and the uncanny sight of tracer bullets disappearing into the airship. The whole event was emphasized by the absence of gunfire. Suddenly a flash of flame leapt out from amidships, followed almost immediately by another from the bows. It all happened so quickly that few people could recall the details. But everyone was sure that this was another fatal fire in the sky when L 32 was alight from end to end She dipped and turned and swung before her nose went down and she began to fall.

She did not plummet to death, but made a slow descent until she crashed at Snail's Hill Farm, Great Burstead, a mile and a half from Billericay in Essex.

Sunday, 24 September was fine and hot. Billericay had never seen such crowds before or since. Local residents and train excursionists trekked across the fields to Snail's Hill Farm. Others came in almost every kind of transport from the humble donkey-drawn barrow, horse-drawn trap and the bicycle, to the latest smart limousines made by Rolls-Royce, Daimler, Lanchester and others.

Enterprising stallholders were there as well to provide food and soft drinks for the sightseers. This was a rare day out, like the traditional working-class beanfast, and even the superior classes caught the spirit of fiesta. The cause of the celebration was clearly visible to everyone who could press close enough to the armed sentries.

No one minded that L 32 did not look at all like a Zeppelin. No one cared if the battered, burnt-out wreck was a control-car or a gondola or some other part of the main structure. It was enough that the huge twist of wire and aluminium was another defeated German airship.

The mood at Snail's Hill Farm was different from that at Cuffley. If the crowds at the farm had then known of the casualties in the previous night's raid, their jubilation would have been even greater.

Some spectators at Cuffley had found time to ponder on the awful fate of SL 11's crew. It was perhaps no more than a morbid feeling, prompted by the tarpaulins covering the dead men, which the early visitors had seen. At Snail's Hill Farm, twenty-two of the scorched bodies—only one of which could be identified—were hidden in a nearby barn.

Three days later the crew of L 32 were buried in the churchyard of Great Burstead Church. About a mile away the wrecked Zeppelin was still there, a reminder of Sowrey's skill and bravery—for which he was awarded the Distinguished Service Order—and the twenty-two men for whom the challenge of death or glory was now over.

The funeral was almost a secret ceremony. Only a handful of local people watched it, in sharp contrast to the thousands who had thronged the fields three days earlier. Royal Flying Corps officers, as pall-bearers, carried Peterson's coffin to the churchyard. The coffins of his crew were carried by other ranks of the Corps. Peterson, whose identity was temporarily mistaken for his executive officer, was buried in an individual grave. His comrades shared one alongside it. The pall-bearers stood to attention as *The Last Post* was sounded.

There were loud protests when it became known that L 32's crew had been buried with full military honours. It was outrageous, some critics said, that 'baby-killers and murderers of innocent civilians' should have been given this kind of funeral. A Scottish church minister thought they should have been buried in quicklime like the common murderers they were. A member of the team which had interrogated Bocker and his crew was less demanding; he believed they should have been put in unmarked graves, like paupers. Ironically, there was an even more insistent demand for the bombing of German civilians.

As usual the pilots and observers of the RNAS and the RFC were less belligerent and more tolerant. Furthermore, they knew that Britain did plan to attack Germany with heavy bombers. Handley Page had almost completed his first bomber, the 0/100. It had been in preparation since December, 1914, following a request from Winston Churchill and Murray Sueter for an aeroplane large enough to bomb Germany.

The indignation about the funeral was increased by another raid which had taken place on the night after the two Zeppelins had been destroyed. Nine airships had taken off on 25/26 September. Details of the previous raid were unknown; but the crews on this mission did know that two ships had been brought down, in one of which all hands had perished.

Only two of the nine Zeppelins—the 'big thirties' L 30 and L 31—had orders to attack London, and then only if there was good cloud cover. The sky over the capital on 25/26 September was cloudless with a canopy of stars.

Of the two southern airships, von Buttlar, in L 30, was the first to reach England. The clear sky caused him to cut short his attack on London. He did not try for an alternative target. Typically he reported, falsely, that he had bombed Margate and Ramsgate.

Mathy, in L 31, came in over Dungeness. He, too, decided to avoid London; but he would not leave England without dropping his bombs somewhere. He chose a very special target indeed—Portsmouth. Although it was in the 'safe' area of the South Coast, the famous naval base was heavily defended. Mathy hoped to take it by surprise. He flew high and fast above the Kent and Sussex seaboard to Selsey Bill, and then to the Isle of Wight. From there he turned to cross the narrow roadstead of Spithead. Portsmouth was only a moment away.

This could be the most spectacular prize of his career. Portsmouth was the Royal Navy's biggest arsenal and its premier home. 'Pompey' lived for, with and off the Navy. Its harbour could accommodate the Grand Fleet. Its dockyard—granted a Royal Charter in 1194 by Richard Coeur de Lion—covered an area of 300 acres. A devastating attack would cause havoc to warships and installations, and might even put the base out of action. It would cause more dismay than the first raid on London.

Blinding searchlights and a heavy barrage of gunfire forced Mathy to drop his bombs wildly and inaccurately. He reported that he had bombed Portsmouth itself and the dockyard, but the missiles fell harmlessly into the sea. L 31 escaped and left England over Hastings and St Leonards.

Nelson's famous flagship, HMS *Victory*, was then, as now, moored in the harbour. In their first action the Portsmouth defences had lived up to his historic signal: 'England expects every man to do his duty'. Between them the gunners and the searchlight crews had been unable to trap and kill L 31. But they had saved the base and the people of the city.

Of the seven Zeppelins ordered to attack 'England middle and industrial areas' only four crossed the coast. Bombs from two of them, L 21 and L 22, killed forty-three people and injured thirty-one others in raids on Sheffield and Bolton.

Martin Dietrich, in L 22, just missed turning the raid from failure to success. His main target was Sheffield, then one of Britain's biggest and most important munitions centres. It seemed impossible to miss the armaments and components factories in that compact and inevitably well-lighted city. But the factories escaped, at the expense of people. Twenty-eight were killed, nineteen injured and several working-class houses wrecked or damaged.

With the conspicuous exception of the Portsmouth defences, there had been a poor response to the raiders. Only one aeroplane, from Calshot in the Solent, had seen a Zeppelin, and it made a hopeless pursuit of Mathy.

Yet, despite the loss of two airships in one night, the aerial bombardment of England was not finished.

CHAPTER 14

The Vanished Dream

For the High Seas Fleet Command the loss of L 32 and L 33 brought an abrupt end to self-deception. The campaign's worsening record of failure could no longer be ignored.

In August Strasser had told Admiral Scheer that 'the airships offer a certain means of victoriously ending the war.' Less than two months later optimism had been replaced by harsh reality. Even Strasser had to face the possibility that Zeppelins alone might not win the war. Instead they would become weapons of intimidation, a much-needed symbol of a still-resilient Germany. They would deprive the British Expeditionary Force of urgently-needed fighter aeroplanes, pilots and observers, anti-aircraft guns and their crews.

The British official history, *War in the Air*, gives authoritative endorsement of the strength which, at the end of 1916, was confined to Britain to meet Zeppelin attacks. The army had 17,341 officers and other ranks who were used exclusively for anti-aircraft defence. Some 12,000 served the guns and searchlights. Ten RFC squadrons absorbed 110 aeroplanes, approximately 200 officers and other ranks.

Set against what had so recently been the highest hopes this was, for Germany, almost an irrelevant detail. Hindsight suggests that this was the moment when the High Seas Fleet Command should have cut its losses. But there were other factors to be considered. It was imperative that Germany showed no signs of weakness. There was still no indication that America would abandon her neutrality. But there was increasing hostility, despite the unspoken support of many commercial interests and the undisguised support by people of German descent, the Irish-American population, and the incessant anti-British attitude of the German-language newspapers.

No foreign diplomat could have been better placed to judge American political and public opinion than the German ambassador, Count von Bernstoff. His soft, persuasive answers had turned away much wrath about 'barbarity' in Belgium at the beginning of the war, the 'frightfulness' of a U-boat campaign which had since been modified, and the indiscriminate bombing of England. Von Bernstoff had snidely insinuated to an outraged American Government that the *Lusitania* had been torpedoed because she was carrying a secret cargo of munitions.

A behind-the-scenes spymaster and organizer of strikes and sabotage by German and Austro-Hungarian workers, von Bernstoff had been the plenipotentiary at Washington since 1908. He was married to an American, moved in the highest social circles and was close to the business world, to which the war was bringing unprecedented prosperity. In August, 1916, he had successfully evaded sensational allegations about his clandestine espionage and sabotage activities. It was the Austro-Hungarian ambassador who was expelled and not the astute, suave von Bernstoff. No country has ever been better served by her ambassador. He realized, however, that even he might not stop the American people from demanding positive action that could lead to war.

There had already been some ominous signs in respected and influential quarters. In a speech to the Republican Convention at New York City, in February, 1916, Elihu Root, former Secretary of State under President Theodore Roosevelt, said:

> American democracy stands for something more than beef and cotton and grain; it stands for something that cannot be measured by rates of exchange . . . Peace and liberty can be preserved only by the authority and observance of rules of national conduct founded upon the rules of justice and humanity; only by the establishment of laws among nations responsive to the enlightened opinion of mankind.

They were unwelcome words to a party which was, to say the least, unenthusiastic about the war. But von Bernstoff knew that the sentiments had a wide, if sporadic, support.

The ambassador had played the intriguer's role in a serious

dispute between the United States of America and Britain. The British Government had announced that it was no longer bound by the Declaration of London, made in 1909. The Declaration set out international regulations for the mutual rights and obligations of belligerents and neutrals in war. Among the sensitive and controversial points was the question of the carrying, landing and ultimate destination of cargoes which might—or might not—be contraband goods. By August, 1914, Britain had not ratified the Declaration, but then agreed to adopt it with modifications. After the outbreak of war Britain modified it again by various Orders in Council, and finally cancelled her obligations with the Maritime Rights Order of 1916.

America had been opposed to any change and the rejection infuriated the copper, cotton, lumber, grain and meat interests. To Count Bernstoff's satisfaction, relations between Britain and America were tense. Even more important to him and to Germany, the possibilities of a negotiated peace were being considered by Germany herself, the United States and the Allies. In the summer and autumn of 1916 Germany was not to know that formal negotiations were never to begin. Expectantly, however, she was determined to be the nation with the strongest cards at any conference table. She might not win the war but she would not lose the peace.

Thus the aerial bombardment of England was now essential to her political strategy. The morale of the German people was part of that strategy, too. The public still would not accept anything less than a maximum effort by the Zeppelins. There were complaints that it was not being made. The years of propaganda had produced a rich but embarrassing harvest. An impatient lust for revenge followed the loss of the two airships. People were greedier for news of death and destruction. Even the strictly-controlled newspapers hinted that these greater efforts were needed. Together with the now routine propaganda that 'London trembles before their attacks', the newspaper *Neueste Nachrichtel* added 'which it is hoped will be more frequent'.

But the Zeppelins were certain to face greater dangers. Even the forthcoming 'height climbers' would not bring a decisive result. At best they might reduce the losses. In the meantime the risk of further losses was inescapable.

They began with the next raid on 1/2 October, when 11

Zeppelins took off for England. The caution, uncertainty and lack of resolution shown on the raid a week earlier—except for Mathy's abortive attack on Portsmouth—was even more evident on this latest sortie. Significantly, only one airship had London as its principal target. The main effort was directed against the North and Midlands.

In contrast to the weather conditions elsewhere in England, the night was dark and sharply-clear in and around London. Two ships—one of which was diverted there by the conditions—attempted to reach the capital. Four did not cross the coast. Five lost their way over Lincolnshire, Northamptonshire and Norfolk.

Inevitably it was Mathy, in L 31, who made the thrust for London. He came in over Lowestoft at 9 pm and flew via Chelmsford towards the capital. The searchlights picked him up almost immediately between Chelmsford and Brentwood. We can only speculate on the reason for the course he took after the searchlights found him, or, indeed, why he chose to attack London over its strongly-defended northern approaches. Because of the surprise he had achieved when he took the south-eastern route to the capital he may have assumed that the British would expect him to do so again; to outwit any such assumption he might have decided to switch back to the conventional approach.

Whatever his reason, his decision was based on a faulty appreciation of the situation. He knew that the raid itself was no surprise to the British, who had long since been able to detect incoming airships while they were over the North Sea. Even if some of the air defences were diverted to the main effort elsewhere, it was most unlikely that L 31 could reach London by stealth. The northern frontier guns and searchlights extended well beyond the capital and could bring a powerful concentration on a single airship; even if some aircraft were diverted to the main effort, the route to London, and the one he took instead, would bring him within the patrolling zones of aeroplanes from 39 Squadron at North Weald Bassett, Hainault Farm and Suttons Farm. There was no doubt that he knew his position precisely, having identified it by calling for radio bearings.

His intention to take the conventional passage was foiled by the searchlights. But he had avoided them on previous occasions, even if they had helped to rob him of success of Port-

smouth. Why did he apparently retreat from them now, instead
of taking avoiding action? Why did he take a circuitous route
which must bring him within the patrolling zones of 39 Squadron?

It was an inexplicable manoeuvre and almost certainly a
fatal error of judgment. He turned away from the flight path to
London and passed over Harlow, Hertford, Buntingford—
where he began his turn back—Ware, Hertford again, and then
to Cheshunt. It cost him precious time.

When he retreated from the searchlights no aeroplanes had
yet gone up to find L 31, although duty pilots were standing by.
The searchlights and anti-aircraft guns would put them on
course for the Zeppelin within minutes. If, however, Mathy had
gone straight to London, he certainly could have flown safely
above the height of the B.E. 2cs, at any rate until he was over
the city; and he might have outdistanced them as well.

Did even the boldest of all the Zeppelin captains lose his
resolution? The diversion seems to be out of character with a
man so skilful and brave. It can be argued that, by making it,
Mathy hoped to persuade the defenders that he had broken off
the engagement and surprise them with a swift return. But he
knew that the approach of even one airship to London alerted
all the air and ground defences. Furthermore, he can scarcely
have deceived himself that his circuitous flight would have gone
unobserved. If he was to win the race to London, time was
everything; but he threw it away.

At Cheshunt L 31 was again caught by searchlights and
heavily attacked by anti-aircraft fire. Among the pilots who
were on patrol was Second-Lieutenant W. J. Tempest. He was
over central London, some 15 miles away, when he saw L 31,
first in a concentration of searchlights and then almost girdled
by bursting shells. The gunfire was so extensive that Tempest
was in danger from it as he flew to attack the Zeppelin.

Mathy saw the B.E. 2c, as well as three or four other
aeroplanes—two of which were piloted by Leefe Robinson and
Sowrey. Again, untypically, he decided not to stand and fight.
In an attempt to reach a safer altitude he unloaded all of his
bombs and turned about.

Tempest pursued L 31 through the barrage of anti-aircraft
fire. His fuel pump failed and he used the hand pump. When he
was within attacking range the airship was at a height of about
12,000 feet. He climbed above her, safe at least from the

bursting shells, 'for which', he wrote some years later, 'I was very grateful.'

He dived and flew beneath her. His Lewis gun used the Brock-Pomeroy-Buckingham mixture as well as .303 bullets. Two attacks had no apparent effect. Fired on by L 31's machine guns, he turned and raked her again when he was astern of her.

The sight of a Zeppelin caught in the searchlights had again brought thousands of people on to the streets. They were confident as they saw her trapped in the beams, but they could not know of Tempest's cool, calculating courage. In his later account he dismissed his close-quarter gallantry with considerable understatement: 'I sat under her tail safely sheltered from her own machine guns, which I could see were firing tracer shells in all directions.'

With his third attempt he knew that he had won the duel. L 31 exploded in flames and finally crashed into a field near Potters Bar in Hertfordshire. Everyone in her perished.

SL 11 had gone down slowly. L 32 had also fallen slowly on her descent to Snail's Hill Farm. L 31 plummeted seemingly straight to the ground. 'Suddenly,' said one spectator, 'it wasn't a Zepp any more but just a sheet of flame.'

The exultant crowds could not know, either, that Tempest had narrowly escaped being hit by the falling airship. 'I did a frantic nose dive with the burning wreckage bearing down on me . . . Only by putting my machine into a spin did I manage to corkscrew out of the way as the blazing mass roared past me, but I managed to right my machine.' He was awarded the Distinguished Service Order.

When the crowds arrived at Potters Bar the next day they saw only half of L 31, and then as a collection of mangled girders. The other half was a scattered mass of wreckage. There had been one recognizable body, that of Mathy himself. He had jumped out in a desperate attempt to escape. He was still alive when local people found him, but he died within a few minutes.

The destruction of L 31 had a much greater significance than the loss of three airships in a week and four in a month. The most successful and formidable of the captains was dead. To the British he had been one of the principal 'baby-killers'. That, with his arrogant boasting—well-publicized in American newspapers—had made him the popular conception of the Hun. In Germany he was among the greatest of her war heroes. More than anyone else he had shown that the Zeppelin could live up to its deadly reputation. His leadership and gallantry had inspired the whole Naval Airship Division. He was irreplaceable.

Any lingering belief in the strategic power of the Zeppelin died with Mathy in the early morning of 1 October, 1916. Even the forthcoming 'high flyers' could only maintain an illusion of invincibility for the German people, reinforce the main war effort and show the world, and particularly the United States of America, that the Fatherland would survive the most daunting challenge.

But the decline of the Zeppelin was to be quicker than Germany anticipated. There were to be more raids on England; only one of them was to cause heavy casualties. With the absolute certainty that there could be no victory for them, and knowing that every sortie was a potential death trap, the captains and crews did their duty to the end.

A gap of nearly eight weeks between the loss of Mathy and the next raid gnawed at the outer edges of their morale, but on 27/28 November, ten Zeppelins were ordered to attack the supposedly less dangerous North of England and the Midlands. Two of them turned back. Six failed to reach their objectives because of mechanical troubles, very heavy anti-aircraft fire and the now dreaded sight of a blazing Zeppelin.

It was L 34, with Max Dietrich in command. She was one of two airships which brought another double loss on one mission. Searchlights held her as she came in over Hartlepool about 12.30 am. Dietrich's reaction was now typical of a normally brave captain with faltering confidence. He went out to sea, but on his way dropped bombs on West Hartlepool where four people were killed and eleven injured. But he was caught before he could escape to a safe height. At 9,500 feet he was attacked by Second-Lieutenant I. V. Pyott of 36 Squadron. Pyott climbed above her and then went beneath her. He reported that he and the Zeppelin 'flew on a parallel course for about 5 miles, firing about 71 rounds at the Zepp.' Finally, he dealt her a fatal burst and she fell into the sea. There were no survivors.

The other loss was that of L 21, commanded by Kurt Frankenberg. She was hit by two RNAS pilots, Flight-Lieutenant E. Cadbury and Flight Sub-Lieutenant E. L. Pulling. The Zeppelin caught fire and disappeared into the sea off Lowestoft with the loss of all her crew. Cadbury's bullets hit her first and set her alight. She was already doomed when Pulling fired the last rounds, and it was his name which was added to the Roll of Honour of pilots who had destroyed a German airship.

The British people were now certain that the aerial bombardment was virtually over; at its worst it would be no more than a nuisance.

Just before midday on 28 November, while everyone in Britain was celebrating the loss of two more Zeppelins, a German aeroplane dropped six bombs on London. A few people heard small, and in some places muffled explosions. Later, when the official bulletin gave sparse details of the attack, some Londoners said they had seen the single-engined LVG (Luft-Verkehrs-Gesellschaft) biplane, 13,000 feet above the capital.

Scarcely anyone, not even Home Forces Headquarters, foresaw that this fleeting raid was a prelude to a new phase in the aerial bombardment of England. Those who did were like 'voices crying in the wilderness'.

CHAPTER 15

A False Dawn

Although only a few people had heard those small explosions on 28 November, rumour raced across London. Spies had tried to sabotage Buchingham Palace; German aeroplanes had singled it out for attack; Irish rebels had tried to emulate Guy Fawkes at the Houses of Parliament.

Early editions of the evening newspapers printed the official bulletin:

> Between 11.50 and noon this morning six bombs were dropped on London by a hostile aeroplane flying at a great height above the haze.

It added that 'material damage is slight' and that four people were injured. Later an amendment corrected the figure to eleven injured.

Despite the bulletin's vague statement about bombs having been dropped 'in London' everyone soon knew that six 20-lb missiles had caused minor damage in the Brompton Road–Knightsbridge–Belgravia–Victoria Street areas.

The visit by the LVG was thought to be just another of the German aeroplanes and seaplanes which had made twenty-two sorties since those of Christmas, 1914. This one, it was believed, had merely been bolder than the rest. There was even grudging admiration for a raid on London in 'broad daylight'. Almost all of the previous sorties had been restricted to the Kent coastal areas. All, except one, had been during the day. Twenty people had been killed and fifty-seven injured.

The only serious attack had been on Dover, Deal, Ramsgate

and Margate in March, 1916. Fourteen people had been killed, including four children on their way to Sunday school, and twenty-six injured. Two German aircraft had been shot down in the sea. There was, of course, grief and distress over the individual tragedies, and complaints about inadequate defences, but raids on ships in the Channel and on places such as Folkestone and Dover were to be expected.

In 1916 the British public's attitude to the aeroplane had undergone a swinging change. Victories against the Zeppelins and recent hard-won successes at the Battle of the Somme had brought respect and acceptance. But it was inconceivable that aeroplanes, British or German, could be more deadly than the Zeppelin. A few dissenting voices were ignored in the excitement of the airships' defeat. Raids meant Zeppelin raids, and now that they were all but conquered the aerial battle was won.

During 1916 Lord Northcliffe, through his newspapers, had warned that heavy bombers would eventually attack Britain. After that daylight sortie over London his sober and restrained *Times* said, 'It is wise to regard it as a prelude to further visits on an extended scale and to lay our plans accordingly.'

The indefatigable Charles Grey went straight to the point in a frank article in *The Aeroplane*: 'When the aeroplane raids start, and prove more damaging than the airship raids, the authorities cannot say that they have not had fair warning of what to expect.'

There were a few other vehement critics, including the veteran Zeppelin scaremongers. Those in Parliament had been joined by Pemberton Billing, the unhonoured hero of Friedrichshafen, whose shrillness and lack of discretion too often spoiled a sound argument.

The warnings were ignored, understandably perhaps by the public, but inexplicably by the Government and almost everyone at Home Forces Headquarters. The Government, as the overall authority, was to be guilty of neglect because of ignorance and a hostile attitude to its critics. To the public, the critics' worst forecasts about the Zeppelin had proved to be wrong.

The British people had no reason to believe in an 'aeroplane menace'. Except for the lone raider over London, almost all the German aeroplanes and seaplanes had been small, single-seater aircraft. Their bombs had not been remotely comparable to the Zeppelins' devastating missiles. But Charles Grey and his fellow critics had not forgotten that as early as October, 1914, Germany had intended to attack England with aeroplanes. A squadron of two-seater machines had been set up at Ghistelles, near Ostend, from which it would move to Calais and establish a base for raids against England. When the German army failed to capture the Channel ports, the squadron was withdrawn.

Its aeroplanes, each of which could carry four 20-lb bombs, would not have been much more effective than those aircraft which did cross the Channel. The intention, however, was different. From Calais, some twenty-one miles from England, the aeroplanes could have flown deeper into the hinterland and been the pathfinders for the heavy bombers of the future, whose exclusive objective would be London. By the autumn of 1916 plans to achieve this were being prepared in the greatest secrecy.

Although the critics of Britain's aerial warfare policy knew nothing of this latest activity, we have seen that they realized that the advent of the heavy bomber was inevitable. And it would not be confined to the Handley Page 0/100. The second 0/100 to be sent to France made a forced landing behind the German lines at the end of 1916. That could have provided the Germans with a model for a heavy bomber; but the Handley Page was not the inspiration of the Gotha bomber, although some people, including those in official quarters, maintained that it was. The G I and the G II were already on active service with the German army, but production difficulties and the demands of the Western Front delayed the Gotha offensive against England until May, 1917.

The 'single hostile aircraft' was soon forgotten by almost everyone. The few gloomy forecasts of dangers ahead were ignored. But the six bombs, ostensibly aimed at the Admiralty and other Whitehall buildings, were a by-product of the main object—a photographic reconnaissance of the Thames Estuary, the docks and London itself.

The absence of any serious aeroplane or airship raids for six months increased the conviction that the aerial bombardment was over. The intervening, and unsuccessful, airship attacks were dismissed as 'sideshows'. One of them, on 16/17 March, 1917, went almost unnoticed. Four Zeppelins crossed the coast and bombs were dropped without serious results. To Peter Strasser, however, the sortie had a special significance. It was the first by his 'height climbers'.

After the airship losses of the previous year, he had fought a stubborn battle for a Zeppelin which could fly even higher and still bomb effectively. There had been complex, frustrating technical arguments in the German Admiralty, the Naval Airship Division, and with the designers. In the end Strasser's demand for height at the expense of speed was met. After many experiments, modifications and changes of mind, L 42 became the first of the 'height climbers'.

Her design was basically the same as that of the 'super Zeppelins' but some major weight-saving alterations included the use of five engines instead of six; a reduced fuel load which cut endurance from 36 hours to 30; the exclusion of machine-guns and machine-gun platforms (although they were restored in later versions); a smaller bomb load because some of the bomb releases and bay doors were omitted; the removal of the crews' quarters; a smaller control car and the minimization of skin friction on the outer cover. The underside was painted black to counter the effect of searchlights.

In prospect L 42 and her sister ships were certainly more formidable than the older Zeppelins, although the bomb load was reduced to eight 660-lb, sixteen 220-lb explosives and about sixty incendiaries, and there were, temporarily, no machine-guns. Safety, however, could be found beyond the reach of British fighters. At anything above 13,000 feet the new ships could drop bombs leisurely if not accurately.

Not for the first time too much faith was placed in theory at the expense of experience already gained. In short, the 'height climbers' needed almost everything to be in their favour—which had never happened before. And now there was a new hazard, one for which the crews were insufficiently trained and prepared.

Strasser flew with Martin Dietrich on L 42's first test flight. She reached a ceiling of 19,700 feet, and even then only some of the crew used the compressed oxygen stimulant. Active service operations were soon to reveal that this and other test flights had provided too little experience of the physical and mental effects of the sub-stratosphere together with those of extreme cold.

Although L 42 was the original 'height climber', the four other Zeppelins which took part in the raid of 16/17 March had been modified to make them 'height climbers' as well: L 35, L 39, L 40, L 41 and L 42.

Strasser accompanied Martin Dietrich in L 42. Once again he was an ill-omened passenger. Dietrich never reached England. Engine trouble and high winds forced him to turn back. The raid, scheduled for London, was a total failure. The weather confounded the forecasters; and at such high operational ceilings it was impossible to warn the captains of unpredictable changes.

The other ships dropped bombs in Kent and Sussex. Seventy-nine missiles caused only minor damage and there were no casualties. The crews of three of the four Zeppelins survived extreme physical distress because of the altitude, mechanical troubles, bad weather and loss of direction.

One did not survive. L 39 (*Kapitänleutnant* Koch) was destroyed, with the loss of all hands, by French anti-aircraft gunfire at Compiègne.

The now familiar false claims to have bombed London—this time by Ehrlich in L 35 and Sommerfeldt in L 40—were of minor importance. We do not know if Strasser accepted them, but this irrepressible optimist was satisfied with his 'height climbers'. On their first mission they had flown between 17,000 and 19,000 feet. Sixteen RFC aeroplanes had, inevitably, been unable to intercept them. Anti-aircraft fire in England had been equally ineffective. It would seem that the enemy's recently-acquired defence supremacy was already useless.

Strasser put aside the loss of L 39, the serious altitude troubles, the seemingly incurable mechanical problems and the bad weather. If conquest was not now possible, his personal reputation would be safe as his airships took a different but important part in the war.

But, like England's hopes that the aerial bombardment was finished, faith in the 'height climbers' proved to be a false dawn. We have followed the decline of the Zeppelin. We shall see also its rapid fall, both metaphorically and in reality. By a cruel twist Strasser was to watch the despised Army Air Service bring a new terror to England and set hitherto unconsidered problems for her defences.

Meanwhile there was some alarm in Whitehall over the new 'high flyers'. Even if any pretence of accuracy had been abandoned, London was again naked to attack. Colonel Simon, the anti-aircraft defence commander, did not share the Government's previous complacency and weakness which had allowed too many pilots and observers to be sent to France, and badly-needed anti-aircraft guns to join the Merchant Service for protection against U-boats. There was only one way to meet this new threat: to attack the Zeppelins before they could reach their bombing altitudes. The Home Defence Squadrons needed to be strengthened and not weakened by the demands of Sir Douglas Haig.

Even Lord French was spurred to vigorous protest. As Commander-in-Chief, Home Forces, he was little more than a figurehead. The real work was done for him—rather than delegated by him—but he was responsible for policy recommendations and, reluctantly, for occasional decisions. His subordinates, and in particular Colonel Simon, suffered accordingly. A more determined man was needed to defend London's defenders. His protest was rejected by the War Office.

The weakening of the Home Defence Squadrons worried Colonel Simon for another reason. He, too, shared those fears about the heavy bombers. But vague fears were no substitute for information on which to base a sound military appreciation. Neither he nor anyone else knew that Germany was assembling the England Squadron—whose formal title was first Kaghol 1 and then Kaghol 3—to revive the strategic plan to bomb England by aeroplane. This time, however, only the intention was the same. The Gotha IV and a unique tactical formation were about to open a new chapter in the history of aerial bombardment.

After the Royal Flying Corps had inflicted a severe defeat on German aeroplanes over the Somme battlefields in July, 1916, the Army High Command reorganized its air force. General von Hoeppner was appointed to carry out the reorganization and to command a newly-named *Luftstreitkräfte*. One of his main objectives was to create the England Squadron.

A soldier with no flying experience, Hoeppner was not a popular choice with the *Luftstreitkräfte*. But he was recognized as an outstanding staff officer who could instil the principle of strategic bombing into a service whose aeroplane operations had been exclusively tactical.

Hoeppner's deputy, and commander of the England Squadron, was *Kapitänleutnant* Ernst Brandenburg, a former infantry officer who, having been wounded in 1914, had transferred to the air force as an observer. Like Peter Strasser, he was a dominating leader who was instantly accepted by Kaghol 3.

His active service experience offset the misgivings about von Hoeppner.

By May, 1917, four flights of Kaghol 3, each with six Gotha IV bombers, were ready for the first attack on England. The Squadron was assembled at Ghistelles before it moved to a permanent base at two aerodromes near Ghent. The Gotha crews were trained on the north German coast at Heligoland and Westerland. From there the bombers were flown to Ghistelles.

The North Sea itself was the vital training area for crews and their aeroplanes. Everything was planned in meticulous detail to ensure that the Squadron would replace the Naval Airship Division as the élite of the German air force. Furthermore, it had to undertake the kind of flying which was done only by the Navy and which, to a lesser degree, had been tried by the Army Airship Service.

Because the campaign was to be entirely different from that carried out by airships there were few lessons to be learned from their failures. Gothas were free of most of the troubles which had beset the airships. Even those troubles which were common had a different application. Navigating over the sea, target location on land and attacks themselves would be easier because the Gothas would raid by daylight. The objective, London, would be explicit, without any ambiguous orders such as 'England South, London if possible'. Alternative targets were to be sought only if a raid on London failed or if the Squadron could not reach the capital. The British could not intercept signals because there were none to intercept—no wireless sets were carried.

Attempts were made to improve the use of compressed oxygen at 14,000 feet and above; but the oxygen supply system was disliked by the Gotha IV crews, whose exposure to high altitude discomfort and distress would be shorter than that of Zeppelin crews. The fatal vulnerability of airships would be avoided by the new formation flying tactics. Even if the so-called squadron raids had ever materialized in the form of several ships concentrating on one target, collective security and control were impossible.

The Gotha IVs of the England Squadron were the pioneers of battle formation flying. The comradeship and collective protection of 20 or more bombers in a tight formation, which could be broken only on the orders of its commander, were a big factor in the morale and efficiency of the crews and the creation of an essential esprit de corps. Less definable, perhaps, was the psychological attitude: crews had to learn to fly as confidently over the water as they had previously flown over land.

The creation and development of the England Squadron ranks as another of the genuinely 'best kept secrets' of the First World War. Britain's failure to discover the long, arduous training, the practice formation flights over the North Sea and the setting up of assembly and operational bases is one of the War's unsolved mysteries. The identity of the England Squadron was to remain a secret until the Gothas' second raid.

Although these training flights took place over German territory, it is curious that, if they were seen, no one gave them any special attention. And, if spies or neutral sources did report the comings and goings of a heavy bomber force, the information was ignored. Even more extraordinary was the failure to observe the assembly and activity of the Gothas at Ghistelles and when they moved to their operational aerodromes at St Denis-Westrem and Gontrode near Ghent.

The contrast in the bombing policies of Germany and Britain after some two and a half years of war shows that little had changed in the respective thinking and attitude about the offensive rôle of the aeroplane. Britain had the means but not the will to create her own strategic bombing command. But the one aircraft type conceived, designed and built for that purpose, the Handley Page 0/100, was never used in a strategic effort. Driven by two Rolls-Royce Eagle 250 h.p. engines, the 0/100 could carry sixteen 112-lb bombs, had an endurance of about eight hours and the undoubted capacity to raid deep into the heart of Germany. Instead it was engaged on North Sea patrols and then for the bombing of enemy targets in Belgium.

The RNAS had some 0/100s at Dunkirk. Even when eight of them were transferred, in October, 1917, to the newly-formed 41 Wing RFC—set up to 'bomb targets of military importance in Germany'—they never were used strategically. People who have not understood the difference between strategy and tactics have wrongly credited 41 Wing—and the 0/100's—with having carried out strategic bombing. Germany was attacked by day and night but with no effect on the course of the war or the morale of the German population. Unlike the Second World War—when the strategic principle was adopted, albeit unsuccessfully—the great industrial and communications centres went unscathed.

The German army, however, had a clear-cut policy for the Gothas. It was unimpeded by differences of opinion and indecisions about its rôle. Events having diminished inter-Service jealousies, there were no attempts to use the same kind of aircraft for different and scattered objectives.

When the Gothas did raid England for the first time in daylight, it was not only the attack itself which was a surprise. Although there had been some fanciful 'artist's impressions' of heavy bombers, very few people had actually seen a Handley Page 0/100. And scarcely anyone could have recognized a Gotha.

It was a biplane with a length of 40 feet and an upper wing span of nearly 78 feet. It had two Mercedes engines mounted on either side of the lower wing, each engine developing 260 h.p. There was a crew of three: pilot, navigator—who was generally the captain—and a rear gunner.

Armament consisted of three machine guns: one, in the nose, was mounted on a turntable which enabled it to fire above, below and on either side. The rear gunner was responsible for the other weapons. One was positioned near the floor and the stern; the third, in the stern itself, could fire downwards, sideways and astern through a tunnel. These two guns were a powerful protection for the underside and the stern which were vulnerable from attack by fighter aircraft.

The bomb load could be varied, but as a rule it was composed of four 110-lb missiles, carried externally under the wings, ten 60-lb bombs, as well as incendiaries which were fixed on internal racks. A Goertz bomb-sight provided some degree of accuracy.

With a speed of about 80 miles per hour, the Gotha was slower than the fighter aeroplanes with which the Home Defence Squadrons of the RFC were then equipped. But their rate of climb was too slow to attack the Gothas, whose height with a full bomb load was between 12 and 15,000 feet. Furthermore, the British pilots would fly individually, with little chance of breaking into the unique, tight formation.

The dangers of the North Sea and its weather were not left entirely to chance. Although neither wireless sets nor parachutes were carried, it was claimed that a Gotha which was not seriously damaged could remain afloat for about eight hours.

To reinforce any lack of faith in this dubious claim, inflatable air bags were provided to break the impact of a heavy landing on the surface.

The one reliable support—which certainly gave the crews more confidence than the carrier pigeons which accompanied each aircraft—was to be given by German naval vessels on patrol to rescue a stranded bomber from the North Sea.

By May, 1917, after months of rigorous training, the England Squadron was ready to begin the campaign which would bring the quick, decisive victory that the Zeppelins had failed to achieve. With supreme confidence in themselves, their aeroplanes and their long-practised formation flying, the crews waited for the first fine day.

CHAPTER 16

The First Fine Day

The afternoon of Friday, 25 May was fine and warm, with almost perfect visibility over the North Sea. Farther south it was one of those days when the English and French coasts, some 21 miles away, could be seen from either side of the Channel.

The balmy weather in London and the coastal towns relieved the gloom of a stoically-borne winter and spring. There were complaints about food distribution, the inequities in the compulsory military service administration, and bitterness about unofficial strikes which defied the Munitions Act of 1914.

Lord Devonport had been appointed Food Controller in December, 1916. He had proposed a voluntary self-rationing scheme and a compulsory 'potatoless and meatless' day a week in hotels and restaurants. The voluntary plan suggested that people would limit themselves to a weekly ration of 4 lbs of bread, 2½ lbs of meat and ¼ lb of sugar. Putting the nation 'on its honour' was a failure. It led to even more grievances and complaints. Greengrocers, grocers, butchers and bakers were accused of having favourite customers who were still on a pre-war supply basis and who saw the tradesmen 'all right' with cash bribes. There was always someone who knew someone else who was never seen in the daily food queues. These privileged people were said to be obtaining extra rations but 'hoarding' as well against the day when starvation was more than a prospect.

Although the prospect never did turn into reality, rumours made many people seek 'extras'. The rumours were increased when the short-lived community kitchens were set up in

March, 1917. There was resentment about the availability of supplies. Country districts were naturally better-off and were the source of a prosperous business in what was known in the Second World War as the Black Market. Hotels and restaurants showed an ingenious dishonesty in avoiding the 'meatless' days.

Many of the complaints and grievances were based on envy. Given the opportunity, most people succumbed to a paid or free offer of 'extras' to supplement the rations. The citizens who accused the 'rich classes' of 'hoarding' justified their own guilt by saying they were 'putting by for a rainy day'.

Among the assortment of rumours the truth was bound to emerge, even if only occasionally. In April 'everyone knew' that the nation had only a week's supply of sugar (the official figure was ten days). It was believed that the Royal Navy was not winning the war at sea and that the U-boats were masters of Britain's trade routes. There would have been even greater alarm if the April shipping losses had been revealed: 526,000 tons were lost, the highest total of any month in the war.

There was bitterness about the unofficial strikes, especially among people with families on active service. There was open cynicism about the 'reserved occupations' and a demand that thousands of these 'slackers' should be 'combed out' and conscripted into the Army.

Nevertheless, the resilience of the population surmounted the tragedies and hardships. Theatres, picture palaces, restaurants, night clubs, pubs and concerts flourished as never before. In the spring and early summer of 1917, with no fears of invasion or air raids, the 'safe area' seaside resorts reported a record number of visitors.

On that 'first fine day' in May there was a feeling that the war might progress from its depressing stalemate. The dynamic 'people's politician' David Lloyd George had replaced Asquith as Prime Minister in December, 1916. He was popularly but wrongly given the credit for having brought the United States into the war. The unlimited material and financial resources of America would more than make up for the imminent collapse of Russia.

One of the minor but immediate results of America's participation was the supply of four Curtiss Large America Flying Boats. They had joined the RNAS at Great Yarmouth and Felixstowe. There had been no serious Zeppelin raids for eight months and the 'menace' was thought to have disappeared with the destruction of L 34 and L 16 on 27 and 28 November, 1916. The destruction of another, L 22, on 14 April, by one of the new flying boats, attracted less public attention when she was shot down in the North Sea with the loss of all her crew. That success may have been received by the British public with indifference but it showed Strasser and the Naval Airship Division that the enemy's outposts were now thrust far out over the sea.

On that fine afternoon of 25 May no one in Britain thought about air raids. During the previous night, to be sure, Strasser himself had flown on a six-Zeppelin attack made by his 'height climbers'. The only result of another demoralizing raid was the death of one civilian in Norfolk and negligible damage.

But morale was at its peak across the North Sea at the England Squadron aerodromes. Sixty-nine crewmen, with their twenty-three Gothas, waited for the Squadron's first attempt to bring death and destruction to London.

The new formation was about to be put to the test. In general it took the shape of a tight 'V'. The commander led from the apex of the wedge. Some of the bombers formed the two outer sides and protected other Gothas inside it. Other aircraft astern, at the base of the wedge, flew higher than those at the apex. Armed with sixty-nine machine guns this was a powerful mutual-support formation and a collective flying fortress.

The formation was not inflexible. It could adopt a diamond shape. It could divide into two or three sections or fly in line astern. Some of the confusing reports about the number of Gothas that were seen from the ground were often caused by the manoeuvring from one formation to another. The principle of mutual support was maintained throughout, so that no Gotha could become an isolated target for fighter pilots, and the pilots themselves could not break up the formation.

At 4 pm the twenty-three Gothas, with *Kapitänleutnant* Brandenburg in the leading machine, took off from St Denis-Westrem and Gontrode aerodromes, moved into the protective formation and set course for London. One aircraft crashed on the way to the coast but the crew was rescued by a patrolling U-boat. Another Gotha developed engine trouble and turned back to land safely at Ghistelles. The remaining twenty-one raiders made their landfall over the Essex coast between the rivers Crouch and Blackwater at approximately 5 pm. The RNAS air station at Dunkirk had neither seen nor heard them.

They were reported, but not identified, by the Tongue Light Vessel which marked the main Thames Channel.

The Gothas split into two groups for the short approach flight to London. But over the capital the weather of that first fine day had changed. Cloud banks and mist made accurate bombing impossible from 12,000 feet. Pride and policy required that the Squadron tried for specific targets rather than drop bombs at random. If a primary target could not be attacked, then the alternative objective must be one of genuine military importance. At Gravesend Brandenburg swung the formation south for a raid on Folkestone, where the first fine day was still living up to its promise, even though the day itself was nearly over.

Folkestone was not a casual choice. It was unquestionably a place of military importance. Its harbour was a major supply link with France and the main embarkation port for the British Expeditionary Force (nearly 10 million British and Allied troops used it during the First World War). Outside the town, at Shorncliffe, there was a big military camp.

Brandenburg led his Gothas across the Weald of Kent and disposed of an imminent counterattack by dropping bombs on Lympne aerodrome. The Squadron reached Folkestone shortly after 6 pm. The complete unexpectedness of the raid and the speed with which it was carried out explains the different accounts of what people believed they saw when the bombers were first sighted in the sunlit evening sky.

There were reports of 'swarms of aeroplanes . . . groups of aeroplanes circling slowly overhead . . . two separate lines . . . groups of three or four aeroplanes flying together.' Some onlookers were so confused by it all that they counted 'at least fifty aeroplanes'. Until the first bombs dropped hardly anyone even thought that these might be enemy aircraft. 'Before the bombs fell,' a woman said, 'I though they were our planes out practising.'

The most reliable eye-witness account was given by an RFC pilot, Captain C. Russell, who was on leave from France. 'I heard them before I saw them,' he said. 'I guessed at once they were Huns. We didn't have anything which made that kind of noise. It was a throbbing hum.'

When he saw the aeroplanes through field-glasses his guess was confirmed. 'Three things surprised me. They looked to be much bigger than I would have expected. They were coming over the land instead of the sea. And if they were returning from a raid on London, I couldn't understand why they hadn't been spotted. But there wasn't any air-raid warning in the town.'

Captain Russell reckoned he saw 'about sixteen Huns. One was ahead of the rest and flying above them. Behind him were about six other machines in line abreast, and they were followed by another group of about six, with some others forming a rearguard. Then they closed to make a 'V' shape like a skein of geese.'

When the Gothas were actually over Folkestone they manoeuvred into one slightly curved line, still with the single aeroplane in the van. Suddenly there was a series of shattering explosions, followed by smoke and flames from the harbour area. A few bombs had fallen elsewhere in the town and at Shorncliffe Camp, but the target had been almost precisely located. The harbour was not put out of action but the main onslaught hit Tontine Street, the crowded, narrow thoroughfare which led from it.

The raid on Tontine Street could not have come at a worse moment. Friday, 25 May was the eve of the Whitsun Bank holiday; the street was packed with late shoppers.

A Canadian army sergeant, wounded at Vimy Ridge only a month previously, was one of the survivors. The havoc was worse than anything he had seen on the Western Front. 'The whole street seemed to explode. There was smoke and flames all over, but worst of all were the screams of the wounded and dying, and mothers looking frantically for their kids. A couple of minutes before, those of us who were on the street were like innocent kids ourselves, as we watched those swine in the sky.'

A greengrocer's, with customers inside and others in a queue outside, was demolished; everyone in it was killed and almost everyone in the queue was either killed or seriously injured. A draper's shop was also among the demolished buildings, with many of its customers fatally entombed.

Amid the crashing of the bombs, the explosively-bursting glass of shop windows and the collapsing buildings, people fled in a desperate but hopeless attempt to escape from that narrow street in the Old Town.

The raid lasted about ten minutes. The twenty-one Gothas flew out to sea in an undisturbed formation. Ninety-five people were dead and 195 reported injured.

Although there had been no air raid warning of any kind in Folkestone, everyone was at action stations at Dover as the

Gothas crossed the coast. But at a height of some 14,000 feet they were safe from the guns, whose shells burst ineffectually below them. A Wireless Telegraphist of the Dover Patrol summed it up when he said, 'They might just as well have been using pea shooters.'

It is impossible to verify the number of aircraft which eventually went up to meet the Gothas. Some estimates put the figure as high as seventy, others as low as thirty-three. With such a confusion of aeroplanes making futile, un-cordinated interception attempts, it is likely that a correct figure never was reliably recorded. Since most of the pursuit took place when the Gothas were leaving England, or had even left the coast, seventy seems an improbable total. Including machines from RNAS Dunkirk, it is reasonable to settle for between thirty and forty aircraft.

None of the pilots was successful, but Flight-Lieutenant R. Leslie, from RNAS Dover, was unlucky not to have destroyed the first Gotha. He pursued the Squadron, now in line ahead, across the Strait of Dover. The trip back to base could be the most hazardous part of a mission. There was an inevitable, if sub-conscious, relaxation after a raid which had been virtually unopposed. Flight-Lieutenant Leslie caught up with a straggler in the rear of the formation. The description of 'overwhelming odds' is a cliché in the history of courage and has been a commonplace in many a commanding officer's recommendation for an award. But it is a strictly accurate description of Leslie's gallantry. Alone, he challenged the possible fire power of sixty-three machine guns. At 12,000 feet he closed with the straggling Gotha and one burst hit it. With smoke and steam showing from engines and fuselage, it was clearly in trouble; another burst of machine gun fire would surely be fatal. The Gotha formation, however, survived its first test. Two of the bombers attacked Leslie from behind and forced him to break off the engagement. He was subsequently awarded the Distinguished Service Cross.

The honour of shooting down the first Gotha might also have gone to the RNAS at Dunkirk. As the formation returned, machines of the Dunkirk Squadron were airborne. In a confused aerial battle one bomber was shot down over the sea, but it may have been hit by a French pilot who was stationed at the RNAS base. A second Gotha crashed near Bruges, with the loss of the entire crew.

The Admiralty issued a characteristically inaccurate state-ment, part of which read:

> In the evening several enemy aircraft were engaged over-sea . . . An encounter took place between one British and three hostile aeroplanes in mid-Channel and one of the latter was destroyed. Several encounters also took place off the Belgian coast, in which two large twin-engined machines were shot down. All our machines returned safely.

A later communiqué, issued by the German Naval Staff, stated that 'The English profess that three German aeroplanes were lost. Only one of our machines failed to return.'

In Britain there was astonishment as well as fury at this unexpected turn of events. Public anxiety was not matched with official urgency. Conferences were called, meetings held, resolutions passed and some RFC squadrons were moved to cover 'likely Gotha routes'. Lord French protested again at the continuing decimation of the Home Defence Squadrons, and thus being compelled to supplement with 'such machines and pilots as happen to be available at Training Squadrons.'

Poor French was insultingly criticized in a House of Commons debate, when Noel Pemberton Billing asked 'what he did on the night (sic) of the Folkestone raid, or whether he knew anything about it until all the people were dead.' Pemberton Billing demanded, unsuccessfully, that the Commander-in-Chief be relieved of the responsibility for air defence.

Some critics have put official complacency down to a fawning obeisance to the requirements of Sir Douglas Haig, wilful pigheadedness in the face of reality, and muddled ideas about a new kind of warfare—made even newer now by the Gothas.

To a degree all this was true, except that there was nothing wilful about it. With the Zeppelins having ceased to be a serious threat, there was some force to the argument that Haig's demands should be paramount. It was argued that the war would never be won in the air. The defeat of the Zeppelins had surely shown that it would not be lost there either. Victory lay exclusively in France which, with the exception of the Royal Navy's battle against the U-boats, was the central object.

But the 'scaremongers' were not to be silenced, either inside or outside Parliament. They argued that the Folkestone raid had endorsed their forecast that heavy bombers would be more deadly than the airships. Advice and warnings had been ignorcd. Home defence had been run down. The element of surprise had been absolute. Twenty-one Gothas has been within twenty-five miles of London. Leisurely and unchallenged, they had made their way to Folkestone with terrible consequences.

It seemed that nothing had changed since the Zeppelins had had the freedom of the skies, except that the Gothas were indeed more deadly—and could be seen; but not, apparently, by the Home Defence Squadrons, the RNAS and the gunners until the bombers were on their way home.

There was no serving airman to put the case for a strong air defence or to fight for its priority. There was no senior officer who believed in it. Sir Douglas Haig and the Chief of the Imperial General Staff, General Robertson, were supported by the Director-General of Military Aeronautics, Sir David Henderson, and the RFC commander in France, General Hugh Trenchard.

Less than a year later, as head of the Independent Air Force, Trenchard was to demand 100 squadrons with which to bomb Germany into submission. It was a rapid conversion from his insistence in the spring and summer of 1917 that such a policy would weaken the concentration in France.

Although the critics were divided in their aims and objects, there was some agreement about the need for a combined air force and complete agreement that a supreme commander was required to co-ordinate air defence and bring about a fundamental change of tactics. Feats of gallantry, like that of Flight-Lieutenant Leslie, emphasized the futility of solo attacks against a squadron of Gothas.

Lloyd George's five-member War Cabinet were all civilians and had no choice but to listen to the Service chiefs. There was to be one exception. The former Boer military leader, General J. C. Smuts, was about to join it. In May, 1917, at the Prime Minister's request, he was already considering revolutionary changes not only in the air services but also in the air defence of Britain.

Events were to shorten the time between consideration and decision. The 'scaremongers' had a sympathetic and influential ally.

CHAPTER 17

Offshore and Off Target

The sense of outrage and the blow to the morale of a nation awoken out of its complacency was not improved by the inflexibility of the censorship. The suppression of all details, including, at first, the name of the town, was as useless as most wartime censorship of home news. The Germans, of course, knew the identity of 'a coastal town in the south-east'.

As usual rumour fed on rumour. There was natural alarm and anxiety among citizens who had families or relatives in any south-east coast town, or indeed outside that area because some people were not too sure of their geography. For a while post offices could not handle the rush of telegrams, and rather fewer telephone calls, which were sent to towns which might have been bombed.

Instead of the immediate suppression of the town's name, mention of it would, among other things, have reduced the rumours. Even when most people did know, by word of mouth, that Folkestone had suffered, rumour had magnified the casualties into thousands some days before the official announcement named the town. In Brighton, for example, it was believed that Dover and Folkestone had been put out of action: a troopship bound for France had been sunk in Folkestone Harbour, with no survivors; a troopship bringing soldiers on leave from France had been bombed just outside the harbour; a hospital ship filled with wounded soldiers had been sunk and the German bombers had machine-gunned those who had jumped into the water.

· The invasion scare was renewed and nourished with a different set of rumours: a German landing was imminent; the

Germans had landed at Sandgate; Folkestone and Dover had been captured, and so had Ramsgate, Deal and Hythe; some fierce fighting had thrown the Germans back into the sea.

But in the town itself, where rumour was no substitute for reality, there was uninhibited anger. On the evening of the raid Folkestone Council held an emergency meeting and officials in London were left in no doubt about the feelings of a stricken town which was mourning its dead.

Five days later the Gothas struck again. Since the abortive attempt on London, for which Folkestone had been the compromise alternative, the weather had been unfavourable. To keep them alert and to maintain their confidence it was essential for the Gotha crews to be in action. Furthermore the Army High Command and the German people demanded proof of the Squadron's killing power—against London.

On the late afternoon of 5 June, twenty-two Gothas, in formation, with Brandenburg leading them, set out from their aerodromes for the second raid on England. Because of the prevailing weather London was not the objective and the raid was not part of the master strategy. It was, however, part of the policy that any other objectives must be of military importance. So Sheerness, where the Medway joins the Thames, was to be the target. With some sixty acres of naval dockyards, three basins, five docks, barracks, an arsenal and a large harbour, it was unarguably a strategic objective. A subsidiary tactical target was at nearby Shoeburyness, five miles away on the Essex bank of the Thames, with its important artillery ranges.

Every man of the Gotha crews knew that this raid would relegate Folkestone to the equivalent of a training flight. There would surely be no surprise. The Dunkirk Squadron was certain to be alert after its previous failure to intercept the Squadron on its outward flight. And the Thames and Medway areas were heavily defended by aeroplanes from adjacent aerodromes and clusters of guns.

Brandenburg led his bombers over the North Sea on the same course as that of the previous raid. They made their landfall shortly after 6 pm between the Rivers Crouch and Blackwater at a height of 14 to 15,000 feet. This time the Dunkirk Squadron had seen them, but the bombers were too high and too far away for any effective action; four RNAS machines tried to overtake them. The Thames and Medway area defences, however, were warned of their approach.

L 33 was forced down by anti-aircraft gunfire at Little Wigborough, Essex. Her captain and crew were captured after they had tried to set her ablaze with parachute flares. But L 33 was basically intact and was to become the genesis of the post-war British airships R 33 and R 34.

Aviation history has relegated the Gotha and Giant aeroplanes to comparative obscurity. They were, however, the first successful bomber aircraft. The Gotha crews originated and almost perfected formation flying. A flight of some twenty Gothas with sixty-odd machine guns and a variety of bombs was a collective flying fortress. The photograph above shows a Gotha G.V.

By contrast, the Giants flew on solo missions, and one Giant could be more formidable than a flight of Gothas. Three versions were operational against England: Staaken R. IV, Staaken R. V, and Staaken R. VI. All of them had a huge wing span of 138 feet 5½ inches, and nearly all of those which attacked England were powered by four 260 horse-power Mercedes engines. The largest of all the Giants, R. 39, had five Mercedes engines. Pictured below is a Staaken R. VI.

When they had made their landfall, Brandenburg signalled the Gothas to turn for Sheerness. They seemed to manoeuvre with the slow symmetry of a ceremonial parade. But there was nothing slow about the subsequent attack. It was so swift and unexpected that there is no authentic record of the sequence of events after the Gothas had emerged from light cloud over Shoeburyness. There was a heavy barrage of gunfire. Some sixty aeroplanes were said to have attacked.

People on Sheerness beach and in the town did not realize that German aeroplanes were overhead until, simultaneously, they saw the smoke puffs of bursting shells and 'hundreds of aeroplanes'. There was a long history of artillery firing and testing on the Shoeburyness ranges and the joke that 'I only notice the guns when they stop' was certainly true of that part of England. But this sudden, intense outburst and thundering crack overhead was something new.

When the raid was over 'eye-witness accounts' differed extravagantly. Watchers on the ground had been enthralled by the unique spectacle of an aerial 'dog fight'. They hardly saw anything else until the pressure of questions later on prompted some attempt to recall the total experience. There had been so much to watch that it resembled a three-ring circus.

Some observers were convinced that the formation was broken almost immediately. There were others who were equally certain that the formation was unchanged until the Gothas broke into smaller units just before they attacked Sheerness. Some people could not recall any kind of formation. Some were sure that the British fighter aeroplanes broke up the 'V' shape and forced the Gothas to drop their bombs in a hurry and escape as quickly as possible.

One of Lord Northcliffe's journalists, H. W. Wilson, was emphatic in a description he wrote, more than four months later, in a weekly publication *The Great War*, of which he was joint editor:

> The Germans followed their usual tactics. Of their three lines one steered for the town, and the second made a great sweep to attack the dockyard. They dropped their bombs with the greatest possible speed from an extreme height, and made swiftly off.

Those on-the-spot observers who were certain that the formation had disintegrated when it was attacked over the Estuary were possibly deceived and distracted by the Gotha which was shot down.

Watchers from the Essex shore had the best view when the bomber was hit by a shell from one of the 3-in anti-aircraft guns which were reported to have fired some 500 rounds. The Gotha crashed into the sea.

Because the Gothas were so large, there was a lasting illusion that they always flew at low altitudes. There is reliable evidence to accept that the doomed bomber dropped away from the formation and was vulnerable between 8,000 and 9,000 feet. It had not then been hit. Some reports said that it had dropped to that level to bomb Sheerness. It is an unlikely theory. Since at least one part of the formation, if not all of it, was going to attack Sheerness anyway, there was no reason for just one Gotha to make a solo effort. We have seen that the discipline of formation flying was rigid. That unwelcome enemy on board, mechanical trouble, was almost certainly the cause, although it was not then generally accepted in Britain.

The raid lasted for about five minutes, although it seemed longer than that to those who watched it. From a confused action two things were certain: twenty-seven bombs were dropped inaccurately and harmlessly on Shoeburyness, although two soldiers were killed there, and the line of Gothas which attacked Sheerness dockyard released their missiles with pinpoint accuracy. But the raid was a failure.

The sound of heavy explosions in the dockyard area exaggerated people's impressions of the damage; many of the bombs were, to use the contemporary word, 'duds'. Although the British post-raid announcement underestimated in its statement that 'the damage was practically negligible', work in the dockyard continued. Sixty-four bombs were known to have fallen. Thirteen people were killed in the raid, including the two soldiers who lost their lives at Shoeburyness, and thirty-four injured.

An unusually restrained German communiqé was general rather than particular. It said that more than five tons of bombs had been dropped and that 'good hits' were made.

The returning Gothas were attacked by ten aeroplanes from the Dunkirk Squadron and their formation was disrupted. With German fighter aircraft providing reinforcement cover, another confused aerial battle took place. At least three bombers were seriously damaged, which led to an inaccurate British claim that two had been destroyed and four forced down, 'of which two are considered to have been destroyed'.

Differing statements from the War Office and the Admiralty, together with some imaginative newspaper reports, left the public with the impression that the battle over the Estuary had been something of a famous victory and that the returning Gothas had been badly mauled by the Dunkirk Squadron.

There was a comforting belief that ten or twelve bombers had been destroyed; but only that one Gotha had been successfully hit. When the rescue boats arrived off Barton's Point it had sunk. One of its crew was already dead. Two others were brought ashore, one of whom died almost immediately. From the third man, interrogating officers learned of the existence of a squadron whose exclusive object was the demolition of London.

Meanwhile, in Belgium, the England Squadron waited for another fine day.

CHAPTER 18

Death in the Daylight

Britain had no opportunity to act on the startling discovery of the England Squadron before the next fine day gave it a clear run to London. On the morning of 13 June twenty-two Gothas took off from St Denis-Westrem and Gontrode but mechanical troubles reduced the final strength to seventeen. Two bombers made forced landings before the Belgian coast was crossed; another turned back near the Isle of Thanet and released five bombs as it flew over Margate. Two more Gothas dropped out near Foulness Island and bombed Shoeburyness and Gravesend. None of these incidental attacks was successful but they helped to warn the London defences.

Brandenburg's assault force, now reduced to seventeen Gothas, flew steadily over Essex and approached the capital from the north-west. The outer London guns were soon in action, but with the raiders at 14–15,000 feet the effect was noisy and spectacular rather than effective. From the ground the anti-aircraft shells bursting overhead looked like artificial puffs of smoke against a mostly blue sky. It was almost as pretty as a picture postcard and seemed to be as harmless.

The sound of the Mercedes engines, which had seemed like a 'double thrum' to Captain Russell at Folkestone, was clearly heard. Not everyone, however, saw the Gothas on their approach flight, although very few people were to admit it. Not to have been in London on Wednesday, 13 June was unthinkable. Those who were innocent enough to confess ignorance were bored with a variety of vivid stories.

Despite the Folkestone and Sheerness raids and the strange sound in the sky, only a few people believed that the aeroplanes might be German. And most of those who thought they were felt safe from the remote, apparently slow-moving machines. Some observers saw them as 'small dots in the sky'; one newspaper reporter saw them as 'little silver birds'. Another journalist described them as 'dead black against a filmy grey sky'. Like so many people who saw Gothas for the first time, he was misled. 'They were flying so low,' he wrote, 'that people with glasses could make out the pilots and the black crosses on the wings . . . I think at this time they were from three to four thousand feet high.'

He saw them from his garden in a north-western suburb when, in fact, they were at 14,000 feet or more, with light cloud hiding them from continuous view.

Again, there was uncertainty about the kind of formation; but this was understandable because it changed several times when the Squadron reached the suburbs and then London itself. We do know that it made a wide sweep from Brentwood which brought it on course for the capital. Thousands of spectators saw it, but although the shape may have changed from wedge, 'V' or arrowhead to diamond, line astern, or, as some people reported, 'in three separate lines' the principle of all-round defence was never weakened.

Except when bombs fell nearby, most spectators ignored the 'take cover' warnings, although there were crude arrangements for children in schools to seek safety under desks, against inside walls, or some other improvised protection.

For most adults this was an occasion not to be missed. It was London's first daylight raid. Even some Victorian-style employers relaxed their strict rules and allowed staffs to watch out of office windows; more daring workers took advantage of the excitement, risked the sack and sneaked on to the streets. With so many Gothas in the clear, sunlit sky there was more to see than when the Zeppelins attacked by night. Some watchers reckoned they counted as many as thirty bombers.

The first bombs fell soon after 11.30 am on the Royal Albert Docks and East Ham. Eight people were killed and there was serious damage. From there the Gothas were so safe and Brandenburg was so confident that he broke the rigidity of the formation. They fanned out to attack in a radius of about one mile from Liverpool Street railway station. More than seventy bombs were dropped, but the most horrifying results came from just two missiles on the terminus itself.

Three or four bombs struck the station. One failed to explode. One exploded on a platform. A third hit the midday express train which was waiting to leave for Cambridge. The two front coaches were set on fire and the dining car was wrecked. The crashing sound of the explosions was immediately replaced by the cries, screams and moans of the injured and the dying.

A first-hand account of the raid appears in Siegfried Sassoon's *Memoirs of an Infantry Officer*. On convalescent leave from France, Sassoon was at the station ready to join the Cambridge train:

> While I stood wondering what to do a luggage trolley was trundled past me; on it lay an elderly man, shabbily dressed . . . This sort of danger seemed to me to demand a quality of courage dissimilar to front line fortitude . . . In a trench one was acclimatized to the notion of being exterminated and there was a sense of organized retaliation. But here one was helpless; an invisible enemy sent destruction spinning down from a fine weather sky.

For such a ferocious and concentrated attack, the fatal casualties were astonishingly small. Only thirteen people were killed; the number of injured was never confirmed. There were heavier casualties elsewhere; the deaths and injuries were, emotionally and in total, even worse than those in Liverpool Street station. At nearby Fenchurch Street a 110-lb bomb demolished the top floors of a ten-storey building, killing sixteen people; about the same number were believed to have been injured. At the Royal Mint, by the Tower of London, the casualties amounted to thirty-four dead and injured.

Every death brought personal tragedy and grief, but there was a collective horror about the attack on the Upper North Street Schools in Poplar. A 110-lb bomb crashed through the roof and three floors before it exploded on the ground floor and in the basement, bringing the first floor down with it. Sixty-five infants, out of a total attendance of some 600 pupils, were on that ground floor. Fifteen were killed almost instantly and thirty others were seriously injured. The astonishing escape of some 550 children was over-shadowed by the peculiar horror of the forty-five infants who were dead, maimed and injured.

In 1917 most elementary schools were neighbourhood

schools. Homes were seldom very far away. There were no 'bus passes' or (with rare exceptions) no school dinners. When the bomb hit Upper North Street distraught mothers rushed to the nearby school. Those whose children could not immediately be found fought and clawed their way past policemen, spectators, fire and ambulance men.

The Gothas departed as safely as they had arrived. Despite many unsuccessful attempts by RFC and RNAS pilots, they landed at their aerodromes precisely at their estimated time of arrival.

Back in England 162 people were dead and 432 injured. The outburst of public anger was made worse by the 'outrage perpetrated on innocent children' at the Upper North Street Schools. It was not merely another protest but a dangerously short fuse of fury. No one cared about the financial cost, later estimated at nearly £130,000

In Germany the conviction that the war would be won over the skies of England regained a peak of hysteria. *Kapitänleutnant* Ernst Brandenburg became a new national idol who could rank with Strasser, Mathy and even the great fighter pilot 'ace' Baron Manfred von Richtofen. He was given the very special and distinguished award, *Pour le Mérite*, by the Emperor himself. But then his luck ran out. The Albatros in which he was a passenger crashed as it took off from an aerodome near Supreme Headquarters. The pilot was killed. Brandenburg was gravely injured and was not to return to active service until the aerial battle was already decided.

His coveted post as leader of the Squadron went to *Kapitänleutnant* Rudolf Kleine. He already had an impressive record as commander of a reconnaissance squadron and had taken part in tactical raids as a flight leader with the original Kaghol I. But even this qualification, and his founder-membership of Kaghol, would not by themselves make him acceptable to the England Squadron. He had to follow a man who was almost revered. Although there had been only two raids on enemy territory, a bond of comradeship had been forged in the heat of battle. They had trained together to form a very private, exclusive little world. Kleine would have to prove himself and forge a new bond. He did not have to wait long to serve the first part of his apprenticeship.

The German army's raid communiqués were not merely restrained, they showed a curious reluctance to give details of casualties, or even to mention them at all. It was as if the Army High Command wished to preserve a hypocritical dignity and leave the propaganda and the newspapers to relish the facts.

In Britain the Admiralty and the War Office still had an endemic dislike of the press, although they, together with the Press Bureau, were always ready to make use of it with selective stories. Editors, severely rationed by the censorship, were eager to dress up the material handed out to them.

In Germany the wartime press accepted forced-feeding more easily. The undertone of official statements became melodramatic overtones in the newspapers. A typical example is this extract from the *Frankfurter Zeitung*, published after the daylight raid on London and allegedly written by someone who took part in it:

> Our first greetings dropped in rapid succession; we gave them more and still more. Then we proceeded coolly and calmly over the suburbs, as we wanted to hit the centre . . . I pressed the bomb release and followed instantly the greetings of the German people to the English. We gave them plenty—blow after blow from bursting bombs in the very heart of England. The sight over Central London was wonderfully impressive. High up, between us, were bursting shells. The Squadron turned. We took a last glance at the City—'good-bye 'till next time'. We had attained the object which not long ago was the unfulfilled dream of German airmen.

In Germany the England Squadron was already replacing the Zeppelin on the pedestal of honour.

In Britain press, politicians and public castigated a helpless and hapless Government. Pemberton Billing, Lord Montagu, Charles Grey and the other scaremongers now had a wider, more serious audience both inside and outside Parliament. They spoke from a position of undisputed strength. Five hundred and fifty-eight casualties from a mid-morning raid were macabre justification of their long-heralded warnings. Even more important than this wider acceptance was that of General Smuts.

Jan Christian Smuts has an enduring place in the history of aerial warfare. The former Boer commando leader against Britain in the South African War of 1899–1902, he became a minister (and for a while acting Prime Minister) in Louis

Botha's Government until the British made him a Lieutenant-General in February, 1916. He took over a force which had failed to conquer German East Africa.

Smuts failed too. He was out-manoeuvered by the wily General von Lettow-Vorbeck and left 'German East' to return briefly to South Africa in January, 1917. A month later he became that country's representative at the Imperial War Conference in London. He was also a member of the Imperial War Cabinet and, when its short life was over, Lloyd George invited him to join his War Cabinet.

Although he was the only Service member, his credentials scarcely lived up to the extraordinary reputation which a well-prepared public relations exercise created for him. His arrival in London was notorious for a statement which had become a classic in the history of military failures. In a reference to 'German East' he said that 'the campaign may be said to be over'. In fact the redoubtable and brilliant von Lettow-Vorbeck held out until the war was over.

Smuts's failure was presented as a splendid military success by just the man of action the country needed. He had been a courageous, daring and skilful Boer commando leader. He had acted with ruthless speed in the suppression of a general strike in 1913. The following year he put down a rebellion in the Western Transvaal with methods which did not endear him to everyone. In 1915 he played a minor part in Louis Botha's decisive defeat of the Germans in South-West Africa.

As soon as he arrived in England, he seemed to be the most famous and experienced of all the Allied generals. He was courted by almost everyone. King George V listened to him with respect. His advice was eagerly sought and given. Virtually every opinion he gave was accepted as if it were divine wisdom. The public did not have to seek another national hero. It was presented with a ready-made one. He mesmerized people who were not given to extravagant praise. That old realist, the inconoclastic 'Jackie' Fisher, wanted him to replace Haig as Commander-in-Chief of the British Expeditionary Force.

But if his military reputation was slightly fraudulent, he certainly had qualities which made him an invaluable Cabinet Minister. He was intellectually superior to most contemporary politicians. As a young man he obtained a first-class honours degree in law at Cambridge University and was outstandingly successful in the Bar Finals. He was a skilled administrator, a deviously-clever negotiator and a positive decision-maker.

He was resented by the Allied generals, and especially by those in the British Army, who objected to the claim that he was the first successful general of the war. He was hated and rejected by many South Africans for his 'disloyal' association with Britain. But to a war-weary British public he was almost as great a figure as Marlborough, Nelson, Wellington and the still-mourned Kitchener.

The few politicians who did protest at his inclusion in the War Cabinet were silenced by his popularity and by Lloyd George's determination. The Prime Minister wanted him as an ally against what he believed was a cartel of conspiracy by the generals, and as someone whose untrammelled background could overcome prejudice and tradition.

This, then, was the kind of man who was to have a profound effect on the history of aerial warfare. Ultimately he became one of the founders of the League of Nations, a delegate at the Versailles Peace Conference and Prime Minister of South Africa. None of these achievements excelled his contribution to the history of British aerial warfare. Its starting-point came on 7 July, 1917.

Aerial bombardment was a new experience for him. When he arrived in London the Zeppelin was no longer a serious threat. If further evidence was still needed, Strasser provided it. Four days after the Gotha raid on London, he ordered L 42, L 44, L 45, L 46, L 47 and the newest of the 'height climbers' L 48 to attack the capital. Viktor Schütze was in command, but he arrived over England with only two airships—his own L 48 and L 42 (Martin Dietrich). L 46 and L 47 were unable to leave their sheds. L 45 and L 44 returned with engine trouble before they crossed the coast.

Dietrich dropped three bombs on Ramsgate, which he mistook for Dover and Deal. Three people were killed and sixteen injured. Although pursued by an aeroplane, a seaplane and a flying boat, L 42 left England unharmed.

But as they left the crew saw the now ominously familiar 'red ball of fire'. It was the blazing L 48. Delayed earlier by a frozen compass and engine trouble, and hampered by accurate anti-aircraft fire, Schütze had dropped bombs on a field near Harwich. A request for bearings, and the reply he received, were probably intercepted. L 48's setbacks had left her fatally exposed at daybreak over enemy territory. She was attacked by

Lieutenant L. P. Watkins of 37 Squadron RFC and crashed in flames at Holly Tree Farm, near Theberton in Norfolk.

Three of the crew escaped, although one died two days later. The three men had been in the bow, which was almost undamaged. Schütze died with the others.

L 48 was the last Zeppelin to be destroyed on British soil; but despite growing opposition in the Navy, Strasser pressed on with a policy which, increasingly, became almost a sentence of death to his crews. The Zeppelins were now in danger everywhere. Two days earlier, and a day after the Gotha raid on London, a Large America Flying Boat had caught L 43 off Vlieland, in the West Frisian Islands, and shot her down in flames with the loss of all her crew.

Meanwhile in London Smuts observed the collective indecision of a Government faced with a sustained press campaign and a public whose anger was implacable after the Gotha raid. The official claim that targets in Germany were being bombed satisfied no one. The attacks were against tactical, military objectives and were not killing civilians. In the Government, and among some Members of Parliament, there were genuine doubts about the morality of 'revenge bombing'. There were equally genuine doubts about its value, other than as a sop to popular clamour. But no close Government supporter, let alone a Minister, dared express them. And not the least of the factors to be considered was the effect on American opinion.

Public confidence was not improved by some feeble answers from Lord Derby, who was now Secretary for War, in a House of Lords debate on the London daylight raid. He said that it had no military significance and made the incredibly insensitive remark that 'not a single soldier had been killed'. This obtuse addition rebounded spitefully and unfairly on a man who was sensitive but unimaginative. He was deeply hurt by the accusation that dead civilians were less important than live soldiers.

The Home Secretary, Sir George Cave, was belaboured for the lack of a real air-raid-warning system. More than sixty years later it is easy to accept the criticism. In the Spring and early Summer of 1917, however, the Government was still convinced that aerial bombardment was no longer a serious threat. Stubbornly, and in the face of considerable advice to the contrary, it would not accept that the Gotha raids were the beginning of a new onslaught and, so far as Britain was concerned, the continuation of an interrupted campaign.

Even if the existence of the England Squadron—revealed only a week earlier—had been accepted as evidence of a new phase, there had been no time to reorganize a casual, uncordinated warning system. Furthermore there were misgivings about its usefulness. The Home Office shared the view of many employers that staff would stop work for air raid alerts which might prove to be unnecessary.

There were differing opinions, too, about the effect on the rest of the civilian population: an early warning system might cause uncontrollable panic. Conversely people would crowd the streets to watch the aerial battles and be in danger from bombs and anti-aircraft shrapnel.

The air defence plan which had been evolved to defeat the Zeppelins was useless against high-flying, well-armed Gothas in their disciplined but flexible formation. But even if there had been co-ordinated early warning systems from Dunkirk to London, the RNAS and the RFC did not have the fighter aircraft to outmatch the Gothas.

Lord French continued to be aggrieved that his home Defence Squadrons were denied aircraft which could meet the Gothas on equal terms. But they were with the RFC in France and the single-minded Sir Douglas Haig was adamant that they should remain there. His decision and opposition were based on sound military principles and on the inflexible conviction that, although London might be severely damaged and its citizens suffer grievous casualties, the war could be won only in France. There was also a personal element which made him more than unsympathetic to any proposal that came from Lloyd George.

Some two months after he had become Prime Minister in December, 1916, Lloyd George had agreed to Haig and the British Army in France being put under command of General Nivelle, who had succeeded General Joffre in December, 1916. In the following February Nivelle became the supreme commander. Haig had not forgiven Lloyd George. As it happened, Nivelle himself was relieved of his post three months later after a disastrous failure at the Battle of the Aisne, and Haig was, temporarily, his own master again.

Now, in the summer of 1917, he was determined not to weaken any part of his army for another of the 'sideshows' which he despised. And he was desperately short of fighter aeroplanes, pilots and observers. But the uproar at home could not be denied. Even his staunch ally, the Chief of the Imperial General Staff, General Robertson, was obliged to endorse the War Cabinet's demand for the withdrawal of two fighter squadrons. Robertson's frank opinion that the defence of London should receive only the minimum attention is emphasized in his casual, almost offhand 'order' to Haig:

> You should send over for a week or two one or two squadrons . . . and the machines would then be returned to you.

Haig took Robertson at his word. No. 56 Squadron was sent to Bekesbourne, near Canterbury, and No. 66 Squadron went to Calais. He insisted that they must be returned to him by 5 July.

No. 56 Squadron was the first to be equipped with the Farnborough-produced S.E. 5. In June, 1917, it had been operational for just two months, but, as J. M. Bruce writes of it in his authoritative work *Warplanes of the First World War*, Volume Two: 'In combat it soon proved itself to be a considerable weapon.'

It had a 150 h.p. Hispano-Suiza engine, a maximum speed of 122 miles per hour at 3,000 feet, 110 miles per hour at 6,500 feet, and 114 miles per hour at 10,000 feet. It could climb to 10,000 feet in 14 minutes 15 seconds, had a ceiling of 19,000 feet and an endurance of 2½ hours. It was armed with a .303 Lewis gun (but a .303 Vickers was used on some machines).

No. 66 Squadron flew the famous Sopwith Pup, which J. M. Bruce described as 'a masterpiece . . . few could equal its performance on the 80 h.p. Rhône engine.' This 9-cylinder rotary engine gave a maximum speed of 102 miles per hour at 10,000 feet. The aircraft had a ceiling of 17,000 feet and could climb to 10,000 feet in 14 minutes. It had an endurance of 3 hours.

The bargain with Sir Douglas Haig was kept. The squadrons were returned to him on 5 July, one day after Rudolf Kleine led the England Squadron on its fourth raid, to Harwich and Felixstowe. Seventeen people were killed and thirty injured. The RFC reinforcements from France never fired a round—one of them did not even take off—and went back to the British Expeditionary Force after what was in effect fourteen days' rest. And two days later, on 7 July, Kaghol 3 made an attack on London that was to have significant consequences.

CHAPTER 19

A Thread of History

Rudolf Kleine had waited three weeks before he led the fourth Gotha attack on England. Even then the unfavourable weather which had prevented an immediate reinforcement of the 13 June raid kept the Squadron away from London.

The three-weeks delay was bad enough for the tense glory-seeking crews and for Kleine who was so anxious to justify his worth to them. But there was a more compelling reason for quick action and a decisive success: the RNAS were bombing German aerodromes, although both St Denis-Westrem and Gontrode had escaped their attention.

The first break in the weather came on 4 July. Harwich and the RNAS air station at Felixstowe were chosen as alternative targets to London. The raid had all the familiar features of previous attacks, except that tactical surprise was to be achieved by an early take-off. The sortie had an unpromising beginning. Kleine led twenty-five Gothas from the aerodromes. Seven turned back with engine trouble. The others only just achieved that tactical surprise.

A D.H. 4 fighter-bomber, piloted by Captain J. Palethorpe RFC, on a test flight over the North Sea, saw the eighteen Gothas. Although not then in fully operational condition, the D.H. 4 was already proving to be one of the most powerful machines in service. It had a 200 h.p. RAF 3a engine, could climb to 17,000 feet, and, with extra fuel tanks, had an endurance of fourteen hours. It generally carried four machine guns, two forward and two aft.

On that morning, however, it was no match for the Gothas, whose protective formation prevented Palethorpe from pressing home an attack. Combined machine-gun fire from the bombers hit the D.H. 4 and killed Air Mechanic J. O. Jessop, who was in the rear cockpit. Palethorpe broke off the action, returned to the Experimental Station at Martlesham Heath in Suffolk, reported the presence of the raiders, and took off again with a replacement for the dead Jessop.

But he and the other aircraft which went up were too late. The Gothas crossed the Suffolk coast at 7 am. Ten minutes later they bombed Harwich and Felixstowe. Seventeen people were killed and thirty injured; the damage was extensive but not serious. It included the loss of a flying boat at Harwich and damage to another at Felixstowe.

Throughout the raid the Gothas were well beyond the range of the anti-aircraft fire. More than eighty British aircraft, including those from 56 Squadron, made unsuccessful interception attempts.

The RNAS Dunkirk Squadron gave the returning Gothas 'a warm reception'. An official naval report said they 'were assisted' by the RNAS and claimed that two enemy bombers were brought down in flames and a third was 'seen to be damaged'.

Although the report turned out to be inaccurate, it was based on acceptable information. As usual, in the brief, close encounter of aerial battle, it was a natural mistake by pilots to believe that hits were 'kills'. Without doubt the Dunkirk Squadron penetrated the Gothas' formation and Flight-Commander A. M. Shook was awarded the Distinguished Service Cross for a 'kill'. He saw a bomber which he had hit fall in flames. At least two of the Gothas were seriously damaged and disproved the German claim that 'all our aeroplanes returned undamaged'. Nevertheless, the records confirm that no Gothas were lost.

Three days later the England Squadron attacked London in what became the most significant raid of the First World War. There was a widely-believed rumour that the raid was the direct result of German spies having reported the return of 56 Squadron to France some twenty-four hours earlier. Although the movement was certain to have been known, as was that of 66 Squadron from Calais, the information was unlikely to have affected the decision to raid London. Weather conditions were the decisive factor.

Unlike the Harwich and Felixstowe raid, there was no attempt at early morning surprise. It was believed that the maximum impact could be made when London was busy and crowded. The seventh of July was a Saturday, and in 1917 the working week for most people consisted of five and a half days.

The timing was perfect. Twenty-two Gothas made their landfall shortly after 9 am. They were officially reported as having been seen at 9.30 am over the Isle of Thanet and the east coast of Essex. They divided into two separate formations for the approach flight—one followed the north bank of the Thames, while the other flew over the south bank.

Kleine had left Belgium with twenty-four machines. Two dropped out before the Squadron crossed the coast. A third fell out of line, apparently with engine trouble, and bombed Margate, where three people were killed and three others injured. The rest re-grouped into the standard 'V' formation, with Kleine out ahead of and above it.

The bright, early morning sun was partly hidden by grey, drifting clouds when the raiders reached the north-western boundary of London. There, still in immaculate formation, they turned on a south-easternly course.

Even official estimates of the number of Gothas seen before and during the raid differed, but at the end of the day there was an acceptance of 'about twenty'. Unofficial guesses varied wildly from twenty-five to as many as sixty. People were misled by the fleeting cloud cover, which was responsible for some duplicated sightings. When the British pilots were in the sky as well, it was often impossible to distinguish friend from foe, although many self-styled experts were sure they could tell the difference, despite the action being 12–14,000 feet above the ground and over a wide expanse of sky.

Some people believed they saw the Gothas before they heard the gunfire, while others, in the same district, were sure they heard the sound of the bombers before they heard—or noticed—the firing. People in other places claimed to have seen everything at once: the Gothas, the bursting anti-aircraft shells and an aerial battle. There were reports of a spectacular duel over Essex, which 'turned a lot of them away from London'. One 'eye-witness' account saw the bombers over Central London when they had not even reached the north-western suburbs. The 'Essex duel' was one of the many attempted attacks on the Gothas as they were on their way back from the raid.

In the E.C.1 and E.C.4 postal districts there was no opportunity to observe details. The relatively distant gun fire had not caused any alarm. Then, suddenly, bombs were falling. Later, those who were there maintained that there was no nearby firing at all. People in the streets scrambled for safety—to churches, including St Paul's Cathedral where morning service was being held, to underground stations, beneath the railway arches in Pilgrim Street off New Bridge Street, to solid buildings such as Stationers' Hall behind Ludgate Hill.

The guns had been in action since the Gothas were first sighted and reported shortly after 9 am. The fire had followed them all the way to London, but many people did not notice its increasing volume until they heard the bangs of seemingly local guns. Some residents in the Hampstead Heath area were sure they heard the firing close at hand and 'caught sight of the aeroplanes as they fley away towards Central London at about ten 'o clock'. The newspaper proprietor Sir George (later Lord) Riddell, who watched the bombers as they passed over Hampstead, recalled that by 10.40 am 'the guns near us stopped firing'.

The author's father saw the Gothas from an office window. When he returned home he was positive that they had flown over Hyde Park Corner and Piccadilly 'just after eleven'. The crowds in those streets which were not bombed, like the onlookers from office windows, were, apparently, more curious than alarmed even when they realized that the aeroplanes were Gothas. It seems that none of the gunfire was near enough to suggest that there was any danger.

One account, written some months later, said that the raiders left the capital at 10.40 am. The Germans believed they had first attacked it at about 10.00 am.

The earlier of two official announcements, from Home Forces Headquarters, was timed 11.45 am.

> At about 9.30 am this morning hostile aircraft in considerable numbers, and probably in two parties, appeared over the Isle of Thanet and the coast of Essex.
>
> After dropping some bombs in Thanet, the raiders proceeded in the direction of London, moving, roughly, parallel to the north bank of the Thames. They approached London from the north-east, then, changing their course, proceeded north and west and crossed London from north-west to south-east.
>
> Bombs were dropped in various places in the metropolitan area.

The number of raiding aeroplanes is at present uncertain, but was probably about twenty.

They were attacked by artillery and by large numbers of
our own aeroplanes, but reports as to the results of the
engagements, as to damage and casualties have not yet
been received.

A second announcement, issued at 6.40 pm stated that
thirty-four people had been killed in the metropolitan area and
three in the Isle of Thanet. The number of injured was given as
139 in the metropolitan area and two in the Isle of Thanet.

The Admiralty supplemented this with its own account:

The enemy raiding squadron was chased by Royal Naval
Air Service machines from this country and engaged 40
miles out to sea off the East Coast.

Two enemy machines were observed to crash into the
sea. A third enemy machine was seen to fall in flames off
the mouth of the Scheldt.

All our machines returned safely.

Vice-Admiral at Dover reports from Dunkirk . . . that
five flights were sent up to intercept them as they returned.

The raiding enemy aircraft were not seen, but three
enemy seaplanes were encountered and destroyed, and
one enemy aeroplane was driven down into sea and
another enemy aeroplane was driven down.

The machines returned to replenish petrol and left again
immediately.

In the course of the patrol one enemy aeroplane was
brought down in flames and another forced to land on the
beach, damaged, near Ostend.

When more accurate information was put together, it told a
different story, some of it good, and some of it bad.

Meanwhile the newspapers weaved stirring tales. A Saturday morning raid gave the Sunday editions a generous time
margin in which to prepare their stories. The sparse official
details were enlarged by a proliferation of 'first-hand' accounts
from the public, and some of them appeared as journalists' own
'Today I Saw . . .' reports. The communiqués were not consistent with what many people had seen.

Like that other raid over the Thames Estuary, the event was

presented as a famous victory. Yet the RFC and the RNAS certainly deserved the lavish praise they received, even if, inevitably, much of the reporting was imaginative guesswork. Londoners were praised, too, for their 'steadfastness' and cool courage 'under fire'. People were 'amazingly unconcerned . . . they just stood and stared.' Only a 'comparatively few people appeared to run for shelter.'

But there were also rumours of panic and of 'stampeding crowds'. Just how Londoners behaved depended on where they were and a fine (if sometimes misplaced) judgment on where the bombs would fall. Spectators in the West End had 'stood and stared', but a mile or so away, at Ludgate Circus for example, everyone sensibly took what cover they could. The rush to safety could not really be described as a stampede.

Thousands of people did not wait for the Sunday newspapers. They knew where the bombs had fallen and were out early to see the sights and, in some districts, to watch, or take part in, the now familiar attacks on the shops of 'foreigners' and, if they were about, the unlucky owners as well.

Among the sightseers in the East End was no less a person than the Prime Minister, whose presence gave rise to angry calls for revenge bombing. Fifty-seven people had been killed and 193 injured. Material damage was put at £205,000. But these figures, and those of reported German losses, bore no relation to the sense of outrage and the feeling of helpless exposure to danger.

The Gothas had been resolutely attacked by the RFC and the RNAS. Three RFC airmen had been killed. Lieutenant J. E. R. Young went up when the alarm was first given. With his rear gunner, Air Mechanic C. C. Taylor, he made a suicidal attack on the formation, but its combined fire power was too much. Once again supreme gallantry against a well-organized and well-armed foe had wasted two lives. And a third was wasted when Lieutenant W. G. Salmon was killed in an equally gallant attempt.

All but one of the British attacks on the Gothas were beaten off, but success came over the Thames Estuary as the bombers were on their way back. One could not keep up with the rest and two RFC aircraft singled it out. Lieutenant M. A. E. Cremetti hit the straggler, but the credit for its destruction went to Lieutenant F. A. D. Grace and his observer, Lieutenant G. Murray. They, apparently, fired the bullets which actually brought the Gotha down into the Estuary. The three crew members clambered on to a wing and fired a signal flare, but they drowned before help could reach them.

The surviving Gothas arrived back without further combat losses, but four crashed on landing. There was one fatal casualty.

But the loss of five Gothas, and the incidental loss of some supporting aircraft, was no consolation to the public, press and politicians in Britain. The only real success had been the one Gotha destroyed in the Thames Estuary, a poor return for the more than ninety aeroplanes which had counterattacked. And in Germany the Army High Command, realistic as always, considered the re-shaping of its strategy.

The anger in Britain was echoed in a hostile House of Commons secret session debate. Lloyd George told the unwelcome (and, to some MP's, unacceptable) truth that total defence from enemy attack was impossible. But his handling of the debate was masterly. He larded the stark truth with smooth reassurance. He said that Britain 'should soon possess an air fleet in excess of the demands of the Army and the Navy,' and that 'before long we should have an adequate supply for both our own military operations and for home defence and independent attack.' He insisted, however, that the war in France must have first claim on men and machines. With the recalcitrant Sir Douglas Haig and General Trenchard very much in mind, he spoke of the Army's needs with picturesque, emotional exaggeration:

> A sufficiency of aeroplanes means everything to that Army. They are the eyes of the Army, which cannot advance without them. By their means the Army discovers the enemy's trenches, guns, and machine-gun emplacements. To photograph these requires air supremacy, and without that air supremacy it is sheer murder to allow troops to advance . . . The slightest deficiency in the work of observation from the air, a single machine-gun emplacement overlooked, might in a few minutes mean the loss of thousands of gallant lives . . . The second means by which they [the Germans] are attempting to diminish our superiority is by trying to force us to withdraw our machines from France to protect our own towns.

But when Sir Douglas Haig heard of this startling military appreciation and apparent support, he had already, and for the second time, been ordered to return two RFC Squadrons. He did what every soldier should do—he obeyed the order 'under protest' in an acid telegram to the War Office.

Modern historians take sharply different views on the animosity between Lloyd George and the generals, and Haig in particular, but it is impossible not to sympathize with the Commander-in-Chief in this particular situation. He was then preparing the Third Battle of Ypres, the long-promised breakthrough which was to end at Passchendaele, a place which, from almost total obscurity, was soon to become one of the most sombre names in history. But, in July, 1917, hopes were high that the greatest 'push' of the war to date would open the road to final victory.

In his protest, Haig, no mean hand at exaggeration himself when it suited him, warned that the transfer of the two squadrons would 'render our victory more difficult'. And he half won his personal battle with the Government, which was, once again, deflected from its policy by the formidable Commander-in-Chief. It was Lord French who saved it from capitulation, for the Government had to handle his protests as well as those of Haig.

Although Lloyd George had grossly exaggerated the influence of the RFC in France, he had been right about its contribution as a back-up to the British Expeditionary Force. It was regularly engaged in close-support of the ground troops, in reconnaissance of enemy positions, in bombing enemy positions and rear areas; and its photographic interpretation had reached a high standard.

But Lord French had, perhaps, the strongest ally of all, public opinion, aided and abetted by Parliamentary support. A dithering War Cabinet heeded his protest and settled for an immediate compromise—one squadron would be brought back.

Sir Douglas Haig, however, was not deceived by the compromise. He heard, indirectly, that he was to be deprived of twenty-eight new fighter aircraft. This time his protest was ignored, although the Cabinet knew of his forthcoming campaign, but Lloyd George maintained, later, that the War Cabinet was misled by its extent.

The historic consequence of the second daylight raid on

London was its direct lead to the creation of a combined air service. Nine months later, on 1 April, 1918, the Royal Air Force was born.

The story of the fusion of the RFC and the RNAS, and the internecine fight to avoid it, are too famous to need more than the briefest mention. The progress to an independent air force has no part in the story of the bombardment of England, but without that second daylight raid on London the founding of the Royal Air Force would have been long delayed.

But it was only one of the results of the raid. Three days later Lloyd George obtained the agreement of the War Cabinet to form a two-man committee of himself and General Smuts 'to examine the defences against air raids' and, in a deliberately vague phrase, 'the existing general organization and study of aerial operations'.

Smuts was not, as some of his admirers maintain, the 'father' of the Royal Air Force. The idea of a single unit was not new. But he was the only man who could cut away the atrophy of prejudice and self-interest.

Home Defence, however, was the immediate task. The gallantry and success of the RFC on the Western Front, and in other theatres of war, had created a new breed of war heroes, the fighter pilot 'aces', whose mounting totals of individual 'kills' were announced as if they were cricket scores, but the public had no faith in the Home Defence Squadrons of the RFC or in the RNAS.

Smuts had to face a chorus of demands for 'reprisals'. After the first daylight raid on London Joynson-Hicks had gained some easy popularity with a demand that, 'Every time the Germans raid London, the British airmen must blot out a German town.'

Smuts was later to become one of the instigators of a retaliatory bombing policy, but in 1917 he knew that success against the Gothas would reduce the temperature and allow him time to make the best use of his resources.

As with his plans for a combined air force, he earned the credit for welding Britain's first and—as subsequent history proved—only co-ordinated air defence system which was, in effect, under one supreme commander. But, as always, the winner took all, leaving scarcely a consolation prize for its first advocates. They included Sir David Henderson, who had anticipated Smuts's most important decision, to appoint an overall commander for London's defences; and Colonel Simon, who had first suggested siting anti-aircraft guns twenty-five miles round the capital.

The command of all the London defence forces in the new organization, the London Air Defence (LADA), was given to a belligerent individualist, Brigadier-General (soon promoted to Major-General) E. B. Ashmore. There could not have been a better choice. A harsh disciplinarian, a brilliant organizer, and confident to the point of vanity, he had been commissioned into the Royal Horse Artillery, had learned to fly at his own expense before the war and had long realized that anti-aircraft defence must be collective. His transfer from France, where he was a Divisional artillery Commander, was not the sending home of a tired or incompetent soldier to be rewarded with promotion and a soft appointment. The qualities which made some senior officers happy to see the back of this argumentative officer were exactly those which were needed for LADA.

Many people who knew Ashmore thought he was the perfect example of Colonel Blimp, and the impression was strengthened by his famous monocle, which he manipulated with considerable style. When the author of this book met him in 1940–41, General Ashmore, then a Home Guard Commander in West Sussex, was aggrieved because he had not been officially consulted on the Air Defence of Great Britain (ADGB). He complained about the waste of hard-won experience. He was critical of the failure to maintain his First World War legacy of a single leader who cracked a single whip. He did not believe that co-operation and co-ordination could be achieved in any other way.

Although he was dogmatically sure how this could be done ('simply choose the right man, get Churchill to believe in him and leave him alone'), he was generous with his sympathy for the difficulties which faced the Anti-Aircraft Commander-in-Chief, General Pile. But he was stingingly critical as well of gun-siting, co-ordination of guns, quality of the crews and lack of discipline.

In 1917, with the RFC under War Office control, Ashmore had no inter-Service problems to contend with. Smuts had decided previously to leave the RNAS out of the defence plan, but the Navy flyers were to be on call. They became a much-needed asset.

Ashmore's operational team included Lieutenant-Colonel

(later Brigadier-General) Higgins, RFC, who was commander of the Home Defence Squadrons, and Colonel Simon, who continued to be in charge of the anti-aircraft artillery. LADA's air strength was reinforced by three additional squadrons: 44, 61, and 112. Equipped with Sopwith Camels and Sopwith Pups, they were stationed to cover the north-eastern, south-western and Thames Estuary approaches.

In outline, Ashmore's plan was to leave one defence zone to the gunners and another to fighter aircraft. Much of it was still in preparation, and new dispositions had barely been made, when the Gothas attacked again.

CHAPTER 20

Suddenly, By Night

It was 22 July, a typically quiet early Sunday morning in London, when a succession of loud explosions brought the usual mixture of alarm, tension and curiosity. But almost everyone noticed that the noise in the sky was different. A few people remembered official announcements that maroons were to be fired as air raid warnings, but the collective noise of some 250 maroons did not resemble the more familiar sound of those used individually to call out the lifeboat, to supplement firework displays, or even by ships in distress. *The Oxford English Dictionary* describes a maroon as 'a firework . . . intended to imitate in exploding the report of a cannon'. An edition of *The Universal Dictionary of the English Language* defines a maroon as 'a kind of firework producing a loud report'. No one would have associated those sudden, violent, short-lived explosions with fireworks, especially when the noise was intensified as it reverberated through the quiet Sunday morning streets.

London waited for a raid which took place elsewhere.

The weather on that fine Sunday morning gave Rudolf Kleine the first opportunity to attack England since 7 July. A superficial glance at the bare facts and figures suggests that this was another routine sortie, but closer study shows that it was a significant turning point, a switch from what had been an apparently inflexible decision to use the specially-trained England Squadron exclusively for the demolition of London and thus create an epidemic of fear throughout the country. Unknown to Britain, and perhaps unsuspected by Kleine and the England Squadron, it was the first indication of the Army High Command's weakening resolve.

Sir Douglas Haig was about to begin the Third Battle of Ypres. Although Germany would not have known the exact date, neither side could ever hide its preparations for a big offensive. Haig needed more guns, equipment and troops and the German Army High Command decided to bomb his principal supply ports in England.

The raid on 22 July was planned to be the first of several attacks. The British defences were taken by surprise when twenty-one Gothas crossed the coast at 8.00 am and bombed Harwich and Felixstowe. Although thirteen people were killed and twenty-three injured, the damage was small and the object had failed. The Gothas avoided the anti-aircraft fire and the swift response of some 120 aircraft and returned safely, though one bomber crashed on landing.

If the Army High Command had been convinced of its strategy, this was the moment to exploit a potential victory. Six attacks had killed more than 340 people; 900 were officially recorded as having been injured. More than 520 bombs had been dropped and material damage was estimated at £364,370. The Gothas were still virtually invulnerable to Britain's ground and air defences. Of the 121 bombers which had crossed the coast, only nine had been lost, and only two of those had been shot down. The anxiety throughout south-east England was more acute than that caused by airships, not only because of heavier casualties but also because the enemy could be seen freebooting in the sky. The spectacular 'dog fights' had been no more than displays of individual heroism.

But nothing effective, let alone decisive, had happened. The raids had caused serious delays and interruptions, but munitions factories were still in production. Docks and harbours at Folkestone, Dover, Harwich and along the Thames were still working. And like Harwich, the RNAS station at Felixstowe had survived two attacks.

Britain's resistance to the assault, first by airships and then by the Gothas, cut at the root of the strategy. In Germany there may have been different ideas about the application of that strategy, but in the beginning only a few people had doubted its successful conclusion. And until now the Army High Command had been convinced that the Gothas would redeem the airships' failure. Suddenly, after the high hopes of May, the strategic resolve faltered.

The protests and open criticism of authority in Britain were still being mistaken by many for a weakness that would engender collapse, but there were unmistakable indications that the nation was becoming increasingly stiff-backed. At this point of the war, and at the nadir of their fortunes, the people showed no enthusiasm for a negotiated peace. The Gotha campaign began to lose its momentum and an irreversible decline set in, although at the time it was almost imperceptible.

The indecision began with the raid of 12 August. It was ill-conceived, hurriedly put together and seriously under strength. The objective was the Chatham naval base; but, important though it was as a tactical target, its destruction or disruption would have no effect on Sir Douglas Haig's supplies.

Only fifteen Gothas were available for a mission which was fraught with danger. The RNAS, at Dunkirk, might, at last, intercept them. The flight to Chatham should have the maximum protection of a full squadron. To reach the objective the Thames Estuary between Shoeburyness and Sheerness must be crossed. It had been a death trap for one Gotha on 5 June; several others had narrowly escaped being shot down, but then the British defences had been weaker and the Gotha force had been stronger. Now, there were only forty-five machine guns to protect a formation which was, in any event, too small.

From the beginning everything went wrong. Two Gothas returned with engine trouble. A third dropped bombs on Margate as it left for home, only to crash at Zeebrugge. The rest were harassed by British fighters, who drove them away from Chatham—with tragic consequences for Southend-on-Sea.

It was a warm, sunny evening when the town was attacked. Thirty-two people were killed and forty-six injured in a raid which lasted for less than a quarter of an hour. One Gotha was shot down in the North Sea by Flight Sub-Lieutenant H. S. Kerby, RNAS, who had previously tried to pursue the other Gotha which had bombed Margate. But his luck changed as he returned from that abortive chase and he saw the formation still over the North Sea. One of the machines was isolated at about 4,000 feet. For Kerby speed was of the essence if he was to catch the bomber before it could be protected. One Sopwith Pup against an ailing enemy bomber seemed a fair chance. Kerby took his, and the aircraft fell into the sea. He was awarded the Distinguished Service Cross, a not very generous recognition for someone who had followed a Gotha far out over the North

Sea in an aeroplane and not a seaplane and then attacked a still powerful bomber force.

Against a background of public, press and Parliamentary outcry, there was some official satisfaction in the general belief that the counterattack over Chatham had turned aside a raid which had been intended for London.

Several of those who were killed and injured at Southend were Londoners themselves, some struck down in or near the railway station where the Sunday excursion train was waiting to take them back to the capital.

This raid also had its own emotional horror, and not only to the people who were at Southend: a *Sunday* attack on an apparently unprotected town, which was famous and much loved as an excursion and holiday centre, crowds of 'ordinary, decent people enjoying their simple Sunday pleasure' killed and injured without warning. Later there were those who recalled gun fire, first a distance away, and then over the Estuary as the Gothas were leaving.

Southend's neighbours included Sheerness, Shoeburyness, Grain, Eastchurch and Rochford. With their guns, aerodromes, aircraft and military installations they were an open invitation to raiders. Because of that, and because they also guarded the waterway to London, they were in a well-defended area, with Southend at the heart of it. Why, then, had there been no warning, when the authorities must have known that an attempt was being made to raid somewhere nearby? Where were the aeroplanes and why were the guns silent while the Gothas spent nearly a quarter of an hour over the town and the outlying residential areas? The only gunfire came from the Shoeburyness batteries as the bombers flew over the Estuary to the North Sea.

There were only uncomfortable answers to these questions. A warning had been sent to the town, but the air-raid sirens were long out of use. It is easy now to criticize the local decision not to issue shouted warnings to the crowds. But a gamble was taken and lost. Instructions to take cover or to clear the streets would almost certainly have caused a panic rush, with a funnel of people pouring into the relatively narrow Victoria Street and the railway station. The town was packed with day trippers as well as residents. Anyway the raiders might not come to Southend which had been safe from attacks for two years.

But come they did, and people *were* killed and injured when they rushed into Victoria Street. And there was confusion in the still-forming LADA organization. General Ashmore ordered his RFC squadrons to stay on the ground and wait for the enemy to enter the perimeter trap. But the Squadron at Rochford took off after the Gothas had bombed their aerodrome and drove the raiders away from Chatham to Southend.

It remains something of a curiosity, if not a mystery, why no one in the town and the immediate neighbourhood was aware of imminent danger. Rochford was only five miles from Southend, but no one paid any attention to the few bombs which were dropped there or to the aeroplanes which went up to attack. Canvey Island, where Kleine made his fatal swoop over the town, was only four miles away.

There has never been an explanation of the delay in getting the Shoeburyness guns into action, except for the local theory that 12 August was a Sunday and that Sunday afternoon was therefore a day of rest.

Eight days after the Southend raid, on 18 August, there was further proof of unsure planning and leadership in the England Squadron when Kleine ordered a maximum strength raid with no named objectives. Decisions on targets were to be taken when the weather conditions at landfall were known. When the twenty-eight Gothas took off from St Denis-Westrem and Gontrode on the morning of 18 August, he had already ignored advice to cancel the raid because of impending bad weather and there was an ominous diversion when strong winds forced the armada off course over neutral territory in Holland. Finally the Squadron turned back within sight of the English coast. The formation was broken; two Gothas fell into the sea and there were no survivors. Two other bombers were shot down by the Dutch gunners and the crews were interned. Five more aircraft are believed to have crashed on landing, some with fatal casualties.

Only fifteen Gothas were available on 22 August when the Squadron made its next raid. Margate, Ramsgate and Dover were the selected targets. Five of the Gothas, including that with Kleine on board, did not make a landfall. For the remainder the barrage of anti-aircraft fire over the targets was the heaviest the Squadron had met. It was reinforced by fifteen RNAS aeroplanes. The formation broke into disarray. Exposed, without mutual protection, the bombers were easy to pick out. The gunners brought one down in flames in a field near Margate. Two others were victims of the RNAS. Flight Commander G. E. Hervey and Lieutenant A. F. Brandon were each awarded the Distinguished Service Cross for shooting down a Gotha off the Kent coast. Twelve people were killed and twenty-seven injured.

There was some misplaced criticism. It was argued that if some of the 120 RFC aeroplanes which were waiting for the Gothas in the London area had reinforced the RNAS, then the entire raiding force might have been destroyed. But Ashmore was not playing the numbers game. Shooting down enemy bombers would have improved public confidence, but the London patrols had one object—to prevent the collective bombing of the capital by waiting for those Gothas which avoided the outposts.

The RFC now had its own strict discipline, and part of it was to avoid a fight which might be a diversion and so leave the fortress without aerial protection. No one knew that the Germans had changed their plans and that, for the time being, London was not the primary objective. If Ashmore was right in thinking that an attack on the metropolis had been broken up at the outposts, then the pursuit of enemy aircraft would have been a waste of still scarce resources. Of the aircraft available, about seventy were effective operational fighters. There was nothing to spare for unimportant action beyond the perimeter. Inside it there was now an interdependent defence system of aeroplanes, guns and searchlights. It was still incomplete, but in essence the plan had worked. The RFC had stayed in their zone and the outer defences, with the indispensable help of the RNAS, had broken up the raiders. Nevertheless, no one overlooked the fact that they were the smallest force to have crossed the coast.

But there was no opportunity to enjoy even modest confidence. The Germans abandoned daylight raids and threw Ashmore's plans into confusion. The Army High Command had made a quick assessment. Nineteen Gothas had now been lost or seriously damaged, ten of them on the fateful mission of 18 August. Daylight bombing had failed in its object. Characteristically, the High Command did not deceive itself, and the harsh decision was quickly taken. The policy change was a bitter turnabout. The Army had changed to day bombing because of the airships' failure by night. There was a touch of despair. The England Squadron had to originate new tactics for a new kind of aerial warfare. On the night of 3/4 September it set out to learn the first lessons, with Chatham again the objective. The sortie was a reconnaissance probe, a tentative first flight and not a full-scale raid, but the result was that of a big attack. Four Gothas made a direct hit on the naval base. One hundred and thirty-two sleeping recruits were killed and ninety-six injured.

This was another of those raids which acquired its own morbid emotionalism: there had been the married couple killed 'in an attitude of prayer' during the first airship attack on London, and the fifteen children who had died in the Upper North Street Schools, and who were buried in a communal grave. Now, 132 young bluejackets had been killed and ninety-six injured while asleep in their hammocks.

Anger and horror at the sailors' deaths were all the greater because no alert had sounded, although the Gothas had previously attacked Sheerness and Margate. No British aeroplanes had intercepted the raiders. Searchlights had been slow to work and failed to catch them in their beams. Anti-aircraft guns had been slow to open fire, and when they did they were no more effective than those which had been used against the first airships.

There had been no special concern when two German aeroplanes had dropped fourteen bombs on Dover the previous night. One person had been killed and six injured. There were some after-the-event complaints that this sortie should have warned the authorities to put the night defences on standby.

But isolated raids by aeroplanes on the south-east coast were the small coinage of aerial warfare. Moreover, the night defence organization had been run down. After the Chatham raid there were alarmist stories of undermanned, even deserted, gun sites, observation posts and aerodromes. Some commanding officers had insisted on eternal vigilance; but for the most part the successful night defence co-ordination for the Zeppelins had been discarded.

The Dover incursion had not caused much excitement at Home Forces Headquarters either. The two aircraft were not part of the England Squadron and there was reason to believe that the pilots thought they were over Calais. All the same General Ashmore called for an air-raid alert, but the Chatham attack took it by surprise.

In spite of the failure to intercept so small a force of Gothas, the raid had significant consequences which, as important events often do, came about almost by chance.

A dozen Gothas were wrongly reported to have crossed the coast and to be making for London. But the inflexibility of Ashmore's policy frustrated pilots who were willing to take what was unquestionably a dangerous gamble.

The Sopwith Camels of 44 Squadron were difficult aeroplanes to handle, even by experienced pilots, whether on take-off, in the air or on landing. At night these difficulties were greatly increased. None of the pilots had the additional help of night fighting; furthermore, neither aeroplanes nor aerodromes were prepared for night operations. Instrument panels were only crudely illuminated, if indeed they were illuminated at all, and only a few aerodromes were now organized for take-off or landing in the dark.

These dangers did not prevent the commander of 44 Squadron, Captain G. W. Murlis-Green, from making a personal appeal to General Ashmore for permission to attack the Chatham raiders. Murlis-Green was a gallant and experienced fighter pilot who had been awarded the Distinguished Service Order while he was serving in Salonika. He had seen Gothas in action. His aggressive persuasiveness made Ashmore change his mind and he allowed three pilots to engage the raiders.

Murlis-Green took off from Hainault Farm, with two other Camels, flown by Captain C. J. Q. Brand (later Air Vice-Marshal Sir Christopher Brand) and Lieutenant C. C. Banks. All three returned safely from a mission which was thought to be doomed. They missed the Gothas, but that one sortie led to an immediate conversion of Camels and some aerodromes for night operations on the assumption that the Germans might try again under cover of darkness.

They did—the very next night.

The attack on Monday, 4 September was more of a reconnaissance in force than a full-scale raid, to discover if the inner defences were as weak as those on the outskirts. Nine Gothas (from eleven originally scheduled) crossed the south-east coast at about 10.30 pm. As on the previous night, the searchlights were ineffective. Lacking the disciplined co-ordination of the Zeppelin campaign, they probed individually for the bombers.

One Gotha was shot down at Sheerness by anti-aircraft gunners. The rest made their way to London. It is uncertain how many actually reached the capital. The first bombs fell as late as 11.30 pm, but they struck streets which were never empty of people. There was severe damage in the Strand area by Charing Cross Station and Charing Cross Hospital, Northumberland Avenue, the Victoria Embankment, and John Street in the Adelphi.

When daylight revealed the results there was a mixed reaction: shock at the damage to familiar places and astonishment that the area was so small. After the crashing noise of the night, it seemed as if London had been demolished by an earthquake. Nineteen people were killed and seventy-one injured.

Five days later almost all the wounds were still visible; but memory recalls the disappointment of a 10-years old boy because there was no sign of the tramcar which had been hit by one of the 110-lb bombs that fell on the Embankment, killed three passengers and injured three others, and because a large crater had been filled in. More than sixty years later, the damage is recalled by the shrapnel scars still to be seen on Cleopatra's Needle which survived destruction from a bomb explosion only a yard or so away from it.

A storm of protest broke against General Ashmore. There were demands for his dismissal. The public was convinced that the home defences had been hoodwinked. The fury was understandable but almost everybody forgot that they, too, had believed that serious night raids were finished.

In his book, *Air Defence*, published in 1929, and in talks with the author of this book, Ashmore maintained that night bombing came as no surprise and was indeed expected because Kaghol 3 was reported to have been carrying out night practice flights. But a close study of all facts confirms without doubt that the new policy was a total surprise.

General Ashmore went on calmly with his adjusted dispositions. Under Colonel Simon's direction, the removal of most of the guns from the inner zone was completed, to cover the flight paths to London. The outer defence was organized into a numbered-squares plan which, together with a sound-location system, could track the Gothas' movements. The Command Post at Horse Guards was the filter for information and all co-ordination stemmed from it. That co-ordination was, on paper at any rate, better but less concentrated.

With nearly all the guns withdrawn from London's inner zone, there were certain to be complaints because their reassuring thunder would no longer be heard. But there would be no complaints from the pilots, whose feelings for the gunners was less than friendly. Even in daylight operations, they claimed to be in danger of being shot down.

In a sincere belief that he could provide a practical alternative, and to offset protests about the absence of the guns, Ashmore set out to prepare a different kind of deterrent. And the deterrent that Londoners were to see was the astonishing sight of barrage balloons 'hanging' over parts of the capital.

Balloons had been used by the Allies at Venice, and had previously been considered by Britain, but on 5 September Ashmore decided to adopt them for London.

There have been some misleading accounts of the barrage balloon scheme, but the official history, *War in the Air*, states that the barrage balloon defence consisted of 'aprons', each of three balloons, which were linked by a cable anchored to the ground, arranged in a straight line 2,000 yards in length. The 'barrage' was formed by wire streamers 1,000 feet long.

Aeroplanes were forbidden to fly at less than 10,000 feet inside the barrage line, which was to operate on the east side of Lewisham, the east side of Plumstead, one mile east of Barking, the east edge of Ilford, the east edge of Wanstead, and the north edge of Tottenham. This left the barrage zone exclusively to the anti-aircraft gunners.

Shortage of suitable material prevented the scheme from achieving its maximum strength. Nevertheless, the balloons had a big effect on the public, if only for a few weeks. Some people ridiculed them, but for a time there was a confident belief that the Gothas would fly into the streamers and crash to the ground. At first the balloons could be positioned at heights between 7 and 10,000 feet, but there were plans to raise the height to 12,000 feet.

For the England Squadron, the reconnaissance in force had exceeded all expectations. Although the Army High Command knew that the enemy's night defences had been run down, there was surprise at the reports of such weak opposition. The most important result of the raid had been the navigational success. With a compass as the only direction finder, without even a wireless link, it was an outstanding feat to have flown over the dark Belgian landscape, the pitch-black North Sea and, until the run-in for London, over a mostly well-dimmed English countryside.

But the Squadron was not misled by this first success; neither was it enthusiastic about night bombing. Britain was scrambling together a reorganized defence. It must soon be as formidable as that which had defeated the Zeppelins. Formation flying, with its mutual protection, was impossible in the dark. Navigation would rarely be so easy. With all its dangers, daylight raids were preferred.

Suddenly the Army High Command changed its policy again. Once more London was to be the central target; but now people were more important than places. The unseen terror of indiscriminate, successive-night attacks by twenty or more Gothas, reinforced by the newly-transferred Giants and a new kind of incendiary bomb, might still breach the fortress. There were real hopes that another Great Fire of London might reduce the city to a smouldering ruin.

In Britain there was another kind of hope. Sir Douglas Haig had begun the Third Battle of Ypres on 31 July. After a desperate struggle during a rain-sodden August, the British army made limited gains. On 20 September a heavy German counterattack was repulsed on the Menin Road. Despite some changes of opinion after 'Third Ypres' had failed, there was political and public confidence that Haig was about to drive the Germans out of Belgium and open the way to final victory.

The exaggerated accounts of the battle were manna to the public in this the worst year of the war. The newspaper correspondents' vividly-written, second-hand stories hid the fact that 'victories' were often no more than the gaining or regaining of a few yards of ground.

But to Londoners the good news was forgotten when the war came back to their doorsteps.

CHAPTER 21

A Fateful Week

When Sir Douglas Haig began the Third Battle of Ypres Gothas from the England Squadron were used to bomb his supply ports on the French side of the Channel, particularly Dunkirk. But this second diversion did not weaken the number of aircraft available for the most concentrated aerial assault of the First World War. It began on Monday, 24 September and ended on Monday and Tuesday, 1/2 October.

All the raids, except one, were on London. Gothas, and their powerful reinforcements, the Giants, dropped 448 bombs. Sixty-nine people were killed and 259 were believed to have been injured. Damage was estimated to have been £137,500. But nerves were so finely stretched that some snapped. Ninety-two Gothas and five Giants were under orders for London; fifty-five Gothas crossed the coast; twenty reached the capital; four were shot down; seven crashed on landing; one was missing, almost certainly hit by anti-aircraft fire; one made a forced landing in Holland. All five Giants crossed the coast and returned safely.

The Royal Flying Corps and the Royal Naval Air Service flew some 150 sorties. Four of their aircraft crashed.

The two previous night raids, with their 318 casualties and the special horror of young sailors killed in their hammocks, had left a postscript of acute fear and apprehension—and a positive reaction. Precautions which had been taken for the Zeppelin raids were used again, but this time more widely and with greater effect. In the London mansions and big houses, there were more elaborate preparations to protect families and servants. Cellars and basement rooms were strengthened with good quality and expertly-stacked sandbags. In more modest houses people could do little more than pile up additional furniture, mattresses, or anything else that was solid enough to give a rather desperate feeling of safety against direct hits, blast, shrapnel and splinters.

It was not until after the sustained onslaught was over that the Government provided sandbags free of charge, and then only after the cancellation of an instruction that local authorities must buy them. Before then, however, there was a ready sale for sandbags 'off the barrow'. The entrepeneurs fixed their prices according to the prosperity of the district. They ranged from two-pence (about one penny in today's money) to a shilling (now five pence) a bag. Many of the bags did not survive the stacking.

There was scant protection for the multitude of slum houses, tenements and other ramshackle properties in parts of the East End. In some houses as many as a dozen people lived. But ever since the first of the night raids by Gothas thousands of residents in the poor and vulnerable areas knew exactly what they would do when the next raid came. And when it did, they wasted no time. Those within walking distance—and often it was a long distance—of Underground railway stations moved into them. Some occupied the tunnels under the Thames, while others trekked to the fields or local public parks.

It was spontaneous, infectious and unorganized. It defied policemen, the Underground railway staffs and park keepers. Officials were scandalized. It simply would not do. Parks closed at dusk, Underground railway stations between midnight and 1 am. 'At no time must platforms be used except by passengers alighting from, entering, or waiting for a train.' This hurriedly-prepared instruction was issued from at least one station on the morning after the first of the raids—and was completely ignored.

Thousands of citizens soon established what were, in effect, squatters' rights in the stations and tunnels. Some people stayed stubbornly in the parks. In one North London public park, the keeper—whose authority was never challenged except by small boys at a safe distance—was affronted by the refusal of people to leave his little kingdom. He fetched a police constable, who found himself in a situation that was beyond the simple rules by which the police then worked. He could not arrest a crowd and charge them under a by-law. He hit on the bright idea of telling them that the 'parkie' would lock them in for the night if they did no leave before dusk. He was dumbfounded when they chose to stay, and walked away with as much dignity as he could muster to make the strangest report of his career.

The invasion was not always settled so amicably or tolerantly. Loud, officious voices ordered the squatters out of the stations. Policemen tried to stop the invaders. There were some ugly scenes as attempts were made to evict those already in the stations or those trying to enter them.

The London 'bobbies' were then rarely accused of violence, even when they were regularly handling drunks or street fights. But some of their respected tolerance gave way in the face of what was officially regarded as trespass. And some of the trespassers were not tolerant either, especially those who had moved out of their East End homes. Most refused to leave the stations, even when the last train had left or when the raid was over. Confronted with this massive resistance, the police were helpless. Their reputation suffered from self-important Special Constables who over-enjoyed their temporary authority.

By the end of the series of raids, some 300,000 people were said to have occupied the stations. Like birds seeking their roosts, they did not wait for darkness. They arrived every evening well before nightfall to cause resentment, indignation, and aggravation among passengers who struggled in and out of the trains.

The squatting soon became unhygienic and occasionally dangerous. The Metropolitan and City of London police were diverted from more urgent duties. The immediate official response was to allow the public to use suitable buildings such as government offices, police stations, and the larger town halls. But these were not intended for all-night lodgers with their coats, blankets, cushions, pillows, mattresses, dogs, cats and cage birds.

Although free accommodation was available in the designated buildings, with their prominently-displayed 'Air Raid Shelter' signs, space was also made available in some safe, undesignated buildings. But there were eager customers for the ubiquitous entrepreneurs who offered dubious safety at a price. Competition dictated that price. Five shillings or more was willingly paid for protection until a raid was over; but there were rival offers of half that figure in some districts, and, if the accommodation was large enough to show a handsome return, as little as a shilling a session was demanded.

In contrast to the nights of the airship raids, residential

streets outside Central London were almost deserted. The Gothas brought a different kind of fear. There was a feeling that their bombs were more dangerous and more accurate. The machines were rarely seen; there was only that eerie sound, coming, as it were, through the clouds. And there was nothing for the sightseers either.

During the first raid, the West End and Strand areas were as busy as usual, until the bombs hit Piccadilly, the Thames Embankment and Southampton Row, when the crowds suddenly rushed for safety. Some went into the Royal parks; some tried to seek refuge in theatres, cinemas and restaurants.

Although fewer people were reported to have been in Central London after that initial attack, it was scarcely noticeable. Theatres, restaurants, cinemas offered bomb-proof shelter, and the magnet of pleasure and entertainment made no significant difference to the crowds.

The casualties in that first raid were the heaviest of the series; and yet surprisingly small. One hundred and eighteen bombs had killed twenty-one people and injured seventy-one others.

Kleine followed up that attack on the following night, when bombs from fourteen Gothas killed nine people and injured twenty-three. Bad weather prevented further raids until Friday, 28 September; but the capital escaped because the North Sea weather again proved to be an implacable liability for more than half of the Gothas which took off for London. The raid was a disastrous experience for the England Squadron. No fewer than twenty-five Gothas, as well as two Giants, left the aerodromes. Unpredicted cloud forced fourteen of the Gothas to turn back. Three were shot down by anti-aircraft fire and six were to crash on landing.

Only three Gothas and the two Giants took part in the attack. A thick ground mist blanketed the English countryside and prevented the raiders from finding London. Forty-five bombs were hurriedly released over Suffolk, Kent and Essex. There were no casualties and the damage was only slight.

The two recently-transferred Giants were among the survivors. The eventual course of the battle for London deprived this outstanding type from a place in the gallery of famous bombers, and its sophisticated superiority over all other contemporary aeroplanes, including the Gothas, has been neglected.

Three versions were used in the raids against England: Staaken R. IV, Staaken R. V, and Staaken R. VI. The name is that of the German town where they were built, and the prefix indicates that they were a Reisen(R)-type, derived from the full name of the Giant Squadron, *Riesenflugzeugen.*

The Giant was truly named. It varied in crew numbers, armament, bomb loads and specifications. One of the earlier versions had six engines; another had five. Nearly all those used in operations against England were powered by four 260 h.p. Mercedes engines and had a speed of about 80 miles per hour. They all had a wingspan of 138 feet 5½ inches.

The most powerful was R. 39, which had five Mercedes engines and a range of some 300 miles. It could carry as much as two tons of missiles—a complete selection from fire bombs to 660-lb explosives. The bomb sights and release were electrically operated. It was armed with six Lewis guns, although all six were not invariably carried on operations. Most of the other Staakens had three machine guns.

The crew in all Staakens was never fewer than seven and never more than nine. The standard complement was seven: the commander—who was also the navigator and bombardier—two pilots, a wireless operator, two flight mechanics, and a fuel mechanic. The flight mechanics each occupied a small cockpit, where they were in charge of the engines which were mounted in streamlined nacelles.

The control cabin, forward, was equipped with a variety of instruments which were then uncommon in aircraft aids. They included an air speed indicator, altimeter, fuel gauge, variometer and an artificial horizon. A unique position-finding method consisted of an apparatus which could send out a call-sign to two ground stations; they fixed the aircraft's position and transmitted it back.

On Saturday, 29 September three Giants and seven Gothas set out for London. Three of the Gothas never arrived over England. Bombing, however, was not the only object of the mission, which was also to provide another, and immediate, opportunity to test the effectiveness of the Giants.

Although only two of them, and two Gothas, reached London, the sortie justified the Army High Command's belief that a few—perhaps only one at a time—of these flying fortresses could kill and injure at least as many people, cause more damage and be less vulnerable than a flock of Gothas. The Mercedes engines deceived the British listening posts, which reported that a large force of Gothas had arrived over England.

Home Forces Headquarters did not know that a new, more powerful bomber type had been secretly filtered into the identifiable England Squadron.

Fourteen people were killed and eighty-seven injured in London and Sheerness. One Gotha was shot down and another forced down in Holland. But there was no complacency now at Home Forces Headquarters. This was clearly a critical stage in the aerial bombardment, with three raids having been made on London, and a fourth which had missed the capital.

The public had an instinctive feeling that the worst was yet to come. Descriptions which have tried to recreate the mood of that significant week give the impression of a people seized with panic. Again, the word was misused. As usual there was some panic at the heart of a raid, but the general mood, especially in those parts of the capital most likely to be attacked, was of growing tension, angry frustration and nervous expectation. It reached its climax on Sunday, 30 September and Monday, 1 October.

On Sunday night the full moon in a clear sky was a perfect setting for London's fourth raid of the week. The morning communiqué on the previous night's raid stated that a determined and simultaneous attack had been made on London by three groups of aeroplanes, which had approached from three different directions and been broken up by anti-aircraft fire.

No one knew that only four aircraft had been over the capital. Rumour even exaggerated the number of bombers which were supposed to have been repelled; the statement said that 'at least eighteen aeroplanes flew in over Essex and Kent'. On the now well-established belief that every communiqué magnified successes and minimized dangers, it was widely believed that probably twice that number of Gothas had been involved. There was small comfort to be found in the reassuring words that the groups had been broken up by anti-aircraft fire. And there was small comfort, either, in the knowledge that the Germans had chosen the harvest moon period for this sustained assault.

As it was a Sunday the streets were quieter than usual, and even in Central London there were fewer people about. On the Saturday night the bombs had been widely scattered on places as far apart as Waterloo and London Bridge railway stations, Kensington, Notting Hill and north-east London. In the suburbs, at any rate, if it was impossible to return before darkness, then it was stay-at-home Sunday. So far the war had had little effect on the universal habit of family visiting on the Sabbath.

But not on this Sunday, unless Mum and Dad or Grandma were nearby.

Going to church was something of a national habit too. On 30 September morning services were more crowded than usual. Some churches cancelled evensong or held it before nightfall. A woman in the North London suburb of Palmers Green remembered that early Sunday evening as the quietest she had ever known. Footsteps of the few people who were out could be heard several streets away. Some residents heard, for the first time, the rumbling rhythm and clanging of tramcars on a distant and mostly deserted main road.

When most people were indoors or had made their nightly trek to safety, the abnormal silence was shattered by maroon warnings and anti-aircraft guns, which fired unceasingly for more than an hour. The raiders had come early and were reported at 6.42 pm. All London and the neighbouring counties which lapped its boundaries heard the guns. Even as far away as Sussex, on the other side of the North Downs, there was the persistent sound of rumbling. And in and around the capital, everyone was convinced that this was to be the heaviest barrage of the war.

Although no raiders were shot down or, apparently, seriously damaged, the 14,000 rounds which were reported to have been fired that night were a successful deterrent. Ten Gothas, but no Giants, crossed the coast and all of them returned safely. Six are believed to have reached London, where bombs were dropped on the eastern suburbs. The four aircraft which failed to find the objective caused some fatal casualties in Margate. In all, fourteen people were killed and thirty-eight injured.

Although nearly all of the London guns were on the perimeter, the sound of the heavy barrage had been both reassuring and alarming. The greater the volume of fire, the more people were convinced that the capital was being attacked by a much larger force. This, together, with the ordeal of four raids in a week, put a noticeable strain on those who endured them.

There would be temporary relief as the moon waned, but there was at least one more 'good moon' night on the following Monday before the series could end.

It was a troubled population which went to work or did the shopping and the housework on that Monday morning. There were strict instructions, requests and appeals to the working members of families to be 'home before dark'. Many offices and shops closed early. Some offices persisted in 'business as usual' and there were stentorian reminders that employees should show the same courage as the boys at the front.

Although there was considerable desertion from the ranks of nightshift munitions workers, there was no militancy or rule-breaking in offices and shops, where still-prevalent Victorian rigidity was unquestioned. In a publishing company in Paternoster Row it was agreed to make a personal appeal to the managing director for the staff to leave half an hour earlier. A senior member was persuaded to present the humble petition, but when he arrived at the great man's office he had gone. The staff stayed until closing time.

There was some relief in Whitehall that Monday because the raids had not been more severe. Indeed, on readily-produced figures, London had escaped lightly, perhaps miraculously. Five raids carried out by forty-nine bombers had killed fifty-eight people and injured about 220 (including the Sheerness and Margate casualties). The material damage, however, was severe. Its value—later put at just over £90,000 for the five nights—was irrelevant, but it was a sombre warning of what might have been and what still might be. It was a painful shock to all who passed it by or who lived with it.

And it was the people who caused acute anxiety in Whitehall on the Monday morning, anxiety which overshadowed any feeling of relief that things might have been worse. The events of the week had shown that smooth statements about enemy aeroplane groups having been broken up, or reports of German losses, were no substitute for a solution. The raids could not now be left to Lord French and General Ashmore, both of whom faced mounting criticism. The embattled home front demanded the attention of the Prime Minister, the Minister of Munitions, Winston Churchill, the Chief of the Imperial General Staff, General Robertson, and, of course, Lloyd George's peripatetic adviser, General Smuts.

The strain was telling not only on the population of London but also on the anti-aircraft gunners, the fighter pilots and the fire services. Many of the guns had literally shot themselves out of action. There was a shortage of ammunition. Night-shift work had been even more seriously disrupted; in some factories, when a raid was over, the shift was over too.

Almost every aeroplane type had been used. That great Zeppelin conqueror, the B.E. 2c, had been useless against the

Gothas and Giants. There were not enough experienced pilots to fly that excellent but hazardous night-fighter, the Sopwith Camel.

Mundane things had as much effect on civilian morale as did the bombing itself. For many Londoners who were out and about during the evenings of that fateful week, it was difficult, and occasionally impossible, to find their usual transport, or any transport at all. Even when there was only a warning, or when a raid was taking place anywhere in the capital, many buses, tramcars and suburban and Underground trains stopped. Taxicabs became scarce and the bolder drivers who kept their meter flags up demanded illegal, exorbitant fares.

Grievances begat grievances. Five nights of raids brought protests about casualties and damage from anti-aircraft fire, something which would have been accepted if the guns were shooting down the bombers.

On the last raid of the series, on the Monday night, Gothas dropped more than seventy bombs in an attack which lasted nearly two and a half hours. But again a thick mist reduced the severity of the raid. No Giant took part in it and only eleven out of eighteen Gothas reached England. Five of them are believed to have bombed the metropolis. The casualties were small, with eleven people killed and forty-one injured. Damage was estimated to be about £45,000, but again it was the effect on morale rather than results which concerned the Government.

The wounds of aerial warfare were now painfully and tragically evident. The damage was so bad in some districts that streets were temporarily closed. There were more departures from the capital, mostly by the prosperous middle classes, whose wives and children went to safe areas. Working-class families clung to their environments, and it would never have occurred to them to expect an official evacuation scheme.

The aristocracy and other wealthy citizens were comparatively secure in their strong town houses or country residences, where nannies cared for the young children, while the older ones were protected in their boarding schools.

But despite the hardships and fears of those who stayed in London, there was no sign of despair. Some foreign observers detected a swaggering pride after the most concentrated raids of the war. The German Army High Command realized that something even more concentrated would be necessary to subdue people who had confounded every expectation about human survival. The dream of surrender had turned into the reality of an aggressive demand for revenge. 'If they can do it to us, why can't we do it to them?' was not a rhetorical question but one which required a definite answer.

Lloyd George, like Winston Churchill in 1940, inspired the nation during the grim months of 1917. Unlike Churchill, he was, as he frequently proclaimed, a 'man of the people'. Like Churchill, who was nothing of the kind, he had a sure instinct for the public mood.

On the morning of 2 October he visited areas which had been bombed a few hours earlier. Always the man to tell his audience what it most wanted to hear, he said: 'We shall give it all back to them, and we shall give it back to them very soon. We shall bomb Germany with compound interest.'

He was confident that his personal popularity would carry a pledge which he knew could not immediately be redeemed; and indeed it never was, although he proved to be half as good as his word when Germany was eventually bombed, tactically but never strategically.

Raids by the RNAS on 25 September, the day after the sustained offensive began, forced the Gothas out of St Denis-Westrem and Gontrode, though no bombers were destroyed or damaged. But this was no substitute for the impatient demand for devastating attacks on the German people and their homes.

If the RNAS raid had succeeded, the England Squadron would have been incurably paralyzed and the demand for revenge would have been silenced. As it was the Gothas lived to fight another day, although the sustained assault had failed. The realistic Army High Command would not accept that the campaign had failed. Uncharacteristically, it had a seemingly last hope for sucess: a new incendiary bomb which, scattered in large numbers indiscriminately, might engulf the capital in flames, the like of which had not been seen since the Great Fire of London some 250 years earlier.

Almost a month went by before they were used. And waiting with them were the Giants, ready to drop their mightly load of explosives into the furnaces.

In the meantime the capital was grateful for the lull. People were now experienced at watching the sky in high-risk periods and looked forward to at least three weeks of untroubled nights.

The lull ended earlier than expected, with an unexpected result.

CHAPTER 22
Last Orders

Shortly before midnight on 19 October a 660-lb bomb hit the heart of the West End of London in and around Piccadilly Circus. An earlier raid warning had been forgotten or dismissed as another false alarm. There were no searchlights or the sound of anti-aircraft fire. No one in the immediate area had time to run for cover, yet only seven people were killed and sixteen injured.

To everyone's astonishment the early morning communiqué from Home Forces Headquarters stated that 'hostile airships' had been over England and that 'a few bombs had been dropped in the London area'.

It was inconceivable that one of the almost forgotten Zeppelins could have stolen into London and been free to bomb at random. During the year there had been six scarcely-noticed raids on England. Some 300 bombs had been dropped in Kent, East Sussex, East Anglia and Yorkshire. Five people had been killed and about twenty injured. It was hard to understand why the Zeppelins had come at all.

There was as much curiosity as there was anger. How could a Zeppelin have slipped the defences? But the strange truth was not then known.

When Peter Strasser had ordered eleven 'height climbers' to attack England on 19 October, London was not even an alternative objective. Targets for the night were industrial areas in the North and Midlands.

The British had early warning that a large force of Zeppelins was on its way, but they did not know that upper air winds, increasing to gale force, were driving the airships southwards, hopelessly off course. When it was realized that Zeppelins were heading south, the London defences stood by for a mass attack.

The scattered armada flew at heights which varied between 16,000 to more than 20,000 feet. The sound of their engines could not be heard from the ground and there were fears that they had been cut so that the Zeppelins could drift silently over the capital to make the squadron-type attack which had been expected in 1915 and 1916.

To make it difficult for the airship captains to find the target orders were given for anti-aircraft guns to be silent and for the searchlights to be switched off. When the first bomb fell, north-west of London, at Watford, Home Forces Headquarters and the Anti-Aircraft Command were tense, but hopeful that the undisturbed Zeppelins might glide harmlessly over the capital.

Reports and plottings of bombs having been dropped outside the London defence zone were taken to be further confirmation of a concentration on the metropolis. But far from there being a clear-cut plan, all the airships were struggling to survive. Only *Kapitänleutnant* Waldemar Kölle in L 45 actually flew over London. He had been unable to locate his main objective of Sheffield and, like the rest of the fleet, was blown southwards. All the ships' captains and crews were virtually blindfolded by bad visibility and an inability to recognize landmarks. It was impossible to obtain bearings from the base at Alhorn.

L 45 dropped more than 20 bombs on Northampton, where three people were killed, but for all Kölle and his crew knew it could have been anywhere in the middle of England or East Anglia, although a guess was made that Oxford had been hit. As the upper air gale drove L 45 southwards, it was only by chance that the crew recognized London.

L 45 announced her approach by dropping bombs all the way to the centre, causing damage at various places including Watford, Harrow, Hendon and Cricklewood, before she re-leased the 660-lb missile on Piccadilly Circus. She then crossed to south-east London, where two more 660-lb bombs killed twenty-six people at Camberwell and Hither Green. Figures for the injured are not accurately recorded, but the official history puts them at thirty.

Engine failure, the debilitating effects of high-altitude fly-ing, with its attendant sickness, nausea, vertigo and some disorientation, together with sub-zero temperatures, made the return journey a supreme test of skill and the will to endure.

L 45 was one of the four Zeppelins which did not return from what were almost the last rites of the airship campaign. She made a forced landing on the River Bueche, near Sisteron, in France. Kölle and his crew set fire to their ship and then surrendered to French soldiers.

Franz Stabbert was killed with all his men when L 44 was shot down by anti-aircraft fire at St Clément in France. And it was in France, too, that L 49 made a forced landing. *Kapitänleutnant* Hans-Carl Gayer and his crew were captured. Later that afternoon L 50 (*Kapitänleutnant* Roderich Schwonder) crashed at Bourbonne-les-Bains. Sixteen of the crew, including the captain, were saved; but, damaged though the airship was, her hull took off, became airborne and disappeared without trace. Four men were still on board.

While the naval Zeppelins were slowly dying, Rudolf Kleine led twenty-two Gothas to London on 31 October. They had with them the new 10-lb fire bomb. There was nothing revolutionary about the bomb itself, but it was more reliable (or so the experts confidently predicted) and, because it was so small, could be carried in much greater quantities; so great in fact that the proportion of those which did not ignite would be unimportant. This was to be the first of the 'scatter raids' which would set London ablaze.

In the event more than 270 explosive and incendiary bombs were dropped on London's eastern and south-eastern outskirts. Ten people were killed and twenty-two injured at Erith, Belvedere, Woolwich—where the arsenal was again undamaged—Charlton, Greenwich, Millwall and its dock. Damage was estimated at £22,800.

A heavy barrage, a myriad of searchlights, and more than fifty aircraft met the raiders; but it was the co-ordination of guns and searchlights, as well as some harassment from the aeroplanes, which kept them from the city centre.

Many of the fire bombs did not ignite and the initial hope that this raid would cause a raging blaze was extinguished with them. Disillusion over the incendiaries was compounded by the loss of five Gothas which crashed on landing. But there was a perverse optimism that the next attack would be successful. It took place on 5/6 December.

Nineteen Gothas and two Giants left for London. More than

half of their bomb load was composed of incendiaries. The raid was planned in three phases, but three of the Gothas dropped out, and the first phase occurred at 1.30 am, when two Gothas and one Giant bombed Sheerness with explosive and fire bombs. Five people were killed and about twelve injured. Two hours later the second phase took place when explosive and incendiary missiles were dropped on Margate and Dover by four Gothas and one Giant.

The third phase, and the main effort, consisted of nine Gothas. They were first reported at 4.00 am. Six of them flew resolutely against a continuously heavy barrage and probing searchlights; but when they reached London they unloaded their bombs with the haste of men who were anxious to make the quickest possible exit. Many of the incendiaries dropped into the Thames, in parks and fields. The three phases of the raid had caused only thirty-six casualties: eight dead and twenty-eight injured; of these, three were killed in London, where about a dozen were reported to have been injured.

In all, more than 420 bombs were dropped, of which about 390 were estimated to have been incendiaries. The capital had been saved by the hard-pressed, much-abused gunners and the indispensable London Fire Brigade which was supported by units from outside its area.

No one then realized it, but they had won the battle for London.

The measure of their success, and the narrow margin between that success and failure, can be judged by the damage, which was estimated at more than £100,000, most of it caused by the fire bombs.

Although so many of the incendiaries had been more like squibs than destructive fire bombs, there were no illusions about their potential danger. The London Fire Brigade knew what would have happened if most of them had ignited. Engines and crews were deployed for immediate and versatile action, but in no circumstances could they have dealt with the sweeping blazes if all the incendiaries had burned.

The metropolitan firemen were over-stretched and under stress. By some misguided decision, firemen who had been in the Royal Navy or the Army before the war were recalled from the Reserve. And, later, full-time firemen under 25 years of age were conscripted into the services. Their replacements were not always of the same high standard. But during 1917 London firemen were brought back to strengthen a force which—and not only in the capital—never received the recognition which its courage, skill and devotion to duty deserved.

No one, not even the police, gave Londoners a feeling of greater confidence than the London firemen. And on the morning of 6 December thousands of people who had been in the raid realized that the Brigade and its allies from outside the area had saved the lives of countless men, women and children who might have been trapped in the blazes or caught in a fearful stampede for safety.

Two Gothas were shot down by the anti-aircraft gunners, one near Canterbury and the other near Rochford. The pilot of the first bomber set his aeroplane alight before he and his crew surrendered, but there was only one survivor from the second. A third Gotha was reported missing. Its fate is unknown except that it disappeared over the North Sea, almost certainly the gunners' third victim of the night.

Not even the most optimistic supporter of aerial warfare could now deny that the campaign to destroy England was over. And the tide of the war itself looked as if it were flooding towards the Allies. America's entry on their side had significantly altered the balance of power. The prospects of a negotiated peace had gone. Lloyd George had ordered a reluctant Admiralty to adopt the convoy system for merchant ships, with the result that the U-boats were losing the battle for the nation's lifeline.

As usual, in conventional warfare, when everything else fails, victory or defeat depends on the respective armies. By the end of 1917 there were no signs of an end to the deadlock of trench-bound troops.

There was always a Spring offensive, whose hopes flickered and died. There would be another in 1918. If that, too, came to nothing a negotiated armistice might be the only way out of the deadlock. With both sides bleeding to death, there had to be a limit to this war of limited objectives. And if it came to an armistice, with neither side defeated, then Germany's strategy would be the same as that for the now-forgotten negotiated peace.

At the end of the year, however, Germany had the weaker hand. The losses of Gothas and crews could not be replaced quickly enough to maintain the raids. Attempts to do so meant that new crews, like those of all air forces with heavy losses,

were hurriedly and inadequately trained. This normally unacceptable standard was not confined to operational flying as
such; the landing of the Gothas, for example, required considerable skill even from experienced pilots. Now inexperience was
the main reason for the increasing number of bombers which
were reported to have 'crashed on landing'.

The England Squadron was soon to be withdrawn from the
assault on London. Just nine months earlier they had made that
historic first raid, certain that they would be the conquerors of
England and Germany's greatest war heroes. From 29/30
January to 19/20 May, 1918, the aerial bombardment of
England was carried out exclusively by Giants, flying individually. The Gothas were to attack only once more, in the final
onslaught.

The inevitability of withdrawal followed the raid of 18
December and 28/29 January. In the first of these thirteen
Gothas and one Giant attempted to attack London. Because it
was a moonless night the raid was unexpected, but a heavy
barrage, an accurate concentration of searchlights, and some
disruption—with one success by the RFC—broke up the
Gothas; only seven of them reached the capital. More than 140
bombs were dropped. Fourteen people were killed and about
eighty injured. Material damage was estimated to have been
some £240,000, the heaviest of any raid during the war.

One Gotha was destroyed by the indefatigable Murlis-
Green. His persistent gallantry was finally rewarded when he
attacked the bomber over Essex. Having been hit, the Gotha
landed safely on the sea off Folkestone, but while being towed
by a trawler, it was sabotaged by an explosive charge set off by
the crew to ensure its destruction and their own deaths—or so it
seemed. In the event only one of the three-man crew was lost,
by drowning.

Seven more Gothas crashed on landing in Belgium.

Although the material damage was the heaviest caused by
Zeppelins or aeroplanes, the raid was a bleak beginning for the
England Squadron's new temporary commander, *Oberleutnant*
Richard Walter. Rudolf Kleine had been killed when his
aircraft was shot down by a Canadian pilot, Captain Wendel
Rogers, RFC.

Kleine's death was another blow to the weakening morale of
the Squadron. He could not be blamed for the failure of the
campaign. He had led the Gothas with skill and bravery, and

had been decorated with the *Pour le Mérite,* at a personal investiture, by the Kaiser.

Kapitänleutnant Ernst Brandenburg was still not fit enough to resume command after his serious accident, so the leadership went to Richard Walter.

Now, at the turn of the year, two new Home Defence Squadrons, 141 and 143, were formed in Britain, and a new fighter aeroplane, the Bristol Fighter, was brought into service. It had a speed of 125 miles per hour, a height of 20,000 feet and was armed with two, and sometimes three machine-guns.

More anti-aircraft guns and searchlights were made available for the inner defences and the approaches to the capital. General Ashmore made further changes in his dispositions and tightened up the liaison between observer posts and control.

In December General Trenchard was appointed Chief of the Air Staff to the newly-forming Air Ministry, under the direction of Lord Rothermere, a union which soon turned to disunity. It was to end with Trenchard's resignation at the war's most critical moment and only a fortnight after the creation of the Royal Air Force.

The last raid before the withdrawal of the Gothas had an inauspicious beginning. Defying thick ground mist over their aerodromes, which persisted over the North Sea and developed over England, thirteen Gothas took off early in the evening of 28 January. Later they were followed by one Giant.

Six of the Gothas turned back over the North Sea. Seven overcame the weather conditions and made their landfall, but only three of them and, eventually, the one Giant, were able to penetrate the London defences. The four other Gothas bombed Ramsgate, Margate and Sheerness. The casualties in the capital were heavy—and yet relatively small. Of the sixty-seven people who were killed fifty-two were the result of three related, macabre incidents; and those same incidents accounted for about 100 of the 166 who were believed to have been injured.

Londoners were still not accustomed to the sound of warning maroons and when they were fired on the evening of 28 January many people mistook them for bombs. There had already been an air-raid alert and crowds were waiting for the Bishopsgate railway goods depot to open; it was an officially-designated air-raid shelter. When one of the gates was partly opened there was a frantic rush for the shelter. One person is believed to have tripped and other people fell over the prostrate body. Suddenly there was a heap of struggling, fighting men, women and children. Some were suffocated; others were pushed inescapably against the walls. The entrance was blocked.

By a tragic coincidence there was a similar collective panic at Mile End Underground station in the East End. The casualties were unbelievably small: the total for both places was only fourteen dead and fourteen injured.

But the greatest tragedy of the night took place at Long Acre, north of the Strand. The Gothas had gone, but at midnight there was another alarm as the lone Giant flew towards the capital. It was the biggest of them all, R. 39, and it dropped a 660-lb bomb outside Odhams Printing Works. The missile exploded under the pavement and the three-storey building shuddered under the impact. Fire took hold of newsprint reels in the basement. A wall collapsed and overturned printing presses.

More than 500 people were sheltering in the basement and only one exit remained open. There were to be many worse horrors during the Second World War raids, but the carnage at Odhams was then unique. Amid the flames and smoke of burning newsreels and the danger of being drowned by the water from the fire hoses, people fought and clawed their way towards the one exit. An entrance was made for doctors to give anaesthetics, do some amputations and relieve the worst of the injuries caused by the panic.

At the end of it all thirty-eight people were dead and eighty-five injured. But the casualties were incomparable to the peculiar horror of the incident. And it confirmed a well-held conviction that the one place not to be in an air raid was the basement of a building, even a seemingly safe one.

A dispassionate tribute has to be paid to the Giant's captain, Richard von Bentivegni, and his crew. They had been attacked relentlessly on the run to London. R. 39 had counterattacked its pursuers and forced one Bristol Fighter to retire with a punctured fuel tank and a wounded observer; in addition, the Giant had a remarkable escape when it hit, and wrenched away, the steel cables of a barrage balloon.

The Giants made four more solo raids which were directed at London. Five made up an attack on 29/30 January, five on 16 February, one on 17 February, and five on 7/8 March. Sixty-six people were killed, eighty-seven injured, and material damage was put at £109,600. None of the Giants was shot down, but two crashed on landing at the end of the four-raid sequence.

They made only one more attack on London, when they joined the Gothas on the last aeroplane raid of the war.

Ernst Brandenburg had resumed command of the England Squadron. Almost a year previously he had led it on the first mission to reduce London to ruins. Now the aerial bombardment seemed to be no more than an extension of the war to the enemy's homeland. Nevertheless, he was determined that even a demoralized Squadron would do its duty to the end. But events changed that extension from a series of tactical raids to an essential part of a great strategic object, with the prospect that the England Squadron would end the war on the wings of victory.

The setting of what proved to be the last aeroplane raid had all the makings of a planned final act of a spectacular drama. In March General Ludendorff had begun his historic offensive on the Somme, in a great gamble to crush the British and French Armies before the Americans were ready for a maximum effort. Peace with Bolshevik Russia had released thousands of German troops to the Western Front.

The March offensive and its consequences are immortal, but a brief reference to its first weeks is required to appreciate the high optimism with which the England Squadron looked forward to raiding London again. The German army offensive began on 21 March. In a thick early morning fog, the British lines were broken. In a few hours the long war of attrition was over. In a few days the Germans advanced forty miles. The British Expeditionary Force was caught flat-footed in its trenches before it left them in a headlong retreat.

Lloyd George acted instantly and Lord Milner replaced Lord Derby as Secretary for War, a change which was no more than a routine gesture.

The German army regained positions it had not held since 1914. In this sudden whirlwind of battle, 90,000 British troops were made prisoners. The Fifth Army, victims of muddled orders and objectives, retreated with the loss of almost an entire Corps. Some 1,300 guns, 4,000 machine-guns, 200,000 rifles, 70,000 tons of shells and 250 million rounds of small arms ammunition were lost.

The first phase of the German offensive ended on 28 March, but was resumed on 9 April. It had lost some of its momentum, but the British Army still faced defeat. At home the public were under no illusions, especially when they read Haig's order: 'With our backs to the wall and believing in the justice of our cause each one of us must fight to the end.'

For the first time there were fears that the war might be lost. Some of the more pessimistic citizens mistook Haig's words 'fight to the end' for an indication of defeatism.

There were other causes for alarm. On 14 April Marshal Foch was made supreme commander of the British and French forces in France. Apart from a chauvinistic resentment that the Army had again been placed under a 'Frog', there was dismay that the long-serving Haig had apparently failed. On 15 April that dismay was compounded by the announcement that Trenchard had resigned as Chief of the Air Staff, only a fortnight after the formation of the Royal Air Force; and it was on that same day that Haig's grave order was issued. On 25 April Lord Rothermere also resigned.

To make up for the losses in France, American troops, together with 300,000 British soldiers from the United Kingdom and Palestine, reinforced the Western Front.

But if the German advance had lost some of its momentum, the Allies' situation was still perilous. When the England Squadron was scheduled to strike new hammer blows on London, it was a critical hour for Britain's fortunes in France and at home.

The Squadron had taken an active part in Ludendorff's offensive, but, by the time it was withdrawn for the raids on London, the German Army had begun to overreach itself. Brandenburg was unaware of this. The news from the Western Front was still good as he made his plans for the renewed attack on the capital, a few days after the Squadron had been detached. With reason he believed that this was, after all, his greatest opportunity; and the old fantasy persisted that England was cowering with fear.

But as the German Army widened its front, its lines of communication were weakening. With the help of American troops, the Spring offensive was soon to turn into the Allied counterattack which led to final victory.

Nevertheless, on 19/20 May Brandenburg assembled a monstrous force of thirty-eight Gothas and two reconnaissance aeroplanes. It was reinforced by three Giants, and formed the biggest aerial armada ever launched against England. But the last act of the drama ended in tragic anticlimax.

Ten of the Gothas never arrived over England, and of the twenty-eight which did, only thirteen, together with the three Giants, got as far as London.

It was a haphazard operation, which, despite Brandenburg's intention, was without inspiration. The confident touch of leadership could not be found. There was neither control nor co-ordination. Attacked relentlessly by guns and aircraft, the Gothas at any rate were at bay from the outset. The great set-piece design never materialized.

One Gotha, which had dropped bombs on south-east London, was shot down by Lieutenant E. E. Turner and his gunner, Air Lieutenant H. B. Barwise. There was one survivor. It was already in trouble, having been hit by Major Sowrey, who had destroyed the Zeppelin L 32 at Billericay in September, 1916. Another Gotha, also on its way back from London, was brought down by anti-aircraft fire as it was leaving the coast. It disappeared into the sea and not a piece of wreckage was found. A third Gotha, trying to reach the capital, was destroyed by Captain C. J. Q. Brand; all three of the crew were killed. A fourth was shot down by gunfire off the Maplin Sands as it crossed the coast at the beginning of the operation; a fifth was forced to land with engine trouble near Clacton. A sixth was shot down over East Ham by Lieutenant A. J. Arkwell and Air Mechanic Stagg; there were no survivors. To complete a night of total failure, anti-aircraft guns destroyed a seventh Gotha; it crashed into the sea off Dover with the loss of all three of its crew.

The twenty-eight Gothas and three Giants dropped 159 bombs on London, Southend, Ramsgate, Dover and Rochester. Forty-nine people were killed, 177 injured and damage was estimated at £170,000.

The aeroplane campaign was over. It had failed to subdue London, and its effect, like that of the Zeppelin, was negligible. In retrospect, it is easy to believe now that it could ever have been otherwise, but almost to the end, the continuing anxieties about aerial bombardment were not misplaced. In his *War in the Air*, H. A. Jones wrote:

> An aerial onslaught at this time [1918] might have had results leading to a popular clamour which the Government might have found themselves unable to withstand.

The Zeppelins made only four raids during 1918, in which nine people were killed and fifty-nine injured.

With victory running swiftly away from Germany, the raid on 5 August was not only the end of a campaign which had lasted for three years and seven months, it was also the end of Peter Strasser's life.

On the morning of 5 August, the eve of a new moon, he ordered L 53, L 56, L 63, L 65, and L 70 to attack 'south and middle.' London was excluded unless Strasser changed his mind. It was L 70's maiden operational flight. She was the newest and most ambitious of the Zeppelin line, having been commissioned in July. She was 693 feet 11 inches long, had a capacity of 2,195,800 cubic feet, was driven by seven Maybach engines and had a maximum speed of about 80 miles per hour.

One of the least experienced captains commanded her. *Kapitänleutnant* von Lossnitzer was on his maiden operational flight to England as well, although Strasser was on board with him.

L 56 and L 63 made their landfall elsewhere, but we are not concerned with them or, indeed, with the others, except L 70. The East Coast defenders were alert after a report from the Leman Tail Lightship. Thirteen aeroplanes went up. Three of them flew out to sea to engage L 63, L 65 and L 70.

Two veteran Zeppelin fighters were the first into action— Major E. Cadbury and Captain R. Leckie. In theory, if not always in fact, the Royal Air Force, now four months old, had abolished distinctions between naval and military flyers. There are still many stories and legends of undying pettiness and jealousies which prevented the efficient welding of the RAF, but there were no such feelings when Cadbury and Leckie climbed into a D.H.4. Leckie had been in the RNAS when, as one of the pilots in the Large America Flying Boat, he had helped to shoot down L 22 in May, 1917. Cadbury had been a RFC officer when he had taken part in the destruction of L 21 in 1916.

The de Havilland aircraft was well able to take on one of the airships, even though it was cruising at about 16,000 feet. The D.H. 4 had a Rolls-Royce Eagle 375 h.p. engine, a ceiling of 22,000 feet and a speed of 122.5 miles per hour.

Cadbury and Leckie approached the airships in about forty minutes and took it by surprise. It turned north. Ten minutes later, at 10.20 pm, Cadbury manoeuvred the D.H. 4 into a position where Leckie could open fire. A burst of the Pomeroy explosive bullet hit the underside of L 70. In less than a minute she was ablaze from end to end and plunged into the sea. Every one of her crew died with her. The other Zeppelins escaped, but six days later Flight-Lieutenant S. D. Culley was to destroy L 53 when he shot her down off the Dutch coast. He was awarded the Distinguished Service Order.

Cadbury and Leckie were each awarded the Distinguished Flying Cross, a recently-instituted decoration for officers and warrant officers in the RAF. One British aircraft, A D.H. 9, was lost at sea.

Although he was dead, Strasser was not forgotten. He remained a German folk hero up to the Second World War. He has a well-deserved place in history but not as the folk-hero and a model for German youth, as some writers have made him out to be. Without doubt he was an inspiring and brave leader. He cannot, however, be acquitted of his perverse faith in the Zeppelin long after it had failed in its object, and of an unwillingness to make a military appreciation which did not fit his ideas.

He was a prisoner of the early veneration of the Zeppelin. It had to have a hero to go with it, and when he was appointed to command the Naval Airship Division he became, inescapably, that hero. But his passionate conviction, personal ambition, vanity and a refusal to admit errors kept him on a virtually static course of tactical action.

Moral standards and successful military leadership do not always go together. If the end justifies the means, all can be forgiven, if not always forgotten. Conspiracy with his captains to exaggerate and even to falsify reports were means that failed to justify an end. When there were no answers to the failures, his seemingly infallible reputation, his experience, which could not be shared by the High Command, led to wrong policies and the squandering of Zeppelins with devoted men inside them.

It is his place in aviation rather than military history which is deservedly secure. He was neither a trained engineer nor a designer, but he quickly acquired technical knowledge and professional skill which put him among equals. He was the inspiration behind many of the wartime changes, and left a permanent influence on future airship progress and evolution.

It is perhaps impossible to speculate on Britain's fate if the Naval Airship Division had not been held back by the

Kaiser's fumbling indecision and the ambivalence over the strategic and tactical use of the Zeppelin. These prevented an all-out assault and a concentration of effort when the enemy was most vulnerable to, and ignorant of, the horror of aerial bombardment.

There were fifty-seven airship raids on England. Some 5,800 bombs killed 564 people and injured about 1,370. The total damage came to about £1,527,500. The Gothas and Giants made twenty-seven day and night attacks, dropped approximately 2,400 bombs, which caused 835 deaths and more than 1,900 injuries. Damage amounted to an estimated £1,400,000.

Nearly 1,400 deaths, some 3,340 injuries and damage reckoned to be almost £3 million from approximately 8,200 bombs are figures whose significance has been diminished in the reducing-glass of time. Behind them, however, is an unparalleled story if endurance and survival by people who, at the beginning of the war, never imagined that bombs on that scale could ever be dropped at all.

Despite the failure of the campaign, the prospect of what might have happened encouraged the conviction that strategic bombing would destroy civilian resistance and bring decisive victory.

But only Hiroshima and Nagasaki were decisive, with bombs of a very different kind.

BIBLIOGRAPHY

Air Raids. Air Ministry intelligence reports compiled by GHQ Home Forces. 1915–1918.

Armstrong, H. C. *Grey Steel: J. C. Smuts. A Study in Arrogance.* 1937

Ashmore, E. B. *Air Defence.* 1929

Bruce, J. M. *British Aeroplanes 1914–1918 (1957). War Planes of The First World War: Fighters, vol 2.* 1968

Churchill, Winston S. *The World Crisis 1911–1914,* vol I. 1923

Fredette, Raymond H. *The First Battle of Britain 1917/1918.* 1966

Gibbs-Smith, Charles H. *Aviation: An Historical Survey from its Origins to World War II.* 1970

Hancock, W. K. *Smuts, the Sanguine Years.* 1962

Imperial War Museum. *Pilots' Reports Relating to Destruction of Zeppelins.* 1915–1918

Joynson-Hicks, William. *The Command of the Air.* 1916

Lloyd George, David. *War Memoirs.* 1933–1936

Manchester Guardian History of the War. 1914–1919

Morris, Joseph. *The German Air Raids on Great Britain.* 1925

Morison, Frank (Albert H. Ross). *War on Great Cities.* 1937

Raleigh, Sir Walter and Jones H. A. *The War in the Air.* 6 vols. 1922–1937.

Rawlinson, A. *The Defence of London 1915–1918.* 1923

Robinson, Douglas H. *The Zeppelin in Combat.* 1962.

Sassoon, Siegfried. *Memoirs of an Infantry Officer.* 1930

Scott, Sir Percy. *Fifty Years in the Royal Navy.* 1919

Slessor, Sir John. *The Central Blue.* 1956

Sueter, Sir Murray. *Airmen or Noahs.* 1928

Taylor, A. J. P. *English History 1914–1945.* 1965

The Times History of the War (1914–1918). 32 vols. 1914–1919.

Wilson, H. W., and Hammerton, J. A. (ed). *The Great War.* 13 vols. 1914–1919

APPENDIX

Raid Records 1914–1918

Notes: (i). *Except when they have some historical interest, aeroplane/seaplane sorties, as distinct from squadron raids by Gothas and solo attacks by Giants, are excluded.*

(ii). *Names under Places/Areas are those which proved to be the main targets, although other primary objectives may have been given in operation orders.*

YEAR	DATE	AIRCRAFT USED	AREAS/ PLACES	BOMBS DROPPED	CASUALTIES
1914	21 December	Seaplane	Dover	2	Nil
1914	24 December	Aeroplane	Dover	1	Nil
1914	25 December	Seaplane	Thames	2	Nil
1915	19/20 January	Zeppelin	Yarmouth East Anglia	23	4 killed, 16 injured
1915	14 April	Zeppelin	Tyneside/ Northumberland	31	2 injured
1915	15/16 April	Zeppelin	Essex	78	1 injured
1915	29/30 April	Zeppelin	East Anglia	76	Nil
1915	10 May	Zeppelin	East Anglia	122	2 killed, 1 injured
1915	17 May	Zeppelin	Southend Ramsgate	53	2 killed, 1 injured
1915	26 May	Zeppelin	Southend	70	3 killed, 3 injured
1915	31 May/1 June	Zeppelin	East London	120	7 killed, 35 injured

YEAR	DATE	AIRCRAFT USED	AREAS/PLACES	BOMBS DROPPED	CASUALTIES
1915	4/5 June	Zeppelin/SL	Kent		
			Essex		
1915	6/7 June	Zeppelin	Yorkshire	23	6 injured
			Hull		
1915	15 June	Zeppelin	Grimsby	59	24 killed, 40 injured
			Yorkshire		
			Tyneside		
1915	9/10 August	Zeppelin	Northumberland	60	18 killed, 72 injured
			Goole		
			Dover		
			Kent		
1915	12/13 August	Zeppelin	Suffolk	104	17 killed, 55 injured
1915	17/18 August	Zeppelin	Suffolk	47	6 killed, 24 injured
			London		
1915	7/8 September	Zeppelin	Essex	118	10 killed, 48 injured
			London		
1915	8/9 September	Zeppelin	Suffolk	97	18 killed, 38 injured
			London		
			Yorkshire		
1915	11/12 September	Zeppelin	Norfolk	152	22 killed, 87 injured
1915	12/13 September	Zeppelin	Essex	60	Nil
			Suffolk	60	Nil

Year	Date	Type	Location	Number	Casualties
1915	13/14 September	Zeppelin	Suffolk, London, Hertfordshire, Middlesex	40	Nil
1915	13/14 October	Zeppelin	Kent	190	71 killed, 128 injured
1916	31 January/1 February	Zeppelin	Midlands	379	71 killed, 113 injured
1916	5/6 March	Zeppelin	Hull	111	18 killed, 52 injured
1916	31 March/1 April	Zeppelin	Lincolnshire, Suffolk	233	48 killed, 64 injured
1916	1/2 April	Zeppelin	London	58	23 killed, 120 injured
1916	2/3 April	Zeppelin	Sunderland, Edinburgh, Leith	234	13 killed, 24 injured
1916	3/4 April	Zeppelin	Norfolk, Yorkshire, Hull	13	Nil
1916	5/6 April	Zeppelin	Co. Durham	83	1 killed, 9 injured
1916	24/25 April	Zeppelin	East Anglia, Lincolnshire, Suffolk, Essex	107	1 killed, 1 injured
1916	25/26 April	Zeppelin	Kent	107	1 injured
1916	26 April	Zeppelin	Kent	3	Nil
1916	2/3 May	Zeppelin	Yorkshire, Northumberland, Scotland	129	9 killed, 30 injured

YEAR	DATE	AIRCRAFT USED	AREAS/PLACES	BOMBS DROPPED	CASUALTIES
1916	29 July	Zeppelin	Yorkshire, Lincolnshire, Northumberland	65	Nil
1916	31 July/1 August	Zeppelin	Kent, East Anglia, Lincolnshire	100	Nil
1916	2/3 August	Zeppelin	East Anglia, Kent	137	Nil
1916	9 August	Zeppelin	Norfolk, Yorkshire, Northumberland, Co. Durham, Scotland	186	10 killed, 16 injured
1916	23/24 August	Zeppelin	Suffolk, London	30	Nil
1916	24/25 August	Zeppelin	Suffolk, Essex, Kent	102	9 killed, 40 injured
1916	2/3 September	Zeppelin/SL	Hertfordshire, London, Lincolnshire, Nottingham	460	4 killed, 16 injured
1916	23/24 September	Zeppelin	London, Nottingham	368	41 killed, 130 injured

Year	Date	Type	Location	No.	Casualties
1916	25/26 September	Zeppelin	Sheffield, Bolton, Portsmouth, Midlands	127	43 killed, 31 injured
1916	1/2 October	Zeppelin	Eastern England, Hertfordshire	201	1 killed, 1 injured
1916	27/26 November	Zeppelin	Lincolnshire, Northamptonshire, Norfolk		
1916	25 November	Aeroplane	Hertfordshire	206	4 killed, 37 injured
1917	17 February	Zeppelin	London	6	Nil
1917	16/17 March	Zeppelin	Kent	Nil	Nil
1917			Kent		Nil
1917	24 May	Zeppelin	Sussex, East Anglia	79	
1917	25 May	Gothas	Essex	60	1 killed
1917	5 June	Gothas	Folkestone	139	95 killed, 192 injured
1917			Sheerness	64	
1917	13 June	Gothas	Shoeburyness, London	116	13 killed, 34 injured
1917	17 June	Zeppelin	Kent	42	162 killed, 432 injured
1917			Kent		
1917	4 July	Gothas	Suffolk, Harwich	42	3 killed, 16 injured
1917	7 July	Gothas	Felixstowe, London	65	17 killed, 30 injured
					57 killed, 193 injured

YEAR	DATE	AIRCRAFT USED	AREAS/ PLACES	BOMBS DROPPED	CASUALTIES
1917	22 July	Gothas	Harwich Felixstowe	55	13 killed, 23 injured
1917	12 August	Gothas	Southend Shoeburyness	37	32 killed, 46 injured
1917	22 August	Gothas	Margate Margate Ramsgate	50	12 killed, 27 injured
1917	22 August	Zeppelin	Dover	29	1 killed
1917	3/4 September	Gothas	Yorkshire Chatham Sheerness		132 killed, 96 injured
1917	4/5 September	Gothas	Margate London Margate	46	19 killed, 71 injured
1917	24 September	Gothas	Dover London	90	21 killed, 71 injured
1917	25 September	Zeppelin	Kent Yorkshire Lancashire	118	3 injured
1917	25 September	Gothas	London	97	9 killed, 23 injured
1917	28 September	Gothas/ Giants	Kent Suffolk Kent Essex	60	Nil
				45	

Year	Date	Type	Location	Number	Casualties
1917	29 September	Gothas/Giants	London, Sheerness	55	14 killed, 87 injured
1917	30 September	Gothas	London, Margate, Dover	92	14 killed, 38 injured
1917	1/2 October	Gothas	London, Kent, Essex	75	11 killed, 41 injured
1917	19/20 October	Zeppelin	London, Middlesex, Eastern England	273	36 killed, 55 injured
1917	29 October	Gothas	Essex	8	Nil
1917	31 October/1 November	Gothas	London, Kent, Essex	278	10 killed, 22 injured
1917	6 December	Gothas/Giants	London, Sheerness, Margate, Dover	421	8 killed, 28 injured
1917	18 December	Gothas/Giants	London, Margate	142	14 killed, 85 injured
1917	22 December	Gothas/Giants	London, Margate	None officially reported on mainland	Nil

YEAR	DATE	AIRCRAFT USED	AREAS/ PLACES	BOMBS DROPPED	CASUALTIES
1918	28/29 January	Gothas/ Giant	London Sheerness Margate Ramsgate	62	67 killed, 166 injured
1918	29/30 January	Giants	London Kent	69	10 killed, 10 injured
1918	16 February	Giants	Essex London	29	12 killed, 6 injured
1918	17 February	Giants	Dover	16	21 killed, 32 injured
1918	7/8 March	Giants	London	29	23 killed, 39 injured
1918	12 March	Zeppelin	London Yorkshire	38	1 killed
1918	13 March	Zeppelin	Hartlepool	15	8 killed, 39 injured
1918	12/13 April	Zeppelin	Lancashire Midlands Norfolk		
1918	19/20 May	Gothas/ Giants	London Essex	135	7 killed, 20 injured
1918	5/6 August	Zeppelin	Kent Norfolk	159 Nil	49 killed, 177 injured Nil

INDEX

(Notes: (i). To avoid an unwieldy Index, some references have been omitted when they do not have a direct relevance to the text. (ii) Zeppelin airships are not shown under separate identification numbers but can be found in appropriate headings and cross-references.)